UNDERSTANDING THE ISLAMIC SCRIPTURE

A STUDY OF SELECTED PASSAGES FROM THE QUR'ĀN

Mustansir Mir

Routledge
Taylor & Francis Group
LONDON AND NEW YORK

First published 2008 by Pearson Education, Inc.

Published 2016 by Routledge
2 Park Square, Milton Park, Abingdon, Oxon OX14 4RN
711 Third Avenue, New York, NY 10017, USA

Routledge is an imprint of the Taylor & Francis Group, an informa business

Credits and acknowledgments borrowed from other sources and reproduced, with permission, in this textbook appear on appropriate page within text.

ISBN: 9780321355737 (pbk)

Cover Designer: Nancy Danahy

Library of Congress Cataloging-in-Publication Data

Mir, Mustansir
Understanding the Islamic scripture : a study of selected passages from the Qur'ān / Mustansir Mir.—1st ed.
p. cm.
Includes bibliographical references and index.
ISBN-13: 978-0-321-35573-7
ISBN-10: 0-321-35573-3
1. Koran—Theology. I. Title.
BP132.M57 2008
297.1'226—dc22 2007026842

for

Dr. Farida Nawaz Tariq, who is like a mother,

and

Professor Sajid Mir, *murshid-i awwal*

Contents

PREFACE

This book seeks to make the Islamic Scripture, the Qur'ān, accessible to general English-speaking readers. The demand for information about the Qur'ān has led to the production of many works aimed at such readers. Some of the works are introductions to the Qur'ān. Others present the contents of the Qur'ān under a thematic arrangement. Still others provide selections from commentaries written by classical and modern scholars. While all such works are useful, none is very helpful to readers who wish to understand the text of the Qur'ān in some detail but lack the linguistic background to read that text in the original language, Arabic, and to benefit from the primary sources of Qur'ānic exegesis. Hence this book, whose operating assumption is that ordinary readers with a serious interest in the Qur'ān but with no previous knowledge of the scripture would be best served by an intensive study—presented in readable, jargon-free language—of a series of passages from the Qur'ān. The passages included in this volume are, in my view, representative of the Islamic Scripture, though it is certainly possible to produce other volumes consisting of different but equally representative Qur'ānic passages.

This book does not offer a systematic collection, anthology, or summary of the classical or modern commentaries. Such works are full of details that, today, are unlikely to excite much interest on the part of general readers. These readers, Muslim or non-Muslim, presumably wish to know—in an intellectually respectable way, yet in readable idiom—the following: What kind of a book is the Qur'ān? What does it have to say, and how does it say it? Are there—many readers in the West might ask—any correspondences or points of contact between the Qur'ān and the Bible? Questions like these have guided my writing of this book. I have, inevitably, drawn on the rich Qur'ānic exegetical tradition. Since I do not claim to speak for the entirety of that tradition, I have offered what I can describe, with some diffidence, as a personal synthesis of that tradition—that synthesis presented here, again, with the aim of helping a particular audience.

Mustansir Mir
Youngstown State University

Acknowledgments

Dr. Bruce N. Waller, my colleague in the Department of Philosophy and Religious Studies at Youngstown State University, is responsible for this book. After suggesting that I write a book of this kind, he put me in touch with Priscilla McGeehon of Longman, who encouraged me to undertake the project. It has been my privilege to work with her and with her successor, Eric Stano, and I am deeply grateful to both editors for their help and advice. James Sacco, my able assistant at the Center for Islamic Studies at Youngstown, proofread more than one draft of the book and helped in several other ways. I am thankful to him for his meticulous work on the manuscript.

General Introduction

This introduction is intended to serve a twofold purpose: to present information that will help the reader to form a general idea about the Qurʾān and to explain the scope of this work and the approach taken to the subject.

I. Two Meanings of *Qurʾān*

The Qurʾān calls Muḥammad the last prophet—he is "the seal of the prophets" (Q 33:40). As such, the revelation he is believed to have received—the Qurʾān—would be the last, or the "seal," of the scriptures. The Qurʾān occupies a central position in the life and thought of Muslims and is of fundamental importance in understanding the dynamics of Muslim history and culture.

Like the name *Bible*, whose Greek original means "books," the name *Qurʾān* means "recitation" and "reading." These two meanings draw attention to the fact that the Qurʾān is both recited from memory and read from text. The tradition of memorizing the Qurʾān goes back to the times of Muḥammad (570–632), the Arabian prophet to whom, according to Islamic belief, the Qurʾān was revealed by Allāh—that is, God—in Arabic, in small and large portions, over a period of about twenty-three years (610–632). Given in an oral culture, the Qurʾān was memorized by many of Muḥammad's Companions. Qurʾān memorization became a distinctive and enduring part of the religious culture of Islam. In every age, large numbers of people have committed the Qurʾān to memory—they are reverently called *ḥuffāẓ*. Found in all parts of the Muslim world, the *ḥuffāẓ* include laypersons as well as scholars, affluent as well as poor individuals, physicians and engineers as well as artisans and craftsmen, females as well as males, and—not at all rare—children in their early teens. Amazing in itself, this phenomenon becomes more amazing when we remember that the vast majority of the *ḥuffāẓ* do not speak Arabic as their first language—about four-fifths of the world Muslim population is non-Arab. The Qurʾān is about the size of the New Testament, and a non-Arab Muslim's memorization of the Arabic Qurʾān would be comparable to a non-Greek Christian's memorization of the Greek New Testament. Collectively, the *ḥuffāẓ* perform the important function of preserving the text of the Qurʾān through the ages. Theoretically, the *ḥuffāẓ* are supposed to produce on demand—and many can—a complete chain of transmission through which they have "received" the Qur'ān from the earliest times. In fact, compared with its transmission through print, the Qur'ān's oral transmission, if well attested, is, in principle, considered a better guarantee of the accuracy of the Qur'ānic text.

The second meaning of *Qur'ān*, "reading," has a certain historical significance. The advent of Islam in Arabia was marked by, among other things, a strong emphasis on cultivating literacy. Though revealed in an oral setting, the Islamic Scripture calls itself a "book" or "scripture" (for example, Q 2:2; 3:3; 4:105; 6:92; 7:2; 10:1; 16:89; 39:23; 46:12), a concept with which most Arabs were familiar but which, outside the scripture-bearing Jewish and Christian communities, was not part of the lived Arabian culture. By presenting itself as a book, the Qur'ān initiated the process of changing a preliterate Arabia into a literate one. This process eventually led to a transformation of the religious, intellectual, and literary landscape of Arabia. As the selections in this volume will show, the Qur'ān deals with a variety of subjects—doctrine, ethics, history, and law. It was only natural that, in each of these fields, the Qur'ān should become the starting point of reflection and study for Muslims. It is not at all surprising, then, that the Qur'ān deeply influenced the many disciplines of knowledge that arose under its impact.

II. Content

What does the Qur'ān say? Since the commentaries on the passages included in this book will address the question in detail, only a brief answer will be presented here.

Taken as a whole, the Qur'ān is addressed to humanity at large. The Qur'ān's fundamental demand of human beings is that they submit to God. The Arabic for "submission" is *islām*, which, as the familiar proper noun *Islam*, is the name of the religion whose scripture the Qur'ān is. The Qur'ān says that everything in the heavens and the earth submits to God and that human beings, therefore, should do the same. In submitting to God, the universe enjoys peace, order, and stability. Human beings, if they submit to God, will enjoy the same in their lives. Nature's submission to God is involuntary and mechanical, whereas human submission to God is supposed to be conscious and voluntary.

To submit to God is to obey Him and carry out His commandments. The Qur'ān contains a number of commandments pertaining to right belief and right conduct. A commonly occurring phrase in the Qur'ān, "those who have believed and have done good deeds" (for example, 2:25; 3:27; 4:57; 7:42; 13:29; 22:14; 42:22; 84:25), establishes a close connection between belief and conduct. Right belief consists in belief in the one and only God, who created the universe and is actively administering it; who has communicated His will to humankind through certain chosen individuals, called prophets; and who will, one day, resurrect all human beings, pass judgment on their conduct during their terrestrial existence, and, depending on the nature of their conduct, reward or punish them justly in an eternal life, always tempering His justice with mercy. The prophets, raised among all nations and not only in one or some, are the mediums through whom God conveys His will to humanity. The prophets not only present the Divine message, they live out that message in their lives, serving as exemplars to their fellow human beings.

Right conduct consists in carrying out the commandments of God with sincerity and devotion. The Qur'ān contains both legal stipulations and ethical injunctions pertaining to several areas of human life, and details of many of those stipulations and injunctions will be found throughout this book. Here, it is worth noting that, in the Qur'ānic scheme of thought, the religious and ethical perspectives receive precedence over the legal and theological perspectives. In fact, it would be correct to say that, from a Qur'ānic standpoint, religious and ethical considerations constitute the matrix in which both law and theology are grounded.

III. Organization

1. The Qur'ān consists of 114 chapters, called sūrahs, whose length varies greatly: the shortest sūrahs are only three verses long, whereas the longest one has 286 verses. At first sight, one feels that the verses in the individual sūrahs were put together arbitrarily and, therefore, lack continuity and coherence, and that the sūrahs were arranged according to the principle of diminishing length. Many Muslim scholars have argued, however, that the sūrahs are unities and that the verses in them treat identifiable major themes in a methodical manner. Furthermore, several of these scholars have demonstrated that the arrangement of the sūrahs in the Qur'ān also is informed by a certain method: adjacent sūrahs deal with similar themes; one sūrah picks up the theme with which the preceding sūrah closes; and the language, tone, and atmosphere of juxtaposed sūrahs have striking resemblances. Since the present work deals with short Qur'ānic passages, a few remarks about the overall organization of material in the Qur'ān will suffice.

2. Readers of the Qur'ān are likely to notice that, usually, diverse kinds of materials exist in it side by side. For example, within the span of a few pages, the Qur'ān might refer to God's way of dealing with the world and with humanity, state the doctrine about the afterlife, distinguish lawful from unlawful food, tell the story of an ancient prophet or people, comment on the hostile attitude of Muḥammad's opponents, cite a parable and draw a moral, promise reward for belief and threaten punishment for disbelief, emphasize the need for one to ask God's forgiveness for one's sins, and so on. Such diversity of subject is, understandably, quite perplexing to many readers, who may conclude that the Qur'ān is a disconnected work. It becomes especially perplexing to those who come to the Qur'ān expecting to find in it a style of presentation similar to that of the Bible. Generally speaking, chronology is the organizing principle used in the Bible, which follows the historical sequence in narrating events, for example. In the Qur'ān, on the other hand, theme, rather than chronology, serves as the organizing principle. The diverse—at times, seemingly incongruous—materials found in a given part of the Qur'ān can usually be knit together and seen as forming a coherent unit with reference to the theme that runs through them all. But the Qur'ān has its own way of lending coherence to seemingly disparate material. For example, in a given segment of the Qur'ān, the theme of the oneness of God may serve as the common denominator in certain teachings quoted from earlier scriptures, in the reference made to the unity of the laws of nature, and in the observation that, in a crisis, human beings instinctively turn toward the one true God, abandoning the deities they have been falsely associating with Him. In such an example, three types of proofs—drawn one each from scripture, physical nature, and human psychology—would be presented next to each other, and, in keeping with the style of classical Arabic, few overt links between them would be established in the text, with the readers expected to discover on their own the implicitly present theme of monotheism common to the three types of proofs. Discovering such thematic links in the Qur'ān is often a challenging, but not impossible, task. One also needs to add that the alleged case for the "disconnectedness" of the Qur'ān is overstated. For one thing, many of the short sūrahs of the Qur'ān are obviously marked by thematic unity, and the same is true of a number of medium-sized sūrahs. Quite often, on closer study, large segments of long sūrahs also would appear to be marked by continuity and coherence.

3. The sūrahs from which the passages included in this book are taken—in a few instances, the passages are complete sūrahs—are, in each case, identified as "Makkan" or "Madīnan." A "Makkan" sūrah is one revealed in the city of Makkah (popularly, Mecca), where Muḥammad lived for about thirteen years after announcing his prophecy (that is, from 610 to 622); a "Madīnan" sūrah is one revealed in the city of Madīnah (popularly, Medina), to which Muḥammad and his followers emigrated in 622 and where he lived until his death in 632. The two terms, thus, denote both a geographical and a temporal division. A more important division between the two types of sūrahs has to do with the content of their revelations. In the Makkan period, Muḥammad, after he had declared himself to be a prophet who had received revelation from God, faced ridicule, opposition, and, finally, persecution by the Quraysh, the wealthy ruling tribe of Makkah that was also in charge of Arabia's most famous sanctuary, the Ka'bah, built, according to Arabian tradition, by Abraham and his son Ishmael. Given the Makkan Muslims' weak social and political position, the Makkan revelations focus on the fundamentals of Islamic religion and ethics. In Madīnah, the Muslims found themselves in a position of power and established the first Islamic state, and the revelations received in that city, accordingly, deal with social, political, and legal matters at greater length. But Makkan sūrahs sometimes contain verses revealed in Madīnah and vice versa. This is not surprising when we remember that the circumstances through which Islam passed in the early Madīnan period were, in some respects, similar to those of the immediately preceding period in Makkah, the revelation, thus, addressing issues that bore relevance to both the

Makkan and the Madīnan situations. Also, on receiving a revelation, Muḥammad would instruct one of his many scribes to place that revelation, if it consisted of one or more verses, before or after a certain verse or set of verses or to place it, if it happened to be a complete sūrah, before or after a certain sūrah. This, of course, meant that the Qur'ān was being compiled by Muḥammad at the same time that it was being revealed to him, and that the compilatory order of the Qur'ān came to be different from its revelatory order.

The Makkan period of revelations itself is divided, in view of the different stages through which Islam passed in Makkah, into three subperiods, the distinctive character of each subperiod being reflected in the subject matter, language, and style of that subperiod. It is customary to speak of the Early, Middle, and Late Makkan periods (roughly, 610–615, 615–620, and 620–622, respectively). In this book, it is not necessary to indicate that division, all Makkan sūrahs having been identified simply as Makkan.

A word about the names of the sūrahs is in order. In some instances, the name of a sūrah indicates or suggests the sūrah's theme or subject. An example is sūrah 12, *Joseph*, which deals exclusively with the story of the prophet Joseph. Sūrah 4, *Women*, has many injunctions involving women, these injunctions forming a major, though not the sole, theme of the sūrah. Quite often, though, a sūrah's name serves only as an identifier, there being no necessary thematic or logical connection between a sūrah's name and the sūrah's contents. In many cases, a Qur'ānic sūrah is named—following a familiar Arab practice of naming individuals, animals, and objects—after something striking associated with the sūrah. For example, sūrah 2 is called *Cow*, not because the sūrah is a research paper on that animal, but simply because a certain incident narrated in the sūrah involves the slaughter of a cow (verses 67–71), that incident having been found striking enough to supply the sūrah's name. Some sūrahs begin with one or more alphabetical letters that do not form regular words and are, therefore, recited one letter at a time. Since such letters, even when they occur in a combination, are disconnected from each other in enunciation, they may be called "disconnected letters" (they are commonly called "broken letters"—again, because they are broken off from each other in pronunciation). None of the passages included in this book has such letters, though sūrah 20, from which a passage is taken, bears the title *Ṭā-Hā*, the sūrah opening with two "disconnected letters"—*ṭā'* and *hā'*.

4. The Makkan-Madīnan division of the sūrahs is helpful in identifying the various groups of people addressed or discussed in different parts of the Qur'ān, such identification, in turn, helping with the interpretation of the Qur'ān. The Muslims—the followers of Muḥammad—are addressed or referred to in both Makkan and Madīnan sūrahs. Three other groups of people need to be mentioned—the idolaters, the Jews and Christians, and the hypocrites. During the Makkan period, the idolaters of the city, represented by the Quraysh, were the chief opponents of Islam, whereas, after the Muslims' emigration to Madīnah, the Muslims' confrontation with the Jews and Christians, until now implicit, becomes explicit. Consequently, the Makkan sūrahs mainly engage the idolaters of Makkah—or of Arabia in general—whereas the Madīnan sūrahs mainly engage the Jews and Christians. In Madīnah, the Muslims had to reckon with a new opponent—the hypocrites. These were people led by certain affluent and powerful individuals whose hopes of assuming a position of dominance in the city were shattered by the arrival of the Muslims from Makkah, leading them to conclude that they could best protect their political and economic interests by professing faith in Islam. But, suspecting that the new religion had not yet emerged as the decisive winner, the hypocrites hedged their bets and were not averse to conspiring against Muslims. A Madīnan phenomenon, the hypocrites are discussed in a number of Madīnan revelations.

IV. Language

The language of the Qur'ān is deceptively simple. For one thing, the Qur'ān has a rather small vocabulary. Also, even ordinary readers of the Qur'ān will conclude that, at a basic level at least, the Qur'ān yields its meaning fairly generously. And yet, countless scholars have spent their lives analyzing the phrasal construction, the functions of the particles, the deliberate omission of words, the parallel structure, the figures of speech, and other linguistic matters in the Qur'ān. In other words, the language of the Qur'ān admits of study at deeper levels, promising fruitful results. We will offer a few brief observations.

1. The language of the Qur'ān has a markedly religious and ethical character. In various forms and with varying emphases, the Qur'ān repeatedly presents the worldview it espouses, the teachings it wishes to impart, and the modes of conduct it seeks to cultivate in the believers. There is hardly a page of the Qur'ān that does not state, refer, or allude to the most fundamental tenet of Islam—namely, monotheism. The Qur'ān aims to create and strengthen in human beings the realization that they owe gratitude to an all-merciful, beneficent God and that, in order to do so, they must submit to Him. Time and again, the Qur'ān reminds its addressees to obey His commandments, to pray to Him for blessings, and to fear the consequences of defying Him. Statements like the following are frequently encountered in the Qur'ān:

- God has full knowledge of all things. (Q 2:29)
- God does not like the transgressors. (Q 2:190)
- Do good; God likes those who do good. (Q 2:195)
- God is fully aware of what you do. (Q 3:80)
- In God should the believers put their trust. (Q 3:160)
- God is Very Forgiving, Forbearing. (Q 5:101)
- God has power over all things. (Q 9:39)
- God is Mighty, Very Wise. (Q 9:40)

2. The Qur'ān is poetic without being poetry. Rhythm, rhyme, and assonance mark the language of the Qur'ān, making it a highly chantable text, facilitating memorization of it, and giving rise to the unique Muslim art of Qur'ān recitation. The Qur'ān frequently employs imagistic devices—similes, metaphors, and parables—of various kinds. The Qur'ānic images, many of which are drawn from nature or from situations of life familiar to seventh-century Arabs, illustrate the fundamentals of the religion and offer a graphic representation of ideas and concepts.

3. As a rule, the Qur'ān adheres to the principle of verbal economy: terseness and omission are the two main forms taken by the Qur'ānic economy of expression, instances of which will be noted and discussed in this book. One special aspect of Qur'ānic verbal economy may be noted here. Classical Arabic, the language of the Qur'ān, is different from modern languages—including modern Arabic—in an important respect. Modern texts, in order to establish continuity of thought, typically make use of such transitional expressions as "nevertheless," "however," "furthermore," "in other words," and "in view of the above." Such expressions are rarely used in classical Arabic—or in the Qur'ān—with the result that the connecting links between the Qur'ānic verses or passages, especially in the longer sūrahs, are obscured, and this creates the impression that the Qur'ān is disconnected. The ability to supply those links mentally as one reads the Qur'ān is essential to seeing continuities in the text.

4. The frequently occurring shifts of person and number in the Qur'ān indicate that the Qur'ān was given in a live setting. In such a setting, a speaker can move from one topic to another without serving the audience with advance notice of the impending change of subject, and the audience, on whom the speaker relies for supplying important components of the meaning, will have no difficulty in understanding the speaker. Also, there is frequent repetition in the Qur'ān, which calls itself a "reminder," and is, therefore, mandated to repeat its message. A close study of the subject shows, however, that repetition in the Qur'ān is often purposive: for example, repetition may provide the needed emphasis in a place or, by rephrasing a statement, draw attention to different nuances of a thought.

V. Interpretation

Interpretation of the Qur'ān requires certain skills and qualifications on the part of the interpreter.

1. The foremost requirement, of course, is possession of a thorough knowledge of the language of the Qur'ān, and this requirement is fulfilled through a close and careful study of the language of the time at which the Qur'ān was revealed. The major source of knowledge of that language is pre-Islamic poetry, which has survived in large quantities and, despite certain problems of historicity surrounding it, remains both an indispensable source of classical Arabic usage and a mine of information about ancient

Arabia's beliefs, customs, practices, values, intertribal relations, social activities, ceremonies, pastimes, and other matters.

2. Like other scriptures, the Qur'ān has its integrity and must be understood in its totality. A well-known principle of Qur'ānic interpretation is stated as "One part of the Qur'ān explains another." Instead of treating a subject—a doctrine, a story, a legal commandment, an ethical precept, a social obligation—exhaustively in one place, the Qur'ān typically treats different aspects of it in several, even many, different places. A full understanding of the Qur'ānic view of a subject requires, therefore, that the Qur'ān's various treatments of that subject be studied carefully and in relation to one another.

3. Knowledge of the historical Qur'ānic scholarship is important. Muḥammad not only transmitted the Qur'ān, but also expounded it to his followers, who, in turn, expounded it to the next generation of believers, and so on. Muḥammad's explanations of Qur'ānic verses or of issues pertaining to Qur'ānic revelations take the form of reports found in books that make up a record of Muḥammad's sayings and actions. This record is collectively known as *Ḥadīth* (with a capital *Ḥ*), a single report in that record being a *ḥadīth* (with a small *ḥ*; pl. *aḥadīth*). *Ḥadīth*, though it does not provide a detailed commentary on the entirety of the Qur'ān, furnishes important explanations of Qur'ānic terminology and thought. Many of Muḥammad's Companions settled in various parts of the expanding Islamic world, setting up teaching circles in which the Qur'ān often figured as a prominent subject of study. With the passage of time, study of the Qur'ān became both widespread and systematized, giving rise to a tradition of Qur'ānic interpretation that has continued to grow through history and is alive and well today. The number of complete or partial Qur'ānic commentaries written is very large, with many commentaries having acquired the status of classics. There also exist commentaries dealing with specific aspects—such as the legal, theological, or philological aspects—of the Qur'ān. There are many specialized branches of Qur'ānic studies. One branch, for example, deals with the grammar, vocabulary, rhetoric, style, and textual history of the Qur'ān.

VI. The Qur'ān as Part of a Larger Scriptural Tradition

Just as Islam is one of the three so-called monotheistic religions—the other two being Judaism and Christianity—so the Qur'ān belongs to the scriptural tradition of which the Jewish and Christian Testaments are a part. The popular view of Islam as a religion that is radically different from Judaism and Christianity is mistaken. Equally innocent of truth is the popular view that the Qur'ān is completely at odds with the Hebrew Scriptures and the New Testament. It is a well-known fact that Jews and Christians are accorded a special status in the Qur'ān, which calls them "the People of the Book" (for example, Q 2:105; 3:72; 4:153; 29:46), the phrase acknowledging that the two religious communities received scriptures from God. The Qur'ān mentions three pre-Islamic scriptures by name—the Torah, revealed to Moses; the Evangel (Arabic: *Injīl*), revealed to Jesus; and the Psalms, revealed to David—though it leaves open the possibility that scriptures were given by God to other prophets and other religious communities as well.

Undeniably, there exist irreducible differences between the religions of Judaism, Christianity, and Islam—and, consequently, between their scriptures. Nevertheless, in their essential religious outlook and ethical perspective, the Jewish, Christian, and Islamic Scriptures are more similar than dissimilar. The themes of the oneness of God, prophecy, revelation, ethical conduct, and moral accountability are as central to the Qur'ān as they are to the Hebrew Bible and the New Testament. In view of the interaction that necessarily took place, on more than one level, between the various religious communities of pre-Islamic Arabia, it would be logical to think that the Jews and Christians had some knowledge of the religious beliefs and practices of the idol worshippers and, by the same token, that the latter had some knowledge of the religious beliefs and practices of the former. As such, the Qur'ān could assume, and it seems that it does assume, on the part of its initial audience, a degree of familiarity with the religions of Judaism and Christianity. Of this familiarity, we will note several instances later. At this point, we need to note that the close similarity of the three scriptures has a certain practical significance: If the Qur'ān is an integral part of a larger scriptural tradition—one might call it the monotheistic scriptural tradition—then a study of the Bible can be helpful in explicating the Qur'ān at some points. Supporting this thought is the fact that the Qur'ān avowedly engages with the Bible, agreeing with it, disagreeing with it, commenting on it, and critiquing it, an adequate understanding of that engagement requiring a close study of the Bible. In fact, Muslim Qur'ānic commentators often cite the Bible or draw on it, but one feels that there needs to be, on the part of Muslim scholars, a more explicit and more formal recognition of the Bible as an aid to Qur'ānic exegesis. In my commentary on the Qur'ānic passages, I have, in some cases, cited the Bible for comparative purposes, but I have done so with the full realization that I am not a Bible expert. In many cases, I have followed the leads provided by Qur'ānic commentators conversant with the Bible. Unless otherwise indicated, all references to the Bible are to the New Revised Standard Version.

VII. About This Work

1. What This Book Includes and What It Leaves Out. This work presents, explains, and discusses, with reference to the selected Qur'ānic passages, the following:

- some of the foundational stories of the religion of Islam
- many of the basic doctrinal and ethical teachings of the Qur'ān

- a variety of Qur'ānic commandments
- the Qur'ānic view of nature as a pointer to a higher reality
- the relationship between God, on the one hand, and the world and humanity, on the other
- in many cases, literary features of the Qur'ānic text
- in some cases, and, as a rule, only to the extent warranted by the Qur'ānic passage in question, Biblical parallels to the Qur'ān

Like any other great book, the Qur'ān is more multifaceted than an anthology can possibly suggest. This volume, since it studies only a small number of Qur'ānic passages, is aimed at a specific audience; and since it had to be of a manageable size, it leaves many aspects of the Islamic Scripture untreated. Those who expect to find in it an exhaustive or schematic outline of Qur'ānic themes will be disappointed. The legislative material of the Qur'ān is not fully represented in this book, and the same may be said about the narrative aspect of the Qur'ān. Also, no attempt has been made here to present a wide range of exegetical opinions, attributing each to a commentator, supplying grounds for each opinion, and commenting on the relative merit of each. In section V, above, the principle of interpretation of the Qur'ān by means of the Qur'ān was stated. In the commentaries on the passages, however, only occasionally is reference made to other, relevant Qur'ānic verses. A wider application of the aforesaid principle would have added considerably to the volume of the book. Again, because of space limitations, not much of *Ḥadīth* is cited. In brief, the focus in this book is on specific Qur'ānic texts, and it is hoped that a diligent study of these texts will give the reader a fairly good understanding of the Islamic Scripture in several important respects.

2. Translation. In translating the selected Qur'ānic passages (or any other Qur'ānic material cited), I have endeavored to stay close to the text and yet produce a readable translation. Certain characteristic expressions of Qur'ānic Arabic imbue the text with a special flavor or atmosphere, and, in my view, not much is gained either by omitting them in translation or by providing explanatory translations of them in a work like the present one, which aims at retaining the structures and emphases of the original Arabic text. For example, the simple conjunction *wāw*, "and," even when it starts a sentence or a passage, adds a quality of flow and continuity to the Qur'ānic text—and, not infrequently, establishes conceptual links between texts—and is, in most cases, best retained in translation. Again, many Qur'ānic verses begin with the Arabic particle *idh*, "when" (or *wa-idh*, "and when"), which serves to remind the reader of an important event that is, from the speaker's point of view, as good as an established fact and, therefore, can be briefly referred to by means of "when." Grammatically, "when" is an abbreviation of "remember when," which would be an acceptable translation of the Arabic particle. I translate the particle simply as "when," trying to preserve, in translation, the Arabic usage found in the Qur'ān and hoping that the complete meaning—"remember when"—would be clear from the context. I give that translation especially since the Arabic equivalent of "remember when" also occurs in the Qur'ān, and a distinction should be made in the translation if it has been made in the original. Only when absolutely necessary have I supplied in translation a word that is taken as understood but is not expressed in the original text. I have scrupulously avoided using brackets to amplify or nuance the translation.

3. Citation of Qur'ānic Sūrahs and Verses. In citing the sūrahs and verses of the Qur'ān, the sūrah number is followed by a colon and the verse number(s). Thus, in 2:255, 2 is the sūrah number, and 255, the verse number. A semicolon separates two Qur'ānic citations. If a given passage is made up of a complete sūrah, the verse numbers are not given. "Q" stands for "Qur'ān."

4. Commentary. The detailed commentaries on the passages are meant to give readers a relatively in-depth understanding both of what the Qur'ān is saying and of how it is saying it. In writing commentary on a passage, I have tried

- to explain what I thought were the main points made in the passage
- to anticipate and answer the questions that might arise in the readers' minds
- where I could do so without getting too technical, to draw attention to some of the literary features of the Qur'ānic text
- where possible and instructive, to present Biblical parallels

In a citation of a work on the Qur'ān, the author's last name is followed by a reference to the work, a colon separating volume number and page number (for example, Rāzī, 22:30 means that the author is Rāzī, the volume number of his work is 22, and the page number of that volume is 30).

5. Works Consulted. I have used a small number of sources, a list of which is provided at the end of the book. From these sources, some classical and some modern, I have taken, and sometimes adapted, what I thought would be helpful in offering an exposition of the Qur'ān for my intended audience.

6. Notes. I have supplied notes primarily to record my debt to the authorities whose works I have used. Occasionally, the notes elaborate certain points. The notes are kept strictly apart from the main text and can be safely ignored by general readers. They are keyed to the main text by means of descriptive phrases referring to statements or discussions in particular sections or subsections of the text. The notes are not indexed.

7. Glossary. The glossary at the end of the book lists and explains, besides one or two names, the Arabic and other technical terms used in the book.

8. Diacritics. In transliterating Arabic words, I have used diacritical marks to designate certain Arabic characters:

- The macron (a bar over a vowel) lengthens the sound of certain vowels (*ā*, *ī*, *ū*).
- The underdot makes the pronunciation of certain consonants emphatic (*ḍ*, *ḥ*, *ṣ*, *ṭ*, *ẓ*).

- The apostrophe-like sign ʾ represents the glottal stop called *hamzah*.
- The sign ʿ represents the guttural character *ʿayn*.

Needless to say, it is not necessary to master the transliteration system used in this book to be able to follow the discussions or the line of argument presented.

9. Root and Form. Occasionally, reference is made to the "root" or a "form" of a word. A "root" is a set of letters, usually three in number, that has a certain basic meaning that subsists in the words formed from that root. For example, the root *k-t-b* means "to write," some of the many words formed from it being *kātib*, "writer"; *maktūb*, "(that which is) written"; *kitāb*, "book"; and *mukātabah*, "correspondence." These four Arabic words each represent a pattern, or "form," yielded by the application of certain rules of grammar.

1 The Essence of the Qur'ān

1 Opening

In the name of God, the Most Compassionate, the Very Merciful.

[1]Thankful praise is due to God, the Lord of the worlds, [2]the Most Compassionate, the Very Merciful, [3]the Master of the Day of Recompense!

[4]You alone do we serve, and You alone do we ask for help. [5]Guide us into the Straight Path—[6]the path of those whom You blessed, who neither became the objects of wrath nor went astray.

Sūrah 1 is Makkan.

I. Introduction

This is the opening sūrah of the Qur'ān—hence its name, *Al-Fātiḥah* (literally, "The Opener"). It is generally believed to be one of the first sūrahs revealed to Muḥammad. Some consider it to be the very first revelation, making it the first in the chronological as well as in the compilatory order of the sūrahs. On the latter view, a plausible one, the sūrah would be seen as inaugurating, on the one hand, the process of the Qur'ānic revelation and, on the other hand, the Qur'ān in its present arrangement.

One of the best-known sūrahs of the Qur'ān, *Al-Fātiḥah* is an integral part of the obligatory daily prayers. It is also recited to invoke blessings in a variety of situations—for example, in praying over a deceased person.

The invocation, "In the name of God, the Most Compassionate, the Very Merciful," occurring at the beginning of this and all the other Qur'ānic sūrahs except sūrah 9, is best regarded as a self-standing verse that is part of the Qur'ān but not part of any sūrah. In other words, the invocation, called *basmalah*, signals the onset of a sūrah or sets one sūrah apart from another, and, in the case of those passages in this book that are complete sūrahs (chapters 1, 35, 36, and 37), it is given, in italics, at the start of the passages but is not counted as a verse of any of the sūrahs. For an explanation of the phrases "the Most Compassionate" and "the Very Merciful" in the *basmalah*, see section II, verse 2, below.

II. Commentary

Verse 1: "Thankful praise." This is a translation of the word *ḥamd* in the original text. The primary meaning of *ḥamd* is "gratitude," though "praise" is part of the Arabic word's meaning. One may praise a being even if one has not received any favors from it, but one shows gratitude to a being only when one receives some favor from it. Human beings owe gratitude to God because they are the recipients of countless blessings from Him. To offer gratitude is to offer praise as well, hence the rendering "thankful praise."

"The Lord of the worlds." "Lord" (*Rabb*) means "Sustainer" and "Master," or rather, "Master *because* Sustainer." "Worlds" (*'ālamīn*) has, basically, the same sense as "kingdoms" in the expression "animal, mineral, and plant kingdoms," with the qualification that there may be innumerable kingdoms, known and unknown, into which existence, or creation, can be divided. Arabian polytheism recognized God as the Supreme Deity but had set up many "Lords"—that is, beings who were believed to be administering different parts of the universe. This dichotomy between Godhead and Lordship effectively negated the divinity, providence, and other attributes of God. By stating that God is the Lord of all the worlds, the Qur'ān rejects the dichotomy, saying that God is not only the Supreme Deity, but also the caretaking Lord of the entire universe.

Verse 2: The Arabic words for "Most Compassionate" and "Very Merciful" are, respectively, *Raḥmān* and *Raḥīm*. The first of these two words denotes intensity; the second, permanence. In other words, God is *always* merciful, but on some occasions, He is *especially* compassionate. It is like saying that a certain person, ordinarily generous, is, on some occasions, especially generous. Thus, the two epithets—"the Most Compassionate" and "the Very Merciful"—represent two different but complementary aspects of Divine mercy, the second epithet being more than a simple repetition of the first.

Verse 3: God is the Master of all days—of the days of terrestrial life as well as of the Day of Recompense. But the verse singles out the Day of Recompense because, on that day, not even nominal or symbolic power will belong to anyone else, whereas, during earthly life, a degree of power—even if, in actuality, granted by God Himself—may be possessed by human beings.

Verse 4: The opening verse rejected the division between Godhead and Lordship. This verse now reinforces the idea of the unity of Godhead and Lordship by saying that God alone must be served or worshipped (Godhead) and that He alone must be petitioned for help in all situations (Lordship).

Verse 5: In verse 4, the speaker expresses a general commitment to serve God and decides to seek only God's help. In verse 5, the speaker seems to have realized, in more specific terms, that possession of right guidance alone will enable one to translate that commitment into action. Having already resolved to seek help only from God, and being convinced that there can be no better source of right guidance than God, the speaker now prays to be guided to the Straight Path.

Verse 6: This verse offers an amplification of "the Straight Path." The amplification is meant to express the commitment of the human speaker, who, after praying for guidance, now resolves to follow in the footsteps of those people of previous generations who took the Straight Path, earning God's favor, and to shun the example of those who lived a life full of misdeeds, incurring God's wrath, and of those who went too far afield in their erroneous belief or doctrine. The verse subtly suggests that, in its essentials, the Straight Path has always been the same and that those who follow this path are, irrespective of whether they belong to ancient times or to modern times, members of a single community.

III. The Qur'ān in Miniature

Al-Fātiḥah is often called the Qur'ān in miniature—and appropriately. The principal themes of the Qur'ān are three: monotheism, prophecy, and the afterlife (see also chapter 6, "The Throne Verse," section III). All those themes are encapsulated in this sūrah, which takes the form of a prayer uttered by a human speaker, who represents humanity. In verses 1–2, the speaker acknowledges that there is only one God, who controls and sustains the heavens and the earth. In verse 3, the speaker acknowledges that God will one day judge humanity. In verses 4–6, the speaker, having realized that the above-mentioned truths about God must be acknowledged by all human beings, now explicitly speaks on behalf of humanity—hence the use of the first person plural pronoun in this part of the sūrah. After making a commitment to serve only God (verse 4), but not knowing the proper way of serving Him, the speaker asks God Himself for guidance (verse 5). In verse 6, the speaker expresses the determination to join the company of the rightly guided people of the past and to shun the company of those who failed to take the Straight Path. The central verse in the sūrah is the fifth: "Guide us into the Straight Path." The first four verses lead up to the petition made in this verse, and the last verse elaborates the petition.

To this petition made in *Al-Fātiḥah*, the rest of the Qur'ān—divine guidance vouchsafed to the Prophet Muḥammad—may be taken as a response. Thus, *Al-Fātiḥah* is an outline or abstract that finds its elaboration or explication in the rest of the Qur'ān. This understanding of the relationship between *Al-Fātiḥah* and the rest of the Qur'ān lends some support to the view that *Al-Fātiḥah* was the very first revelation received by Muḥammad.

IV. The Sūrah as a Logical Argument

As stated above, *Al-Fātiḥah* takes the form of a prayer, which, taught by the revelation itself, is made to flow on human lips. The tone of the prayer appears to be exclamatory, expressive of emotion, rather than declarative, expressive of contemplative thought. Underlying the emotion, though, is a certain logical argument, which may be stated as follows:

1. The human speaker observes the universe, noting its order and harmony, reflects on the remarkable system of providence that is attested everywhere in the world, and recognizes and appreciates the blessings of which all of existence is a recipient. The speaker reaches the conclusion that the source of all this providential care is a single being—a sovereign who created everything and sustains everything. Having reached this conclusion, and having realized that God is that being, the speaker exclaims: "Thankful praise is due to God, the Lord of the worlds" (verse 1).

2. The speaker next wonders why God is taking such providential care of the universe. Is He under any obligation to do so? A little reflection yields the conclusion that, being under no such obligation, God is doing so out of sheer mercy and compassion on His part. This realization leads the speaker to say: "The Most Compassionate, the Very Merciful" (verse 2).

3. At this point, a question arises in the speaker's mind: "Does God's providential care place any responsibility on me?" The question arises because privilege entails responsibility. Human beings, if they have received divine blessings, must be held accountable for the way they use and respond to those blessings. The thought of accountability leads the speaker to the notion of a day on which all human beings will be called to account, a day on which God will sit in judgment. So, the speaker says: "the Master of the Day of Recompense" (verse 3).

4. If there is going to be a Day of Judgment, then one needs to know exactly what success and failure on that day will consist in. In other words, one feels that one is in need of guidance. But before one can ask God for guidance—and what better source of guidance than God Himself?—one needs to submit to Him and declare one's subordinate status to Him, and one can do so by acknowledging God as the sole being worthy of being served and the sole source of help and support. Accordingly, the speaker, representing humanity, says: "You alone do we serve, and You alone do we ask for help" (verse 4).

5. Having submitted to God, the speaker, still using the plural pronoun, now asks for direction: "Guide us into the Straight Path" (verse 5).

6. The speaker not only prays for guidance to the Straight Path in a theoretical sense, but also expresses a commitment to follow that path in practice by walking in the footsteps of those who took that path and by shunning the example of those who rejected that path or deviated from it: "The path of those whom You blessed, who neither became the objects of wrath nor went astray" (verse 6).

This view of *Al-Fātiḥah* as an argument has some important philosophical implications. It makes religion a conscious and positive response of the human mind and heart to existential reality, thus parting company with theories that view religion as the product of fear or some other negative thought or emotion. On this view, furthermore, the essence of religion would seem to lie in (1) an appreciation of the good, beneficent aspects of reality; (2) a recognition of the need for human beings to establish with the creator of that reality, God, a relationship based on gratitude; and (3) a resolve, on the part of human beings, to accept conscientiously in their life the demands and dictates arising from that relationship.

V. Polar Harmony in the Sūrah

The sūrah sets up certain polarities and then harmonizes them. Some of the resulting complementarities can be seen if we divide the sūrah into two parts, one consisting of verses 1–3 and the other, of verses 4–6.

1. Thought and Action. In part 1, man reflects on the universe and, witnessing a vast providential arrangement, breaks out in praise of God, offering gratitude to Him. In part 2, he decides to serve God and seeks help from Him in the course of his life. In other words, contemplation and understanding lead to action and movement.

2. Emotion and Cognition. Part 1 is emotive: upon reflecting on the universe and his own situation, man cannot help but exclaim how provident, compassionate, and just God is. Part 2 represents the recognition that Divine providence, compassion, and justice require man, first, to submit to God and, second, to translate that recognition into a prayer for guidance so that the submission can take a proper form. In part 2, the affective element is not entirely absent, though the cognitive and discursive elements predominate. In part 1, on the other hand, the reflective element is not completely missing—in fact, it is reflection that leads man to make the exclamatory pronouncement—but reflection is in the background, exclamation in the foreground.

3. Initiative and Response. Part 1 represents the initiative taken by God, who is merciful and just to man and takes providential care of him. Part 2 represents the response made by man: he submits to God and seeks His guidance. Part 2 would appear to be marked by a polarity of its own: man makes a conscious decision to serve God and mold his life in accordance with His commandments. To this initiative, God's response, one can infer from verse 6, is to bless those who follow the Straight Path.

4. Privilege and Responsibility. Part 1 speaks of God's blessings on human beings. Part 2 speaks of the obligation of human beings to serve only Him and seek only His help. This responsibility is entailed by the privileges referred to in part 1.

5. Individual and Humanity. As noted above, the exclamatory tone of verses 1–3 strongly suggests that they are uttered by an individual—the implication being that it is a model individual, and that this is how every human being ought to act in a situation like the one described in the sūrah. The reflective tone of verses 4–6 suggests, and the use of the plural pronoun in the verses seems to confirm, that the verses are uttered by a person representing humanity.

6. This World and the Next. The primary focus in part 1 is on this world, reflection on which leads man to certain theoretical conclusions. The primary focus in part 2 is on the next world, in whose context salvation is sought on the strength of a certain kind of practical conduct. This polarity can also be described in terms of the seen and the unseen or in terms of the concrete and the abstract: The data of the universe on which man reflects in part 1 are primarily sensory or material in character, whereas the notions of guidance and salvation in part 2 are primarily conceptual or spiritual in character.

VI. Literary Notes

1. The discussion in section IV ("The Sūrah as a Logical Argument") should make it clear that this short sūrah is, in terms of the progression of thought that takes place in it, well-knit and coherent.

2. In the translation of verse 5—"Guide us into the Straight Path"—the use of the preposition "into" rather than of the expected "to" is meant to capture a certain emphasis that marks the Arabic text. In Arabic, in fact, the preposition—it would, normally, be *ilā*, "to"—is omitted, and the omission makes the statement quite emphatic. The Arabic text, thus, does not merely mean "Guide us to the Straight Path," but "Guide us to the Straight Path and set us firmly in it, giving us the will and strength to adhere to it against all odds"—hence the translation "Guide us *into* the Straight Path."

VII. *Al-Fātiḥah* and the Lord's Prayer

Al-Fātiḥah enjoys in Islam an importance very similar to that enjoyed by the Lord's Prayer in Christianity. The Lord's Prayer occurs in Matthew 6:9–13 (a version with slight variations is found in Luke 11:2–4):

9 Our Father in heaven, hallowed be your name.

10 Your kingdom come. Your will be done, on earth as it is in heaven.

11 Give us this day our daily bread.

12 And forgive us our debts, as we also have forgiven our debtors.

13 And do not bring us to the time of trial, but rescue us from the evil one.

The Qur'ānic and Biblical prayers differ in some respects, but even a cursory comparison will show that the themes of submission to God, of reposing trust in Him, and of the acknowledgment that God is the source of all good and the granter of petitions are common to both prayers. A closer look will reveal both thematic and structural similarities (in the following paragraphs, "F" stands for *Al-Fātiḥah* and "LP" for the Lord's Prayer):

1. F 1–2 ("Thankful praise is due to God, the Lord of the worlds, the Most Compassionate, the Very Merciful") glorifies God and calls Him a caring God. It is comparable to LP 9 ("Our Father in heaven, hallowed be your name"), in which the phrase "Our Father" makes a pithy reference to God's providential care.

2. F 3 ("the Master of the Day of Recompense!") acknowledges that, on Judgment Day, all power will belong to God, in the sense that even token power will not be enjoyed by anyone else. It is comparable to LP 10 ("Your kingdom come. Your will be done, on earth as it is in heaven"). A more precise determination of the degree of similarity between F 3 and LP 10 will, however, depend on the way the Christian concept of the kingdom of God is interpreted—whether as a this-worldly realm, as an otherworldly realm, or as a realm that spans both this world and the other world.

3. F 4 ("You alone do we serve, and You alone do we ask for help") is a humble acknowledgment that God alone can provide help and comfort. It is comparable to LP 11–12 ("Give us this day our daily bread. And forgive us our debts, as we also have forgiven our debtors").

4. F 5–6 ("Guide us in the Straight Path—the path of those whom You blessed, who neither became the objects of wrath nor went astray") is a prayer for steadfastness on the path of righteousness. It is comparable to LP 13 ("And do not bring us to the time of trial, but rescue us from the evil one").

2 The Story of Adam

2 Cow 30–39

30And when your Lord said to the angels, "I am going to appoint a caliph on earth." They said, "Will You appoint on it one who will work havoc in it and shed blood, when, already, we glorify You, praising You, and proclaim Your holiness?"

He said, "I know what you do not know."

31And He taught Adam the names—all of them—and then presented them before the angels, and said, "Tell Me the names of these if you are right."

32They said, "Glory to You! We possess no knowledge except what You have taught us; indeed, You are All-Knowing, All-Wise."

33He said, "Adam, tell them their names." When he had told them their names, He said, "Did I not say to you that I know the hidden things of the heavens and the earth? And I know what you are expressing and what you have been concealing."

34And when We said to the angels, "Bow down before Adam." They bowed down, except Iblīs: He refused, having become proud; and he became one of the disbelievers.

35And We said, "Adam, reside, you and your spouse, in the Garden, and eat from it anywhere you like, freely. And do not approach this tree, or you will join the ranks of the wrongdoers."

36But Satan caused them to slip with regard to it and expelled them from the state they were in. We said, "Descend—as enemies of each other. And you shall have, on earth, a dwelling place and a provision for a certain time."

37Then, Adam acquired certain words from his Lord, and so He turned toward him in mercy; indeed, He alone is the one Most Accepting of Repentance, Very Merciful.

38We said, "Descend from it, all of you. Then, should any guidance come to you from Me, those who follow My guidance, there shall be no fear upon them,
and they shall not grieve. 39But those who disbelieve and call Our verses false, they
shall be the people of the fire; they shall remain in it forever."

Sūrah 2 is Madīnan.

I. Introduction

This passage is composed of two sets of verses, 30–33 and 34–39. The first set of verses is about God's decision to appoint a caliph on earth and the angels' reaction to that decision; the second is about God's placing of Adam and his spouse (who is not named in the Qurʾān, but whose Biblical name, Eve, is commonly used in Muslim scholarship to refer to her) in paradise, forbidding them to approach—that is, with the aim of eating the fruit of—a certain tree. The incidents narrated in the two sets of verses are interrelated.

II. Commentary

Verse 30: God announces to the angels that He is going to appoint a caliph (the Arabic word *khalīfah* means "deputy" or "vicegerent") on earth. God does not state explicitly whom He will appoint, but the angels seem to have guessed that the caliph is not going to be from among them. As we learn from this and other passages in the Qurʾān, the caliph that God has in mind is Adam, who belongs to a species about to be created—the human species. By definition, a caliph is possessed of certain discretionary powers delegated to him, and it follows that he will have at least some freedom to use those powers. The angels, whom the Qurʾān presents as rational beings, must have wondered about the need for such a caliph, for, they must have thought, the would-be caliph's injudicious use of his discretionary powers might produce evil. But how could God, the source of all good, allow such evil to exist? The angels have figured out that the real purpose of a caliph's appointment cannot be to create a new species that would praise and glorify God and proclaim His holiness, for this is a function they are already performing. So, they decide to ask God about the rationale behind the appointment of a caliph. Hiding their curiosity under a veneer of apprehension, the angels underscore the possibility of evil that a caliph's free exercise of his powers might cause: "Will you appoint on it one who will work havoc in it and shed blood?" To the angels' question, God does not give a direct answer. After saying, "I know what you do not know," He provides what may be called a dramatic enactment of the answer (verses 31–33).

Verse 31: God teaches Adam "the names—all of them." Next, He presents "them"—not the names but, as the Arabic personal pronoun *hum* signifies, the living beings who bear those names—and asks the angels to name "these"—the demonstrative pronoun *hāʾulāʾi*, again, signifies living beings—"if you are right," that is, if the angels are right in thinking that a caliph's appointment will produce nothing but evil on earth. There is a strong suggestion that the angels are mistaken. But if they are, we are not yet told in what way they are mistaken.

Verse 32: Unable to name the people they have been asked to name, the angels admit their ignorance. At this point, we need to understand that the bearers of the names are, like Adam, members of the human species and are, like Adam, caliphs (see section III.1, below). It is reasonable to assume that the angels' question is not about the caliph as a single individual but about the caliph as an occupier of a certain office. In other words, the word "caliph" has been used in the passage in a generic sense.

Verse 33: "Tell them their names," that is, "Inform the angels of the names of the people in question." Similarly, "When he had told them their names" means "When Adam had informed the angels of the names of those people."

Upon the angels' admission of their ignorance of the names of the people in question, God asks Adam to tell the angels those people's names. After Adam has done so, God says to the angels, "Did I not say to you that I know the hidden things of the heavens and the earth?"—a reiteration of the remark made by God at the end of verse 30, "I know what you do not know." But God adds, "And I know what you are expressing and what you have been concealing." This remark suggests that the angels, in asking their question, purposely refrained from expressing their thought fully. Alarmed at the possible negative consequences of a caliphal appointment, they gave expression to their fears. The real intent of their question, however, was to find out the rationale behind such an appointment, and it is this intent that they kept hidden.

Ostensibly, the angels are satisfied with the reply they receive to their question. But what is the point of the reply? How does the dramatically enacted reply address the angels' question? The key to the answer is contained in the word "names" that occurs in the phrase "the names—all of them" in verse 31.

In asking their question, the angels had highlighted the negative possibilities inhering, in their view, in the human beings' use of their delegated powers; they had ignored, or left out of their calculations, the equally strong possibility that human beings could use those powers for good and noble purposes. The angels were looking only at part of the picture, and so it would make sense to apprise them of the positive side of the appointment of a caliph. To drive the point home, God, instead of providing a theoretical answer to a theoretical question, presents before the angels all the people who are ever to be born, and He does so to show them that humankind would consist not only of people who would do evil but also of people who would do good. The verse even seems to suggest that the good done by human beings will outweigh the evil done by them. We can now say that, while the phrase "the names—all of them" in verse 31 refers to the names of all the members of the human race, the demonstrative pronoun "these" in verse 31 refers, more specifically, to the good human beings, for only a reference to such human beings would constitute a complete response to the angels' apprehension-filled question. Incidentally, the statement that it was the members of the human race that God presented before the angels is corroborated by Q 7:172, according to which, in preexistence, God brought forth, from the loins of Adam and his progeny, all members of the human race that were ever to be born and made them attest to His Lordship (see chapter 21, "The Primordial Covenant").

The scene depicted in the next set of verses (34–39) represents a development of the incident narrated in the first set of verses.

Verse 34: God commands the angels to bow down before Adam. The angels comply, but Iblīs, or Satan, filled with pride, refuses to bow down. The bowing symbolizes Adam's—and, therefore, humanity's potential supremacy over the angels—in fact, over the rest of creation—since the angels represented the highest order of creation before God brought Adam into existence.

This verse gives the impression that Iblīs was one of the angels. In Islam, however, there is no concept of fallen angels. According to Q 66:6, the angels do not disobey God, and Q 18:50 explicitly states that Iblīs was a member of the order of creation called *jinn* (sing. *jinnī*), who are made of fire (whereas the angels are believed, on the basis of a *ḥadīth*, to have been made of light) and, like human beings, have been given the option to obey or disobey God. The angels being the highest order of creation until the creation of Adam, God's command to the angels to bow before Adam was also, by implication, a command to all the lower orders of creation, including the *jinn*, to do the same. The angels obeyed the command, but the *jinnī* called Iblīs did not.

"And he became one of the disbelievers" can have one of the following three meanings: (1) Iblīs became a disbeliever—irrespective of whether any other disbeliever existed at that time; (2) Iblīs joined an already existing group of rebellious *jinn*; and (3) Iblīs was one of a number of *jinn* who disobeyed God's command, thus forming a group of disbelievers.

Verse 35: God commands Adam and Eve to reside in the Garden of Eden, permitting them to enjoy themselves in it but forbidding them to eat of a certain tree. The use of the word "approach" in the prohibition ("And do not approach this tree") suggests that Adam and Eve would be well advised to keep a safe distance from the tree, for getting close to the tree might tempt them to eat the fruit of the tree. The Qurʾān does not specify what kind of tree Adam and Eve were instructed to stay away from. It does not seem to regard such specification as crucial to the purpose for which the story of Adam is being told.

Verse 36: Deceived and misled by Satan, Adam and Eve lose the state of bliss in which they have lived until now. The words "[Satan] expelled them" means "[Satan] had them expelled," the act of expulsion having been attributed to Satan because he set in motion the chain of events culminating in the loss of the state of bliss enjoyed until then by Adam and Eve.

The Divine command, "Descend—as enemies of each other," is addressed to the two parties that are the natural enemies of each other—one party consisting of Adam and Eve and their future progeny and the other of Satan and his progeny—and both are being commanded to descend to earth. The statement, "And you shall have, on earth, a dwelling place and a provision for a certain time," is, in the present context, primarily addressed to the human race, though, in principle, it is also addressed to the race of the *jinn* (to which Iblīs, or Satan, belonged), for, according to the Qur'ān, the *jinn* are, like human beings, responsible moral agents, there being good *jinn* and bad *jinn* (sūrah 72), with Iblīs belonging to the latter category.

Satan's "causing" of Adam and Eve "to slip" does not mean that Adam and Eve were passive, helpless playthings in Satan's hands. The Qur'ān holds Adam and Eve responsible for the act of eating the fruit of the forbidden tree. At the same time, the use of the word "slip" strongly suggests that Adam and Eve were not rebellious by nature but succumbed to Satan's temptation in a moment of weakness, and that their violation of the Divine command to stay away from a certain tree lacked the gravity of Satan's violation of the Divine command to bow down before Adam.

Verse 37: Adam's acquisition of "certain words" from God means that Adam learned words of forgiveness from God. Q 7:23 reports those words, spoken by both Adam and Eve: "Our Lord, we have wronged ourselves, and if You do not forgive us and have mercy on us, we will, surely, join the ranks of the losers." On uttering these words, Adam and Eve were forgiven by God. The Arabic verb used for Adam's acquisition of words of forgiveness is *talaqqā*, whose form connotes effortfulness, implying that, after eating the fruit of the forbidden tree, Adam was filled with remorse and actively sought the forgiveness of God, who taught him the right words to use for seeking forgiveness. As Q 7:23 implies, Eve shared Adam's feeling of remorse and joined him in asking for God's forgiveness.

This verse negates the idea of original sin: By eating of the forbidden tree, Adam and Eve committed a lapse, but they asked for God's forgiveness and were forgiven by a merciful God, the forgiveness obviating the need for a redeemer to appear in later history.

Verses 38–39: As in verse 36, so in these two verses, the command beginning with "Descend" (plural in the Arabic) is addressed, on the one hand, to Adam and Eve—and, through them, to the human race—and, on the other hand, to Iblīs—and, through him, to the race of *jinn*. The primary addressees, again, are human beings, who are told that their final destiny will depend on their response to Divine guidance. Acceptance of the guidance will lodge them in heaven, which is typically described in the Qur'ān as a place whose inhabitants will have neither fear of anything untoward befalling them in the future nor regret over anything they may have done in the past. Rejection of that guidance will land the addressees in the fire of hell.

The imperative "Descend" in verse 38 does not signify punishment for Adam and Eve since, understood in light of verse 37, this descent is supposed to have occurred after God's acceptance of Adam and Eve's petition for forgiveness.

In verse 38, the phrase "Then, should any guidance come to you from Me" suggests, in view of the emphatic verb employed in the Arabic (*ya'tiyannakum*), that such guidance will, indeed, be given to humankind—a promise, one might say, that God will use the medium of prophets and scriptures to send guidance to human beings. At the same time, the verse does not imply that human beings will be allowed to go scot free if no Divine guidance reaches them. In Islam, the Divine gift of reason given to human beings makes them subject to basic accountability (see chapter 30, "Luqmān's Advice to His Son"). The fundamental truth upheld by Islam is that of monotheism, and Islam maintains that human reason by itself—that is, even when unaided by revelation—is capable of reaching and appreciating that truth. The implication is that, regardless of whether any revelation is communicated to them, all human beings are expected to hold, if in a broad and general way, the right belief about monotheism.

III. Issues

1. Human Beings as Caliphs. The Qur'ānic passage under study designates human beings as caliphs of God on earth. Since a caliph is one who possesses delegated powers, it follows that, as caliphs of God, human beings have been given the mandate to rule over the earth, using their faculties and abilities to exploit and make use of the earth's resources, but to do so in accordance with the injunctions of God, from whom they receive their delegated powers.

The angels' surprise at the appointment of a caliph suggests that no such office had existed until then. It also suggests the fateful nature of the office: the caliph will have the power to do evil—as the angels fear. But the dramatic enactment of the reply to the angels' question indicates that the caliph will have the power to do good as well. In fact, the elaborate demonstration mounted to provide the reply evinces a certain optimism on the part of God, who chooses to appoint the human being His caliph in spite of the possibility that the caliph might misuse the powers associated with his office.

The nature of the human caliphate is essentially moral. The angels' question suggests that the ability to glorify God does not constitute a sufficient qualification for that caliphate—hence the realization on the angels' part that the caliph will not be chosen from among them. As the concluding part of the passage indicates, the real purpose of the caliphal appointment is to put human beings to the test: those who accept Divine guidance will enjoy a happy fate, whereas those who reject that guidance will suffer a terrible fate. From this, one can infer that human beings are God's caliphs in a provisional and contingent, not in an absolute and permanent, sense. Proper discharge of their responsibilities will confirm them in their caliphate, whereas failure to carry out those responsibilities will result in their deposition from that office.

2. Human Nature. The passage makes a statement about human nature: human beings tend to be drawn to the forbidden. Taking advantage of this human weakness, Satan misled Adam and Eve. That Adam and Eve were given free reign in the Garden of Eden and were only forbidden to approach a certain tree implies that human beings, even when they possess many things that they can enjoy and derive pleasure and satisfaction from, tend to desire what is forbidden to them, thinking that their happiness depends on their possession of the one thing they do not have.

3. Satan as Man's Enemy. Verse 34 says that a sense of pride led Iblīs to disobey God's command to bow down before Adam. Verse 36, which speaks of Satan's causing of Adam and Eve "to slip" with regard to the prohibition of eating of a certain tree, clearly implies that Satan's act was actuated by his hurt pride and that, in persuading Adam and Eve to eat of the tree, he wished to avenge himself by bringing disgrace upon them. The same verse, by declaring that Satan and man are enemies, forewarns all human beings, advising them to be on their guard against the machinations of Satan.

IV. Literary Notes

1. Each of the two sets of verses that make up the passage—30–33 and 34–39—presents a complete, albeit short, story, each story having a proper beginning, a point of climax, and a dénouement. In verses 30–33, the question posed by the angels creates a critical situation, and a similar situation is created in verses 34–39 by the succumbing of Adam and Eve to Iblīs's temptation; each situation finds a resolution—the first, through a dramatic enactment, the second, through Adam's repentance. The dramatic nature of the two situations depicted in the passage is further underscored by the Qur'ān's preference for dialogue over description in advancing the plot of a story.

2. In the first set of verses, the key figures—or characters—are God, the angels, and Adam; in the second, they are God, Iblīs, Adam, and Eve. The roles of some of the characters change from the first set of verses to the second, most notably the role of Adam. In the first set of verses, Adam simply carries out the Divine command of telling the angels the names of certain people; in the second, he figures as an independent and full-fledged moral agent who makes a choice that has consequences.

3. The referential style typical of the Qur'ān is noticeable in this passage. To take only one example: Verse 31 begins with the statement, "And He taught Adam the names—all of them." The reference to "names" is rather abrupt, for, up to this point, we have been told nothing about any names, much less about "all of them." Close analysis of the passage suggests that, since the angels' question was about the species that, in their view, was likely to cause mischief on earth, an adequate reply to that question perforce had to involve reference to that species. In asking God whether He plans to appoint a caliph who would make mischief, the angels had in mind only some of the members of the human species. They needed to be told that the human race would include not only those who might do evil, but also those who would do good. Hence, the significance of the little phrase "all of them" in the Qur'ānic verse. The example just analyzed also highlights the fact that, in many places in the Qur'ān, the apparently simple text hides meaning that only patient study will bring out.

4. In the passage, two kinds of shifts—those of number and person—are notable. First, the shift of number, involving the first person singular pronoun and the first person plural pronoun—with God as the referent in both cases: The singular pronoun is used in verses 30, 31, and 33, and the plural pronoun, in verses 34–36. But in verse 38, the use of the plural pronoun in the beginning is followed by the use, twice, of the singular pronoun, and in verse 39, again, the plural pronoun is used. It seems that, as a rule, the plural pronoun expresses Divine majesty or sovereignty (with connotations of transcendence added), whereas the singular pronoun expresses Divine affection or relationality (with connotations of immanence added). Because of this difference, perhaps, the singular pronoun appears to be more suited to a dialogical situation, and the plural, to a monological situation or to a situation involving assertion of authority. Thus, verses 30–33, in which the singular pronoun is used, report a dialogue between God and the angels, with the two parties interacting with each other at close range, so to speak: "*I* am going to appoint a caliph" (verse 30); "Tell *Me* the names of these if you are right" (verse 31); "Did *I* not say to you that *I* know the hidden things of the heavens and the earth?" (verse 33). In the one-sided dialogue of verses 34–36 and of the first half of verse 38, on the other hand, God asserts His authority, speaking in imperious tones, as in the following: "And when *We* said to the angels, 'Bow down before Adam'" (verse 34); "And *We* said, 'Adam, reside, you and your spouse'" (verse 35); "*We* said, 'Descend—as enemies of each other'" (verse 36). In the second half of verse 38, the use of the singular pronoun ("Then, should any guidance come to you from *Me*, those who follow *My* guidance . . .") suggests a certain closeness of relationship between the Divine sender of guidance and the human recipients and beneficiaries of that guidance; the use of the singular pronoun also serves to reinforce the idea that God alone is the source of guidance. Rejection of Divine guidance calls for a stern judgment on the rejecters—hence the use, in verse 39, of the plural pronoun ("*Our* verses").

The shift of person, in reference to God, takes two forms in the passage: the third person changes to the first, and the first, to the third. In verses 30–33, God is referred to in the third person, as in the following: "And when *your Lord* said to the angels" (verse 30); "And *He* taught Adam the names—all of them" (verse 31). Starting with verse 34, however, the first person pronoun is used predominantly, as in the following: "And when *We* said to the angels" (verse 34); "And *We* said" (verse 35); "*We* said" (verses 36, 38). The rule seems to be that the third person is used for basic narration, whereas the first person implies a relatively direct involvement of the being or person in question.

V. Comparison with the Bible

The Qurʾān tells the story of Adam in many places, highlighting different parts or aspects of it in different places. In the following paragraphs, the comparison with the Bible is made principally with reference to Q 2:30–39.

There are some obvious similarities between the Qurʾānic and Biblical stories of Adam. In both scriptures, we see the conferring of a special status on man (Q 2:30; Genesis 1:26–27); the lodging of Adam and Eve in a paradisiacal setting (Q 2:35; Genesis 2:8, 15); the enjoining upon Adam and Eve of keeping away from a certain tree (Q 2:35; Genesis 2:16–17); and the succumbing of Adam and Eve to the temptation of eating of the tree (Q 2:36; Genesis 3:6).

There are also some obvious differences: in the Qur᾽ān, in the context of a question asked by the angels, Adam names certain members of the human race, God having taught Adam those names, whereas, in the Bible, Adam receives the privilege of naming creatures: "whatever the man called every living creature, that was its name" (Genesis 2:19–20); the Qur᾽ān does not explain the kind of tree from which Adam and Eve were supposed to keep away, whereas the Bible says that it was the tree of the knowledge of good and evil (2:9, 17); in the Qur᾽ān, the tempter is Satan (Q 2:36), whereas, in the Bible, it is the serpent (Genesis 3:1–5). Perhaps, a major difference is that of the dominant perspective. In the Bible, that perspective is historical—hence the situation of the story in a framework of space and time—whereas, in the Qur᾽ān, that perspective is religious, the focus of the story being Adam's moral role as the caliph of God—hence the absence of a spatiotemporal framework. Also, the Biblical account is, characteristically, more detailed than the Qur᾽ānic. One other point requires attention.

In the Qur᾽ānic passage under discussion, God's decision to appoint man His caliph on earth is made quite early—even before the temptation of man by Satan. In the Qur᾽ān, strictly speaking, the event of the temptation is of secondary importance and the event's occurrence or lack of occurrence would not have affected the Divine decision to place man on earth. According to the Qur᾽ān, man, though forgiven for his transgression, was yet sent down to earth, not as punishment but in accordance with an original Divine plan. In the Bible, on the other hand, man is banished to earth for an unforgiven sin that gives rise, in most of Christianity, to the doctrine of original sin. In Islam, such a doctrine has no place since God forgave Adam and Eve, wiping their slate clean for a fresh start on earth. Nevertheless, in the Qur᾽ān, the event of temptation in the Garden of Eden serves a certain purpose. It helps Adam and Eve assess their strengths and weaknesses: In a moment of weakness, human beings may fall and, thus, move away from God, but they have both the opportunity and the ability to come back to God by seeking His forgiveness. For Adam and Eve, then, the encounter with Satan serves as a dress rehearsal for their career on earth. To use an analogy from modern times, just as astronauts, in simulated conditions on earth, get a foretaste of the experience they are about to have in space, so Adam and Eve get, in the Garden of Eden, a foretaste of the experience they will have during their earthly tenure.

3 Abraham Builds the Kaʿbah and Prays for a Prophet

2 Cow 124–129

[124]And when his Lord tested Abraham by means of certain commands, and he
carried them out fully. He said, "I am going to make you a leader of humankind."
He said, "And from among my progeny, too?"
He said, "My covenant does not extend to the wrongdoers."
[125]And when We made the House a center for people and a secure place,
and—"Turn part of Abraham's staying place into a prayer area." And We charged
Abraham and Ishmael: "Purify My House for the circumambulators, those who
would go into retreat, and those who would bow and make prostration."
[126]And when Abraham said, "My Lord, make this a secure land and provide its
residents with produce of various kinds—to those of them who believe in God and
the Last Day." He said, "And as for those who disbelieve, I will provide for them for
a little while, but will, afterward, drag them over to the punishment of the fire. And
a very evil destination is that!"
[127]And when Abraham was raising the foundations of the House, and Ishmael,
too: "Our Lord, accept from us; indeed You alone are the All-Hearing, All-Knowing.
[128]Our Lord, make us submit to Yourself, and raise, from among our progeny, a
community that will submit to You. And show us our rites. And accept our
repentance; indeed, You alone are the one Most Accepting of Repentance, Very
Merciful. [129]And, our Lord, raise among them a messenger from among themselves,
one who will recite Your verses to them, will teach them the Book and wisdom,
and will purify them; indeed, You alone are the Mighty, the Wise."

Sūrah 2 is Madīnan.

I. Introduction

This passage relates the incident of Abraham's building of the Kaʿbah as a center of monotheistic worship and reproduces his prayer for a prophet who would carry on the monotheistic mission in Arabia. The passage is significant in several ways. First, it throws light on some aspects of the character of Abraham, a major prophet in Islam.

Second, it provides a basic insight into Islam's self-understanding. Third, it elucidates the relationship, as conceived in Islam, between this world and the next.

II. Commentary

Verse 124: The verse opens with words of praise for Abraham's devotion to God: God put Abraham to the test by giving him certain commands, and Abraham carried out those commands fully. We are not told what the commands were, but other passages in the Qurʾān furnish some details: (1) in his native city, Abraham was commanded to present the message of monotheism in a staunchly polytheistic society, his own father, an idol maker, being one of Abraham's severest critics (Q 6:74–83; 19:42–48; 21:51–70; 43:26–27); (2) in fulfilling the mission with which he had been charged by God, Abraham, on one occasion, confronted and defeated in a debate the king of his time (2:258); and (3) Abraham was commanded to sacrifice his son (37:102–107). In all these cases, Abraham carried out the will of God, showing unflinching loyalty to God, who subsequently conferred on him the title of *khalīl* ("intimate friend"), according to Q 4:125.

The word "commands" in the text is a translation of the Arabic *kalimāt*, whose singular, *kalimah*, literally means "word, utterance." Since, in giving a command, words are used, *kalimah* here comes to have the meaning of "command." But the use of *kalimāt* in the verse subtly points to Abraham's readiness to obey God's commands: no sooner did Abraham receive a command from God—or rather, no sooner did God utter a single "word" of command—than he set about the task laid on him, and he did so without questioning, objecting, or hedging.

God tells Abraham that He will make him a "leader of humankind." The announcement means that Abraham will have a long line of descendants and a large number of followers, who will proudly associate themselves with him and take him as their spiritual progenitor and as a model human being.

On hearing God's promise, Abraham—a prophet, but also an individual with typical human feelings and aspirations—couches his wish in the form of a polite question: Will his progeny share in the promised blessing? That is, will Abraham's line continue to retain the religious and moral leadership of humankind? In His response, God makes a distinction between lineage and righteousness: God is righteous, and so His covenant will not extend to the wrongdoers, even if they happen to be Abraham's offspring. This warning, ostensibly addressed to Abraham, is actually addressed to Abraham's progeny, who are being told that they must not take their relationship with the house of Abraham as an assurance of Divine approval of their less-than-righteous conduct in this world and as a guarantee of salvation in the afterlife.

Verse 125: The "House," as we learn from several Qurʾānic verses, including verse 127 of this passage, is the building called the Kaʿbah, which Abraham, with the help of his young son Ishmael, built in Makkah, later a major town of Arabia. The Kaʿbah, according to this verse, was meant to serve two functions. First, it was to be a "center"—the Arabic word, *mathābah*, denotes a place that is much-frequented and serves as a point of congregation for people. Since the Kaʿbah is the place that is being referred to, *mathābah* comes to have a religious meaning, with Abraham seen as wishing that, as a house of worship, the Kaʿbah be thronged with worshippers. But the purely mundane aspect of the meaning of the word is not entirely absent, for wherever large numbers of people gather, whether for religious or other purposes, significant social and economic interchange usually takes place. Second, the Kaʿbah was meant to be a place of safety and refuge. Historically, the Kaʿbah has served the two purposes well. On the one hand, the Kaʿbah's association with Abraham and its position as the site of an annual pilgrimage (*ḥajj*) instituted by Abraham is attested in Arabia's pre-Islamic tradition, which Islam later confirmed and built upon. The Islamic pilgrimage has always been a major religious event in the world. On the other hand, the city of Makkah, where the Kaʿbah is located, has been, as a rule, an abode of peace and security (see the explanation of verse 126, below).

"Turn part of Abraham's staying place into a prayer area"—this is addressed to "people," referred to in the verse immediately before this command; the "prayer area" is the Kaʿbah itself. The injunction implies that the prayer is the essential form of worship performed in the Kaʿbah. The Kaʿbah is the prototypical mosque of Islam, with all the other mosques of the world oriented toward it. This fact, too, evidences the Kaʿbah's centrality as a house of worship (see the explanation of the word *mathābah*, above).

Abraham and Ishmael are instructed to purify the Kaʿbah. Purifying the Kaʿbah includes not only keeping its physical premises clean but also guarding its integrity as a center of monotheism. The Kaʿbah is to be kept pure so that (1) the pilgrims can perform the rite of circumambulation at it (the Kaʿbah is the only mosque in Islam that is circumambulated); (2) those wishing to retreat to the Kaʿbah for a period of time for purposes of prayer and meditation may do so; and (3) people may bow and prostrate themselves—that is, perform the prayer—in it. Incidentally, the verse hints that the acts of bowing (*rukūʿ*) and prostration (*sujūd*) were essential elements of the Abrahamic prayer as well. The verse suggests that a clean environment, desirable in itself, is also conducive to worship with concentration.

Verse 126: Abraham prays that God may make Makkah, where the Kaʿbah is located, a safe and prosperous place. But security and prosperity, desirable in themselves, are here made ancillary to the primary mission of Abraham: The success of that mission requires, as preconditions, a degree of political stability and a degree of economic affluence. Both stability and affluence assume a more or less settled life, and so Abraham's prayer can be taken as a prayer for a settled as opposed to a nomadic life (see section III.3, below). In the pre-Islamic as well as in the Islamic era, Abraham's twofold prayer will seem to have been fulfilled in notable ways:

- Four months in every year came to be designated as the months of peace. During these "sacred months," all fighting was prohibited in order to facilitate the pilgrims' visit from various parts of Arabia to the Kaʿbah in Makkah.
- Hunting, fighting, and taking revenge in the vicinity of the Kaʿbah were forbidden.
- Makkah became a center of trade and commercial activity, whose benefits were reaped in later times by the Quraysh, the tribe that ruled the city at the time of the rise of Islam.

Abraham requests that the believers from among the residents of the land be blessed by God with "produce of various kinds" (*thamarāt*). This, as noted above, is a prayer that God may allow the conditions of nomadic life to evolve into the conditions of a settled life.

To Abraham's request that only the believers be allowed to enjoy what the earth yields, God responds that the disbelievers, too, will receive a share of that provision during worldly life. Abraham, in his request, specifies the believers because, after learning that the Divine promise of leadership of humankind does not extend to the wrongdoers (verse 124), he does not consider it appropriate to include the disbelievers among those for whom he had made the request. God, however, tells him that the issue of the leadership of humankind is distinct from the issue of providing sustenance to humankind and that it is not right to analogize from the former to the latter. In other words, no necessary relationship exists between correct belief and economic prosperity. Put differently, affluence is no proof of Divine approbation.

Verses 127–129: As they build the Kaʿbah, Abraham and Ishmael pray to God (1) to accept the product of their effort (verse 127); (2) to make them *muslims*, that is, "submitters" to God's will (verse 128); (3) to raise a whole community of *muslims* from their progeny (verse 128); and (4) to raise, in that community, a prophet who will teach them scripture and scripture-based wisdom and purify their ideas and thoughts, their morals and habits, and their society and culture (verse 129).

Read together, verses 127–129 would signify that, in building the Kaʿbah, Abraham wished to build a house of worship that would endure as a center of monotheistic worship and continue to serve as a source of guidance and inspiration to people. It is this wish that lies behind the prayer of Abraham and Ishmael for the rise, on the one hand, of a community of *muslims* from among their progeny and, on the other, of a prophet who would bring out the full potential of the monotheistic movement launched by Abraham and his son. In Islam, Muḥammad is regarded as the prophet that Abraham prayed for at the time of the construction of the Kaʿbah. Muḥammad, then, is Abraham's heir, and he was raised by God to complete Abraham's monotheistic mission.

III. Issues

1. The Concept of Trial. The passage opens with a reference to an important Islamic concept. One of the fundamental teachings of the Qurʾān is that God has created human beings in order to put them to the test, their true merit, or moral worth, being determined by their performance on the various tests to which they are put during their lifetime. From this general rule of trial, no one is exempt, not even prophets, as Abraham's example shows. A related point is that each generation has to win its own laurels: Abraham is told in clear terms that God's promise to honor him with leadership will not extend to the wrongdoers in his progeny.

2. Abraham's Character. This passage, like several others in the Qurʾān, speaks of Abraham's steadfast submission to God, of his humility before God, and of his sensitivity to Divine command. Abraham's submission is seen in his carrying out of God's commands. His humility is seen in the supplication made by him and his son at the time of the building of the Kaʿbah; note, especially, the humble urgency in the repetition of the phrase "Our Lord," the self-abasement in the appeal made by father and son to God to accept their act of building of the Kaʿbah and to forgive them for any of their shortcomings in fulfilling His command, and the self-effacing acknowledgment made by the two that the modest task started by them will find consummation at a later time. Abraham's sensitivity to Divine command is seen in that, having learned that God's promise does not extend to the wrongdoers, he modifies his later petition for the Divine grant for sustenance, mentioning only the believers as the prospective recipients of that grant. Abraham's prayer for the continuity of leadership in his progeny, for the provision of sustenance for the residents of the land of the Kaʿbah, and for the rise of a prophet in Arabia shows his solicitude for his offspring. According to the Qurʾānic passage, the prayer for the rise of the prophet is made by Abraham and Ishmael both, but it is likely that the prayer was made by Abraham and that Ishmael, a young boy at that time, joined his father in the act of praying.

3. The Original Setting of the Kaʿbah. According to the passage, the Kaʿbah was built by two persons only—Abraham and his son Ishmael. This suggests that the Kaʿbah was built in a sparsely populated area in which, at that time, Abraham had few followers who might have assisted him in the task of the construction. In Q 14:37, addressing God, Abraham first says that he has "settled some of my offspring in an uncultivated valley" and then prays that God may bless them with produce of various kinds (see section II, verse 126, above). In other words, Abraham is praying for a change of the existing nomadic lifestyle to a settled lifestyle since the latter is much more conducive to the propagation of the kind of message Abraham has been charged with spreading.

IV. Literary Notes

1. The Demonstrative "This." The use of the demonstrative pronoun "this" in verse 126 and the omission of the same demonstrative in verse 127 are notable. In verse 126, Abraham prays to God, saying, "My Lord, make *this* a secure land." One might have expected him to say, "Make *this land* peaceful." The absence of a noun that "this" would qualify suggests that the area in which Abraham was building the Kaʿbah did not have much by way of population or resources and was, consequently, best described by means of a nondescript "this." In verse 127, Abraham and Ishmael, referring to the Kaʿbah they have built, pray to God to "accept from us"—leaving out the object of the verb "accept"—namely, "this" (or "this House"). The omission is an indication of modesty on the part of Abraham and Ishmael, for they do not seem to think much of the effort they have put into the construction of the Kaʿbah.

2. Bifurcation of the Subject. That young Ishmael played a secondary, yet significant, role in the building of the Kaʿbah is indicated by the construction of the Arabic text in verse 127: "And when Abraham was raising the foundations of the House, and Ishmael, too." The interposition of the object—"the foundations of the House"—between the two components of the subject—Abraham and Ishmael—assigns to young Ishmael a role subsidiary to Abraham's in the construction of the Kaʿbah: Abraham was the main builder, with Ishmael assisting his father with odd jobs.

V. The Bible on Abraham and Ishmael

The opening statement of the Qurʾānic passage—namely, that Abraham faithfully carried out God's commands—has an obvious parallel in Genesis 26:5, in which God says that "Abraham obeyed my voice and kept my charge, my commandments, and my laws." The Hebrew for "voice" in this verse is *qōl*, which is a near synonym of the *kalimāt* of Q 2:124. The only difference—if it is a real difference—between these two words is that, while, in context, both mean "command," this meaning is embedded in the Arabic *kalimāt* but made explicit in the Hebrew *qōl*. The Qurʾānic statement about God making Abraham "a leader of humankind" is, likewise, paralleled in Biblical verses that speak of Abraham becoming the progenitor of "a great nation" (Genesis 12:2; see also 13:16; 16:10; 18:17–18). Notably, a similar promise is made in the Bible to Ishmael (Genesis 17:20; 21:13, 18). The Qurʾānic account of Abraham building a house of worship in Makkah does not have a Biblical counterpart. As for Ishmael, the Bible calls him "a wild ass of a man" (Genesis 16:14), that is, a nomad. The Qurʾānic mention of Ishmael helping his father build the Kaʿbah suggests, however, that, after the building of the Kaʿbah at least, Ishmael lived a settled life. Muslims regard Ishmael as a prophet. In the Bible, Ishmael, while not called a prophet, receives the favor of his father, who prays to God, "O that Ishmael might live in your sight" (Genesis 17:18), and is, furthermore, blessed by God (Genesis 17:20; also 21:18, 20).

4 True Piety

2 Cow 177

It is no piety that you should turn your faces to the east or the west. Piety, rather, is theirs who believe in God, the Last Day, the angels, the Book, and the prophets; who give money, in spite of their love of it, to relatives, to orphans, to the needy, to travelers, and to beggars, and in the cause of slaves; who establish the prayer and give *zakāh*; and who always keep their commitments when they make them, and, in particular, are steadfast in hunger and illness and at the time of war. These are the ones who have proven truthful, and these are the godfearing.

Sūrah 2 is Madīnan.

I. Introduction

This verse, one of the pithiest in the Qur'ān, provides a fairly complete overview of Islam: After rejecting a certain understanding of piety, it explains what true piety is. In the course of that explanation, it lists the fundamental articles of the Islamic faith, identifies the primary rituals of Islam, underscores the importance of spending one's wealth for social causes, and highlights several aspects of the ideal Islamic character.

The word "piety," a translation of the Arabic *birr*, has the sense of "dutifulness," which, in fact, is the literal meaning of the Latin word *pietās*, the origin of the English word "piety."

II. Commentary

The verse opens with the statement that piety does not consist in facing—that is, while praying—east or west. In other words, piety cannot be achieved simply by performing a few mechanical motions in worship (see section IV, below). The verse lists a few requirements that have to be fulfilled before piety can be attained.

In the first place, one must subscribe to certain articles of faith. In light of the Qur'ān's explanation of them, the five articles of faith listed in the verse may be briefly explained as follows:

- Belief in God means belief in an eternal, living, omnipotent, and omniscient God who is one and unique, who created the world and controls it, who guides humanity and deals with it in accordance with the principle of merciful justice.

- Belief in the afterlife means belief in the Last Day, resurrection, judgment, and heaven and hell.
- Belief in angels means belief in an order of creation that devotedly serves God and diligently carries out the tasks assigned to it by God, including the task of conveying Divine revelation to prophets.
- Belief in the Book means belief in the revealed scripture (the singular "Book" is used generically, meaning "revealed books," that is, all scriptures, though the singular both suggests the unity of the contents of all scriptures and makes a pointed reference to a particular scripture—namely, the Qurʾān—which the People of the Book were invited to accept as Divine revelation).
- Belief in the prophets means belief in certain individuals who were chosen by God to communicate His message to humankind and who lived model lives.

Next, the verse speaks of using one's financial resources for the well-being of several categories of people. The first on the list are relatives—in consideration of the principle that charity begins at home. The very next category to be mentioned is that of orphans, signifying that orphans are not to be regarded as a burden but are, rather, to be cared for as if they were relatives. The needy are those who, besides possessing few resources, lack the ability to engage effectively in the economic struggle. Travelers, being away from home, may find themselves in a situation in which they would need financial help. Beggars, as opposed to the needy, are those who petition for help; they, too, have a claim on one's generosity. Slavery was a deep-rooted institution at the time of the Qurʾān, and Islam, using a graduated approach to implement its program of abolishing slavery, urged Muslims to set free the slaves they themselves had and help slaves owned by others to win their freedom.

The two most important rituals of Islam are the prayer and *zakāh*. The prayer—the reference is to the formal, obligatory prayer—is performed five times a day, at set hours. *Zakāh* is the mandatory donation made by people of some means to help the poor and needy and to serve other social causes. Since the text mentions *zakāh* separately from the spending of one's wealth on orphans and others, it follows that the money to be spent for social causes is above and beyond the money to be given as *zakāh*.

Of the character traits enumerated in the verse, the first is fulfillment of commitments. *ʿAhd*, the Arabic word used in the verse for "commitment," is general in its import and encompasses commitments made to God, to fellow human beings or society, and even to oneself. *ʿAhd* has the clear religious and moral overtones of the word "covenant."

The phrase "who always keep their commitments when they make them" is notable. The Arabic particle here translated as "when" has the force of "once," making the powerful suggestion that the people in question, since they are fully aware of the responsibility attached to making a commitment, are reluctant to make one at the drop of a hat, but *once* they make a commitment, they keep it at all costs.

The last three qualities mentioned in the verse resonated strongly with the Arabian life and culture of the times of the Qurʾān: They consist in remaining steadfast in three representative situations: (1) at a time of scarcity of resources (hunger, when it took the form of famine, tried the patience not only of individuals, but also of clans and tribes), (2) in illness (physical debility rendered it difficult for one to withstand the rigors of a harsh environment or to defend oneself against enemies), and (3) in case of war (which was not infrequent).

"These are the ones who have proven truthful"—that is, it is people who possess all the above-listed qualifications whose conduct is in complete accord with their professed conviction and who can be said to have true integrity of character. And it is these people, the verse adds, who can be said to be truly godfearing.

III. Piety and Godfearingness

The key term in the passage is "piety," a translation of the Arabic *birr*, a much more comprehensive term than its English counterpart. The essence of *birr* is fidelity: *birr* is faithfully to carry out one's obligations. The word is used to denote such acts as keeping a promise, fulfilling an oath, and discharging one's duty to, for example, one's parents by being obedient to them and treating them affectionately. As noted earlier, piety does not consist in facing a particular direction while performing the obligatory prayer (the direction of prayer is called *qiblah*), for God is free from all geographical constraint, and it is wrong to insist that He can be approached only from one direction and from no other. Piety, in other words, is not a function of dry, spiritless formalism (see next section). Having rejected the narrow view of piety, the verse gives details of what true piety is—a synthesis of right belief, right practice, and right behavior. Notably, the verse identifies piety with godfearingness. After giving details of what qualifies people as pious, the verse ends with these words: "These are the ones who have proven truthful, and these are the godfearing." Since most of the verse gives details of the qualities of a pious person, one expects the verse to end with "and these are the pious." The strategic replacement of the expected "pious" with "godfearing" indicates the interpenetration, according to the Qurʾān, of the semantic areas of "piety" and "godfearingness."

IV. Critique of Formalism and Renunciation

The tone of a statement often furnishes a clue to—may even be part of—the meaning of a statement. The tone of the opening statement of the verse ("It is no piety . . . ") suggests that the Qurʾān is being critical of a certain attitude.

One of the issues discussed in sūrah 2 is that of *qiblah*. The performance of the daily prayers had been made obligatory in the Makkan period (610–622), and

Jerusalem was the *qiblah* that the Muslims faced in their prayers, hence Islam's designation of Jerusalem as the first *qiblah*. When the Prophet and his followers emigrated to Madīnah, the *qiblah* was changed to Makkah, where the Kaʿbah, the mosque built by Abraham (see chapter 3, "Abraham Builds the Kaʿbah and Prays for a Prophet"), stood. The change was criticized by the People of the Book—Jews and Christians—and their criticism is reported in verse 142 of this sūrah. To the criticism, the same verse responds with these words: "To God belong the east and the west; He guides whomever He wishes to a Straight Path." The words "east and west" in the verse under study, thus, make reference to the same words in verse 142, and this enlarges the context of verse 177. The Qur'ānic reply to the criticism made by Jews and Christians amounts to saying that, just as the first *qiblah*—that of the Temple in Jerusalem—was appointed by God, so the second *qiblah*—that of the Kaʿbah in Makkah—has been appointed by God, God being free to change the direction of prayer since all directions belong to Him. In other words, the sole reason why a particular *qiblah* becomes sacred is God's appointment of it as *qiblah*. But Jews and Christians are not the only ones who are being admonished; Muslims, too, are being told that, now that Makkah has been declared the *qiblah*, they must not fall into the trap of thinking that all they have to do to qualify as good believers is to face Makkah in their prayers. Facing Makkah is necessary, but not sufficient: the most important thing is to have the right belief, perform the right actions, and cultivate the right attitude.

In saying that piety is not a matter of turning one's face toward the east or the west, then, the verse is saying that religion is not merely a matter of performing superficial rituals, like that of facing a certain direction in prayer, that true religion is form imbued with spirit, or rather, a synthesis of sincere faith and devoted action. The verse is critical of religious formalism.

The verse puts great emphasis on social action. Piety is not reached through renunciation of the world and reclusive worship of God, but through active involvement in society, through meeting one's social obligations, especially through generous spending of one's economic resources for the welfare of others. Thus, faith in God and worship of God must manifest themselves in faith in humanity and service to it, such translation of belief into practice being a true measure of devotion to God and of piety, the essence of religion.

V. View of Wealth

The verse says that the truly pious are those who, among other things, spend their wealth, "in spite of their love of it," on those who need financial assistance. This short phrase gives an insight into the Islamic view of wealth. From an Islamic viewpoint, money is not the root of all evils; rather, it can be the source of much good. In fact, one of the Arabic words for "wealth," used elsewhere in the Qur'ān, is *khayr*, "good." The phrase "in spite of their love of it" also implies that love of wealth in itself is quite natural and, therefore, not blameworthy, that there is nothing wrong with possessing and acquiring wealth as long as one remembers that wealth, being *khayr*, is to be used for good purposes.

VI. Literary Notes

1. The phrase "Piety, rather, is theirs who . . . " is a translation of *wa-lākinna l-birra man*, which, with the word *birru* understood after *al-birra*, could be translated as "Piety, rather, is the piety of those who . . . ." The actual construction of the original text, however, gives a meaning somewhat different from both translations. It would literally translate as "Piety, rather, is those who . . . ." In the Qurʾānic text, in other words, piety, instead of being posited as an attribute of certain people, is identified with them, the people in question being presented as an embodiment of piety, the verse thus saying: If you wish to find out what piety is, then just look at these people, for they are piety incarnate.

2. The phrase "in the cause of slaves" is, in the original text, *fī r-riqāb*, literally, "in necks." "Necks" here stands for the "necks of slaves"—or for "slaves." Since a part (necks) is made to stand for the whole (slaves), the phrase represents a case of metonymy.

5 A Battle Between the Israelites and the Philistines

2 Cow 246–251

246Did you not see the chiefs of the Children of Israel after Moses, when they said to a prophet of theirs, "Appoint a king for us and we will fight in the way of God"?

He said, "Might it be that, if fighting is prescribed for you, you will not fight?"

They said, "And why would we not fight in the way of God when, already, we have been expelled from amidst our homes and our children?"

But when fighting was prescribed for them, they turned away, with the exception of a few of them. And God is well aware of the wrongdoers.

247And their prophet said to them, "God, indeed, has appointed Ṭālūt your king." They said, "How can he be king over us when we have a greater right to kingship than he? And he has not been given an abundance of wealth either!"

He said, "God, indeed, has chosen him over you, and has endowed him generously in respect of knowledge and physique. And God gives His kingship to whomever He wishes; and God is Wide-Ranging, All-Knowing."

248And their prophet said to them, "The sign of his kingship is that the Ark will come to you, in it being tranquility from your Lord and remnants from what the family of Moses and the family of Aaron have left behind; angels will be carrying it. In this, indeed, there will be a sign for you, if you would be believers."

249So, when Ṭālūt departed with his troops, he said, "God is going to test you by means of a river, so those who drink from it are not of me, and those who do not taste it are of me—excepting those who have a scoopful taken with one hand." But they drank from it, with the exception of a few of them. So, when he and those who believed along with him crossed it, they said, "We are powerless today before Goliath and his troops." Those who thought they were going to meet God said, "How often a small group has overcome a large group, by God's will! And God is with the steadfast!"

250When they came out to face Goliath and his troops, they said, "Our Lord, pour out steadfastness upon us, and make our feet firm, and help us against the disbelieving people."

251And so they routed them, by God's will, and David killed Goliath, and God gave him kingdom and wisdom, and taught him of what He wishes. And were it not for God's repulsing of some people by means of others, the earth would be filled with corruption. God, however, is bountiful to the people of the world.

Sūrah 2 is Madīnan.

I. Introduction

This passage narrates an event from the post-Mosaic period of Jewish history. Around 1000 BCE, according to the Bible (from which we can borrow some details to flesh out the Qur'ānic account), the Israelites were sorely oppressed by their enemies, especially the Philistines, and, as a result, had fallen into disarray. In the Qur'ānic account, the Israelites ask their prophet (called Samuel in the Bible) to appoint a king under whom they may fight and defeat their enemies. After some hesitation, the prophet appoints Ṭālūt (Saul, in the Bible) as king. The Israelites object to Ṭālūt's appointment on the grounds that he neither has a distinguished family background nor possesses much wealth. The prophet responds that Ṭālūt has the intellectual and physical qualities of a ruler, and adds that the return of the Ark of the Covenant, which the Israelites have lost to their enemies, will serve as a sign of the Divine approval of Saul's appointment. The necessary preparations made, Ṭālūt sets out to do battle with the enemy (identified in the Bible as the Philistines). First, however, he tests the resolve of his troops by forbidding them to drink from a certain river they have to cross, allowing them to drink, if they must, no more than what they can scoop up in one hand. The majority of the troops fail the test and, on facing the Philistines in the battlefield, are terrified at the prospect of engaging the formidable army led by Jālūt (Arabic for the Biblical Goliath). But a small number of troops, putting their faith in God, express their determination to fight. The Israelites defeat the enemy, with David, who kills Goliath, later becoming king and prophet of the Israelites. The passage concludes with a statement about God's merciful law of keeping the world free of large-scale corruption by counterbalancing aggressor groups by means of other groups.

II. Commentary

Verse 246: "Did you [sing.] not see?" is a translation of the Arabic *a-lam tara*, which, in a context like the present one, expresses surprise. It is not necessary that the event being referred to be one that has actually been witnessed by the addressee. The use of the phrase signifies that the event is well attested and is as good as one witnessed by the addressee, such that it would suffice to call it to the addressee's mind by means of "Did you not see?" Usually, the phrase is used in Arabic to address a group of people, with the singular pronoun "you" signifying, as here, that each member of the group is being addressed individually. Accordingly, the addressee in this verse does not have to be the Prophet Muḥammad; it is the Muslim community—or rather, each member of the Muslim community taken individually—that is being addressed.

As noted above (see section I), the verse refers to the Israelite chiefs' demand that the prophet—whom we can now call Samuel—appoint for them a king under whose command they may fight an organized war to recover the lands they have lost to their enemies and, in this way, restore their national pride and honor. The use of the word "chiefs" (Arabic: *mala'*) is meant to compound the surprise expressed by the phrase "Did you not see?"—for the implication is that the chiefs of Israel, supposedly wiser than ordinary Israelites, should have been the last ones to make the demand for a king, for, as the prophet's response quoted by the Qur'ān suggests, the lack of a king was not a sufficient explanation of the Israelites' reluctance to fight against their enemies. Samuel's question—"Might it be that, if fighting is prescribed for you, you will not fight?"—obviously expresses certain reservations on his part: Samuel knows that the weakness of the Israelites as a nation is not that they lack a king but that they lack the necessary resolve to face the hardships of war, and so his question barely hides his strong suspicion that the Israelites will drag their feet when they actually receive the command to fight. To his question, however, the Israelites reply that they have cause enough to fight against their enemies, who have expelled them from their homes and taken their offspring prisoner, separating parents from children. But the Qur'ān says that, upon facing the enemy in the battlefield, most of the Israelites—here called "wrongdoers"—failed the test.

Between "when, already, we have been expelled from amidst our homes and our children" and "But when fighting was prescribed for them," there is an omission, namely: The prophet prayed to God for the appointment of a king for Israel, and God, granting the prayer, appointed a king.

Verse 247: With this verse begins the detailed report of the event in question. Told by their prophet that God had appointed Ṭālūt their king, the Israelites raise two objections: (1) Ṭālūt does not belong to a distinguished Israelite family, a member of such a family having greater right to appointment as king, and (2) Ṭālūt is not very rich. The irrelevance of the objections is rather obvious, for the need for a king, really, was the need for a competent ruler and general who could win wars for Israel, and, as the next part of verse 247 indicates, Ṭālūt preeminently possessed the requisite military knowledge. Since, moreover, he had an impressive physique, Ṭālūt would have a commanding presence on the battlefield and would be, in terms of physical appearance, an adequate match for the formidable-looking Philistine general, Goliath. Above all, Ṭālūt had been chosen by God Himself. God is Wide-Ranging—that is, He is not subject to the limited perspective to which human beings are hostage—and He is Well-Aware—that is, He knows exactly who would be most competent to fill the office of king for Israel.

In intoning "God, indeed, has chosen him over you," one needs to stress "God" in order to bring out the nuance of Samuel's statement. Samuel is saying: Do not argue with me, for it is *not I but God* who has appointed Ṭālūt king.

"And God gives His kingship to whomever He wishes." That is: God gives rulership to whomever He wishes, for all sovereignty or dominion belongs to Him, and He can put whomever He likes in a position of power. The statement does not mean that God awards rulership arbitrarily, for the verse itself provides the rationale for God's awarding of rulership to Ṭālūt. It only signifies that God's awarding of rulership—or of any other gift, for that matter—should not be judged by the inadequate and skewed yardsticks at the disposal of human beings: being wise, God acts wisely, but people, like the Israelite chiefs in the case of God's appointment of Ṭālūt as king, may not always be able to fathom the wisdom of Divine decrees. The statement also makes the important point that rulership is not by heredity but is for God to award to whomever He wishes.

Verse 248: This verse suggests that the evidence offered by the prophet Samuel in support of Ṭālūt's kingship as a Divine appointment did not convince the Israelite chiefs completely, and that they demanded further proof. In order fully to convince them, Samuel informs them of an objective sign validating Ṭālūt's kingship: The Ark of the Covenant, a wooden chest that contained certain remnants, or surviving objects, from early Jewish periods and was a source of peace and comfort to the Israelites, will be returned to the Israelites. The Qur'ān does not explain what the "remnants" are, but Jewish sources state that the contents of the Ark contained such items as the staffs of Moses and Aaron and parts of the Tablets of the Torah. "[A]ngels will be carrying it" means that the Ark will return to the Israelites without being led by human hands, an indication that it will be brought back, at God's behest, by angels, who will, as if "carrying" it, safely drive it to the Israelites. Since the Ark gave peace and comfort to the Israelites at times of distress, its return would constitute a decisive sign of God's appointment of Ṭālūt as king, provided the Israelites are minded to believe the sign and accept Ṭālūt as king.

Verses 249–250: There is an omission of some detail between these verses and the preceding verse: The Ark of the Covenant arrives; the Israelites finally accept Ṭālūt's kingship; and, under Ṭālūt, the Israelite army makes ready for combat with the Philistines.

As the Israelite troops depart from their land, Ṭālūt, aware of the weakness of Israelite resolve, decides to put the troops to the test: he would like to determine how many of them would fight to the bitter end and how many would turn tail; he wants to separate the wheat from the chaff. His words, "God is going to test you," show that the test was commissioned by God. He instructs the troops not to drink from a certain river along the way, and to drink, if they must, no more than a scoopful taken with one hand. "But they drank from it" means: Most of the troops drank their fill, failing the test.

"So, when he and those who believed along with him crossed it" means: When Ṭālūt crossed the river in the company of those who, like him, truly believed and had given proof of their firm belief by not drinking from the river. Ṭālūt and his loyal followers cross the river, but those who have failed the test and have lagged behind announce, from across the river, that they lack the ability to fight the mighty army of the Philistines. Those who stand by Ṭālūt, convinced that true strength comes from a firm belief in God and in the afterlife, in which martyrs will meet God and be honored by Him, declare that, often in history, with God's help, an outnumbered but determined army has defeated the enemy. On joining battle, these troops pray to God for steadfastness in combat and for victory over their opponents.

"And God is with the steadfast" (verse 249) may also be taken as a Divine comment rather than as an utterance of the small number of troops that passed the test posed by Ṭālūt.

Verse 251: Again, there is an omission between this verse and the preceding verse, namely: God granted the true believers' prayer for victory, pouring out on them steadfastness, making their feet firm, and giving them victory over the enemy.

This verse provides a summary account of the battle: The Israelites rout the Philistines, the highlight of the battle being the killing of the Philistine general, Goliath, by a young Israelite, David, who is later made both king and prophet by God. The verse closes with the following message: A perpetually dominant nation tends to become oppressive of other nations, and so the bountiful God, in order to counter such a menace, eliminates oppressor nations by means of other nations. Of this universal Divine law concerning the removal of tyranny, elimination of evil, and repulsion of aggression, the Israelites' fight against the Philistines is presented in the Qur'ānic passage as an instance.

David's election by God as both king and prophet means that the functions of king and prophet, formerly exercised separately by Ṭālūt the king and Samuel the prophet, respectively, are now integrated in the person of David. In Islam, accordingly, David is known as a prophet-king, and so is his son Solomon.

Elsewhere, the Qur'ān speaks of David as possessing certain distinctions: he developed a special way of melding iron, perfected the art of making coats of mail, and sang the praises of God in a most beautiful voice (21:79–80; 34:10–11). It is these abilities and skills—or gifts from God, in Qur'ānic perspective—to which reference is made in "and [God] taught him of what He wishes" (on the use of "wishes" instead of the expected "wished," see section IV.5, below).

III. Issues

1. The Ark and the Kaʿbah: The Motif of Liberation. In 622, Muḥammad and his followers emigrated from Makkah, where they had been a persecuted fledgling community, to Madīnah, where they became a dominant majority. Before the emigration to Madīnah, Jerusalem, the city of the prophets, had served as the *qiblah*, or direction of prayer, for Muslims. After the emigration, a Qur'ānic revelation (2:142–150) changed the *qiblah* to the Kaʿbah, which had been built by the monotheist Abraham (see chapter 3, "Abraham Builds the Kaʿbah and Prays for a Prophet"), and this change generated fears among the Quraysh that the Muslims, who claimed to be the true heirs of Abraham, would now lay claim to their new *qiblah*, the Kaʿbah. Already in sūrah 2, it had been intimated to the Muslims that they would have to make sacrifices to liberate the Kaʿbah (verses 153–156). With this possibility in mind, Q 2:246–251 now signals to the Muslims that they should be ready to fight against the Quraysh to gain control of the Kaʿbah, their *qiblah*, just as the Israelites fought against the Philistines to retrieve the Ark of the Covenant, which enjoyed the status of *qiblah* among the Israelites.

2. A Divine Law. The second half of verse 251 lays down a Divine law. At different periods in history, different nations have dominated the world scene, but no nation is ever allowed by God to monopolize forever a position of supremacy over the rest of the world, for, in that case, such a nation would forever keep other nations in subjection. From time to time, therefore, God purges the world of evil and wickedness, and He does so through human agency: He removes from the world scene one group of people—one that has become oppressive—by means of some other group, and, if this latter group, too, becomes oppressive, then God removes it by means of yet another group. "These fortunes of time [literally, 'days']—We shuffle them around among people," Q 3:140 represents God as saying.

IV. Literary Notes

1. Syllepsis. Verse 246 contains an instance of syllepsis, in which one word is used with two other words, though it is properly used with only one member of the pair, with the word that would go with the second member indicated by the context. Responding to a question asked by the prophet Samuel, the Israelites say that they have reason enough to fight since "we have been *expelled* from amidst our homes and our children." The underlying sentence is: "We have been *expelled* from our homes and *separated* from our children." The Arabic verb here translated as "expelled" is *ukhrijnā*, which is properly used with "from our homes" but which points to an unexpressed word, such as "separated," that may properly be used with "from our children."

2. Prolepsis. In verse 247, Samuel says to the Israelites, "God, indeed, has appointed Ṭālūt your king." The Arabic sentence employs two intensifying particles, *inna* at the beginning and *qad* in the middle. The resulting emphasis, here rendered by means of "indeed," is meant to preempt an objection by the Israelites, to whom the news of Ṭālūt's appointment as king is being broken. In other words, the Arabic text is proleptically saying: God knows that, given Ṭālūt's humble background, you will be reluctant to accept his appointment as king, but God will appoint him regardless of any reservations you may have, and so Ṭālūt is hereby appointed king, and you are expected to accept him as such.

3. Litotes. One of the objections made by the Israelite chiefs to the kingship of Ṭālūt is that "he has not been given an abundance of wealth either" (verse 247). The phrase is an instance of litotes, or understatement, since the objecters really mean that Ṭālūt is quite poor. By remarking that Ṭālūt does *not* have a great deal of wealth instead of saying that he is poor, the Israelite chiefs foreground the idea that possession of abundant wealth is essential to occupying kingly office.

4. Summary and Detail. The Qurʾān sometimes outlines a story before presenting it in detail, and this is the case in the passage under study. In verse 246, after reproducing the initial interchange between the Israelites and the prophet Samuel, the Qurʾān remarks: "But when fighting was prescribed for them, they turned away, with the exception of a few of them. And God is well aware of the wrongdoers." Without providing too much detail—without giving the show away, so to speak—the verse summarizes a story, details of which are provided in verses 247–251.

5. From Anecdote to Rule. Verse 251 says that, after David had killed Goliath, God made him king and prophet "and taught him of what He *wishes*." One feels that "wished" rather than "wishes" should have been used. Actually, by using the present tense rather than the past, the Qur'ān is universalizing the anecdotal, the underlying sentence being something like this: "and taught him of what He *wished, just as, in all other cases, too, He teaches people what He* wishes." With the italicized explanatory part taken as understood, we are left with "and [God] taught him of what He wishes."

6. Significant Construction. The phrase "and [God] taught him [David] of what He wishes" is significant in two other ways. The ambiguity of "what He wishes" points to the distinction of the knowledge imparted to David: what God taught David was of such special merit that it cannot be explained fully in words, and is, therefore, best referred to in such general terms as "what He wishes." Further, the preposition *of* in the phrase, technically called partitive, signifies that David, though he was taught a great deal by God, received only a very small portion of the knowledge that God possesses. In other words, the preposition underscores Divine omniscience by contrasting it with David's limited knowledge.

V. Comparison with the Biblical Account

Following the sequence of the incidents in the Qur'ānic passage, we will note the similarities and differences between the Biblical and Qur'ānic accounts of the battle between the Israelites and the Philistines.

1. The Israelite Demand for a King. In both the Bible and the Qur'ān, the Israelites demand that their prophet—who, as we noted earlier (section I, above) is unnamed in the Qur'ān but is identified as Samuel in the Bible—appoint a king for them (1 Samuel 8:4–5). In both scriptures, the prophet shows reluctance to accede to the demand. The reluctance, hinted at by the prophet's question quoted in the Qur'ānic passage under study—"Might it be that, if fighting is prescribed for you, you will not fight?" (verse 246)—is evidenced in much more detail in the Bible, where, responding to Samuel's prayer for a king for the Israelites, God says: "Listen to the voice of the people in all that they say to you; for they have not rejected you, but they have rejected me from being king over them" (1 Samuel 8:7; see also 12:17: "and you shall know and see that the wickedness that you have done in the sight of the Lord is great in demanding a king for yourselves"). That the Israelite demand for a king is made under foreign influence and represents a certain lack of faith or trust in God is made quite apparent in the Bible (12:12). Samuel tries to dissuade the Israelites from making the demand, "But the people refused to listen to the voice of Samuel; they said, 'No! but we are determined to have a king over us, so that we may be like other nations, and that our king many govern us and go out before us and fight our battle'" (8:19–20). It can be presumed that the Qur'ān has a very similar understanding of the Israelites' demand for a king and of the prophet Samuel's displeasure at the demand.

2. Ṭālūt's Appointment. In the Qur'ānic passage, when the prophet appoints Ṭālūt king at God's behest, the Israelite chiefs object, saying that Ṭālūt is unqualified to hold kingly office. Their objection—"How can he be king over us when we have a greater right to kingship than he?"—alludes to Ṭālūt's humble family origins. In the Bible, it is made very clear that the king-designate, Saul, does not come from a tribe or clan known to have provided leaders for Israel in the past. In the Bible, in fact, Saul himself is shown to be acutely conscious of his lack of social distinction, and, on being told by Samuel that he is the hope of Israel at this dark hour, says: "I am only a Benjaminite, from the least of the tribes of Israel, and my family is the humblest of all the families of the tribe of Benjamin" (1 Samuel 9:21). In the Qur'ān, to the Israelites' objection to Ṭālūt's appointment, the prophet replies that Ṭālūt more than meets the mental and physical qualifications needed for leading the Israelites and, most important, has been appointed king by God (see section II, verse 247, above). In the Bible, too, the Israelites raise an objection to Saul's appointment as king and Samuel deals with the objection in roughly the same terms as the prophet in the Qur'ān does. Some of the details in the Biblical account are, however, different. To begin with, Samuel presents the king-designate before the Israelites and says, "'Do you see the one whom the Lord has chosen? There is no one like him among all the people.' And all the people shouted, 'Long live the king!' " (1 Samuel 10:24). Samuel's rhetorical question—"Do you see the one whom the Lord has chosen?"—hints that, at least, some people are not happy at Saul's appointment. This is borne out by the report only a few verses later: "But some worthless fellows said, 'How can this man save us?' They despised him and brought him no present. But he held his peace" (10:27). It appears, though, that the objection to Saul's appointment was made by more than a few individuals, that the objecters included some influential people as well, for the Bible further reports: "The people said to Samuel, 'Who is it that said, "Shall Saul reign over us?" Give them to us so that we may put them to death'" (11:12). In view of this widespread challenge to Saul's appointment, Samuel instructs the people to reconfirm their acceptance of Saul as king: "Samuel said to the people, 'Come, let us go to Gilgal and there renew the kingship.' So all the people went to Gilgal, and there they made Saul king before the Lord in Gilgal" (11:14–15).

Incidentally, the name *Ṭālūt* signifies height or tallness, and this is how the Bible describes Saul: "he stood head and shoulders above everyone else" (1 Samuel 9:2). It seems that the Bible uses the proper name Saul, whereas the Qur'ān uses the nickname Ṭālūt.

3. The Ark of the Covenant. The Ark of the Covenant, along with the remnants it contained—remnants associated with some of the most revered figures of Jewish history, such as Moses and Aaron—had a special importance in Israelite religious life.

The Ark was placed in the Tabernacle or in the Temple, and its presence on the battlefield gave courage to the Israelites. Its capture by the Philistines in a battle was construed as the departure of glory from Israel (1 Samuel 4:10–22).

According to the Bible, the Philistines, soon after capturing the Ark, decided to return it to the Israelites because its presence in their lands had caused deadly illness and great panic (1 Samuel 5). Placing the Ark on a cart pulled by two cows, they "send it off, and let it go its way" (6:7–8), and "[t]he cows went straight in the direction of [the Israelite town of] Beth-shemesh" (6:12). In the Qur'ān, the return of the Ark to the Israelites happens much later than it does in the Bible and is called a sign of God's approval of Samuel's designation of Ṭālūt as king, with the Ark's safe return foretold as "angels will be carrying it" (2:248).

4. The Test. Considering the Israelites' performance in recent wars, Ṭālūt thought it advisable to test the Israelites' commitment to fighting. The test, which was meant to mark off the sheep from the goats, consisted in the command to the Israelite troops to refrain from drinking water from a certain river—and to drink, if they had to, only as much as they could scoop up with a single hand. Most of the troops failed the test, giving a clear indication that they would not be able to withstand the rigors of the battle. In fact, they made no secret of their fear of Goliath and his army. A small number of the troops, however, passed the test and expressed their resolve to fight.

The Bible, too, mentions a test to which Saul puts his troops (1 Samuel 14:24). A minor difference between the Qur'ānic and Biblical tests is that, in the former, the troops are asked not to drink water, whereas, in the latter, they are asked not to eat food. A major difference is that, in the Bible, the test is given during the battle and is intended to motivate the troops to concentrate on destroying the enemy and the whole army fails it; in the Qur'ān, the test is given before the battle and is intended to determine the troops' commitment, and a small number of troops passes the test, even though the majority fails it.

5. Israelite Victory and David's Distinction. On setting out to meet Goliath's army, the Israelite troops who pass the test posed by Ṭālūt pray to God to give them strength and bless them with victory. They defeat the enemy, with David killing Goliath. God makes David a king and also blesses him with wisdom—the Arabic word for "wisdom," *ḥikmah*, here denotes prophethood (Q 17:55 explicitly calls David a prophet, to whom was given the revelation of Psalms). Moses had combined, in his person, both the religious office and the political office: he was both a prophet and a leader. Eventually, the two offices were split from each other. Just before David, prophethood was vested in one individual—Samuel—and kingship, in another—Saul. David, according to the Qur'ān, had the distinction of reintegrating the two roles of prophet and ruler in a single person. The phrase "And [God] taught him of what He wishes" in verse 251 refers to the arts and crafts at which David was known to be an expert (see section II, verse 251, above).

VI. Concluding Remarks

This passage highlights, in a striking way, the importance of the Bible as an aid to Qur'ānic exegesis; it shows unmistakably that the Qur'ān has stakes in the Bible. Notwithstanding some notable differences that exist between the Biblical and Qur'ānic accounts of the battle between the Israelites and the Philistines, the two accounts share significant common ground. The passage underscores the need for scholars—especially Muslim scholars—of the Qur'ān to make a systematic study of the Bible in order to make use of this source in explicating the Islamic Scripture.

6 The Throne Verse

2 Cow 255

God—there is no god but He, the Living, the Great Sustainer. Neither drowsiness nor sleep overtakes Him. To Him belongs what is in the heavens and what is in the earth. Who is the one who would intercede with Him—except by His permission? He knows what is in front of them and what is behind them. And they cannot encompass any part of His knowledge, except what He should wish. His throne extends over the heavens and the earth, and keeping watch over them does not overwhelm Him. And He is the Exalted One, the Great.

Sūrah 2 is Madīnan.

I. Introduction

This verse, known as the Throne Verse, is a classic statement of Islamic monotheism. In the immediately preceding verse in the sūrah, the believers are urged to spend of their wealth in the way of God before the coming of Judgment Day, "on which there shall be no trading deal, no friendship, and no intercession"—that is, on which nothing except good actions will salvage one. The idea that intercession, to the exclusion of good actions, is sufficient for salvation is obviously incompatible with the Islamic doctrine of monotheism, which includes the notion that, in the hereafter, God, and God alone, will pass judgment on human beings. This latter notion necessarily excludes the thought that one is assured of salvation as long as one has, in one's corner, certain intercessors whose petition for salvation on one's behalf will not be turned down by God (see section II, below). Thus, the mention of intercession in verse 255 paves the way for a detailed statement about monotheism.

On the basis of several *aḥādīth* and other reports, many consider the Throne Verse the greatest verse of the Qur'ān. Most Muslims memorize it at an early age and recite it on a variety of occasions. It is a favorite with Qur'ānic calligraphers.

II. Commentary

"God—there is no god but He." This formulaic phrase is almost identical to the first half of the Islamic declaration of faith, *Lā ilāha illā llāh*, "There is no god but God." It categorically affirms that no being or object other than God is deity and that God alone is, therefore, worthy of worship. Thus, the verse denies that statues and images can, in any sense, partake of divinity; that God can beget or be begotten; that the Godhead can admit of plurality or division; or that nature or any part of it can be God.

"The Living, the Great Sustainer." God, other than whom there is no deity, is a living being in the sense that He exists by Himself or in His own right and has always existed, and in the sense that He has personality and is not just a philosophical principle or a theoretical abstraction. Not subject to death, He is eternally living. The Divine attribute of life, as understood here, denies that a living God can die, can die and live again, or can go through repeated deaths and live after each death.

"Great Sustainer" is a translation of *Qayyūm*, which means both "one who is self-sustaining" and "one who sustains others." This attribute of God rejects the deification of those beings and objects that are incapable of sustaining themselves, not to speak of sustaining others, or are, in some way, deficient in their ability to sustain themselves or others without the help of other forces or agencies. In philosophical language, *Qayyūm* signifies that God's existence is absolute, whereas the existence of everything else is contingent—contingent on God, that is. The Arabic word is emphatic in meaning, hence its rendering as "Great Sustainer."

"Neither drowsiness nor sleep overtakes Him." Clear in itself, this statement is subtly connected to the preceding phrase—"the Living, the Great Sustainer." In drowsiness, one is at least partly unconscious, whereas, in sleep, one is, metaphorically, if not literally, dead, and God would not be fully living if He experienced drowsiness or sleep. Likewise, drowsiness or sleep would impair God's ability to sustain the universe—in fact, to sustain Himself. The statement means, then, that God, the sustainer of all, is never unmindful or neglectful of His creation.

"To Him belongs what is in the heavens and what is in the earth." God is the creator, owner, and controller of all things, so all things come under His jurisdiction. As such, all those claims are false that attribute creation to anyone other than God, vest ownership of any part of the universe in anyone other than God, or regard anyone other than God as sharing control of any part of existence.

"Who is the one who would intercede with Him—except by His permission?" The question is expected to elicit a negative response: None can intercede with God—except by His permission. God is the only ruler of the entire universe, and His decrees are not subject to repeal, modification, or challenge by anyone else. On the Day of Judgment, He alone will pass judgment, and no one will be able to overthrow His verdict. In fact, no one will have even so much power as to intercede on someone's behalf unless God Himself were to permit the intercession. This permission to intercede does not necessarily mean that intercession will, after all, take place, if only by God's permission. In fact, the exact opposite is implied, for the point of the exception drawn by means of "except by His permission" is that the only possible authorization for intercession could have come from God, and God is not going to give the authorization. It should be kept in mind that the verse is rejecting a specific notion of intercession—the notion, namely, that intercession can serve as the sole and exclusive basis of salvation. But does this mean that the Qur'ān would allow at least some types of intercession? This question will be taken up shortly.

"He knows what is in front of them and what is behind them." This can be taken to mean that, while people have only partial knowledge—at best, they know what lies in front of them, and, even then, only what lies within their immediate field of perception, but are ignorant of what lies behind their backs, especially of what is yet in the womb of time—God's knowledge is comprehensive and perfect. The statement can also be understood as having idiomatic force, in which case it would mean that God knows everything—that is, everything that was, is, or will be, whether it is a sensory object, an abstract notion, or anything else. In either case, the meaning is that God is omniscient.

This statement about Divine knowledge is connected with the statement about intercession. Since God is omniscient, no one may intercede with Him since no would-be intercessor can add to God's knowledge or provide Him with information about the intercessee that God does not already possess.

We asked, above, whether some intercession will be allowed in the hereafter. The answer is a conditional yes. Given the Qur'ānic doctrine of salvation, it can be asserted that, on Judgment Day, God will not allow any intercession that will subvert the principle of justice, turning a "pass" into a "fail" or vice versa, for example. One can, however, imagine certain cases—borderline cases, for example—in which permission to intercede may be given, but such permission will only represent an honor conferred by God upon the intercessor, who, otherwise, will have no power to influence God's judgment.

"And they cannot encompass any part of His knowledge, except what He should wish." Far from possessing all of God's knowledge, human beings cannot acquire even part of God's knowledge, unless He himself were to allow it.

"His throne extends over the heavens and the earth." God's sovereignty extends over all existence, and His jurisdiction is universal.

"And keeping watch over them does not overwhelm Him." God is actively keeping watch over the heavens and the earth, and He does so without suffering any fatigue and, therefore, without needing any assistance in carrying out the task.

"And He is the Exalted One, the Great." This statement can have three meanings: (1) God is "Exalted" in the sense that He is above all imperfection, and He is "Great" in the sense that He is the possessor of all perfection. The two attributes would, thus, complement each other. (2) God is too "Exalted" and too

"Great" to be dependent on anyone else. (3) God is too "Exalted" and too "Great" to be judged or evaluated by the ordinary yardsticks used by human beings to size up one another.

III. Focus on Monotheism

The ten component statements into which we have divided the verse all have monotheism as their focal point:

> God *alone* is deity.
>
> God *alone* is the living deity, the Great Sustainer.
>
> God *alone* is free from the constraints of sleep or drowsiness.
>
> God *alone* is the owner and master of all that exists.
>
> God *alone* has the power to judge.
>
> God *alone* is omniscient.
>
> God *alone* is the source of any knowledge possessed by human beings.
>
> God *alone* has jurisdiction over all of existence.
>
> God *alone* takes care of all of existence.
>
> God *alone* is the Exalted One, the Great.

It is easy to see why the Throne Verse should be regarded as an important formulation of the Islamic doctrine of monotheism. According to a *ḥadīth*, the Throne Verse is the equivalent of one-third of the Qurʾān. This is so because monotheism, the main focus of this verse, is one of the three principal themes of the Qurʾān, the other two being prophecy and the afterlife (see chapter 1, "The Essence of the Qurʾān," section III). In respect of its focus on the oneness of God, this verse is comparable to sūrah 112 of the Qurʾān (see chapter 37, "Serving Only God").

7 No Compulsion in the Matter of Religion

2 Cow 256

There is no compulsion in the matter of religion: Guidance has become distinct from misguidance. So he who disbelieves in the Rebel and believes in God has grasped the Firmest Tie, which will not unravel. And God is All-Hearing, All-Knowing.

Sūrah 2 is Madīnan.

I. Introduction

"There is no compulsion in the matter of religion" is one of the relatively well-known Qur'ānic statements. Immediately after making this statement, the Qur'ān offers a rationale for it: Since the revelation has, through explanation, clarification, and repetition, clearly distinguished the path of guidance from the path of misguidance, it is now up to people to choose the one or the other path. The verse presents the addressees with a choice between offering one's allegiance to God and offering it to the "Rebel" (see section II, below), though the wording of the verse is meant to persuade them to submit to God and deny the "Rebel," since submitting to God would give one a secure grounding in faith and earn one salvation.

II. Commentary

The dictum "There is no compulsion in the matter of religion" means that God, having clearly shown human beings both the right path and the wrong path, has left them free to choose the one or the other. The next part of the verse explains why God has not coerced people to take the right path: Truth and falsehood have been made unmistakably distinct from each other, so there is no point in compelling people to choose the right path over the wrong, for human choice, if not free, would lack all merit. Closely connected in thought with this verse is an almost immediately preceding verse, namely, verse 253. The latter part of verse 253 says that God, having furnished people with manifest signs of the truth, could have forcibly eliminated all disagreement or dissension among people but chose not to do so, even though this meant that, using God-given freedom, people not only differed with one another, but also fought and killed one another. The import of verse 253 is not that it was God's wish that people should disagree with one another and fight and kill one another, but that God allowed people to have freedom of opinion and action, even though this freedom came at a cost. And this is also the import of the opening statement of verse 256. Thus, verse 253 anticipates and provides a sort of advance reinforcement of the idea underlying verse 256, namely, that the very fact that many people choose disbelief over belief, or misguidance over guidance, signifies that they have not been compelled by God to take the path of belief or guidance.

The statement "There is no compulsion in the matter of religion" is made in a specific context—that of the conflict between Islam and other religions in Arabia. As such, the Arabic word in the original text, *ad-dīn*, means, strictly speaking, not so much "religion" in general as "*the* religion"—that is, the particular religion called Islam. The verse is the most explicit and most forceful enunciation of the principle that no one may be coerced into accepting Islam, for to do so would be to subvert the freedom of conscience and action granted to human beings by God.

In the original text, the preposition *fī*, "in," in the opening part of the verse is, perhaps, best translated as "in the matter of" rather than as "in" because "in" may give the impression that there is no compulsion in Islam in the sense that Islamic law is not to be implemented through the use of force. All legal systems need the backing of force, and Islam is no exception. In other words, the verse is not speaking of the coercive mechanisms that Islam, like any other system, has to employ to enforce its stipulations in certain spheres of life, but of coercion applied to convert non-Muslims to Islam.

"Rebel" is a translation of *Ṭāghūt*, whose root, *ṭ-gh-w* (or *ṭ-gh-y*), means "to cross the limits, overstep the boundaries," hence "to rebel." In this verse, the word "Rebel" is used as an antonym of "God." As such, the *Ṭāghūt* is any being or power that defiantly sets itself up in opposition to God, demanding allegiance to itself at the expense of God. The Qur'ānic usage does not specify that the *Ṭāghūt* is necessarily a living being, thus leaving open the possibility that the *Ṭāghūt* may be an object, or even an institutionalized entity, that receives the devotion or allegiance of people in opposition to God. The seriousness of the opposition between God and the Rebel is underscored when one notices that the verse uses the verb "to believe" with God and the verb "to disbelieve" with the Rebel ("So he who disbelieves in the Rebel and believes in God"). In other words, one cannot believe in God and the Rebel both, loyalty to God being genuine only if it is exclusive of loyalty to the Rebel. The opposition between God and the *Ṭāghūt* is also evidenced in a number of other Qur'ānic verses (for example, 2:257; 4:59–60; 16:36; 39:17). Thus, a review of the available evidence suggests that the Qur'ān uses the word *Ṭāghūt* in the sense of "one that, or that which, defies God and assumes the position of a rival of God."

This verse is often cited as enshrining the Islamic doctrine of religious tolerance. That Islam upholds religious tolerance is undeniable, but that is not the main point being made in this verse, which talks of the freedom that God has granted human beings to choose the right or the wrong path. The verse does not refer to tolerance that may be extended by one religious community to another. One can, of course, derive the idea of tolerance among religious communities from the idea of the freedom to subscribe to one or another religion, but such a derivative argument may be open to question. It is, therefore, important to keep in mind the precise meaning and thrust of the verse.

"The Firmest Tie" is the one that will not "crack" (the literal meaning of the word *infiṣām* used in the verse), not to speak of breaking. As such, it affords the most secure and reliable grip. Conjuring up the image of one who is firmly grasping a sturdy, unbreakable rope—for it is to such a rope that the "Firmest Tie" belongs—the verse is saying that those who take hold of the "Firmest Tie" will stay on the right path and will not go astray. The verse also means that God is the sheet anchor of those who believe in Him and will not let them down.

The concluding part of the verse means that those who put their faith in God, turning away from the *Ṭāghūt*, put their faith in a being who hears and knows everything and, therefore, will help them when they call upon Him for help. It also implies that those who worship objects or beings other than God worship those who neither hear their devotees nor know that they are being worshipped by the devotees, and, on the Day of Judgment, those worshipped will, if they are living beings, wash their hands of such devotees and will, if they are nonliving beings, be deaf to their devotees' calls for help.

III. Literary Notes

This verse contains an instance of parataxis. It juxtaposes two statements— "There is no compulsion in the matter of religion: Guidance has become distinct from misguidance"—without explicitly establishing a causal or any other type of relationship between them, whereas, as we noted above, the second statement offers a rationale for the two: "There is no compulsion in the matter of religion" *because* "guidance has become distinct from misguidance."

The verse also contains an instance of reverse parallelism: Since guidance comes from God and misguidance, from the Rebel, therefore, in the verse, *guidance* would pair off with *God* and *misguidance*, with the *Rebel*, yielding the structure ABB′A′, thus:

> *Guidance* [A] has become distinct from *misguidance* [B].
> So he who disbelieves in the *Rebel* [B′] and believes in *God* [A′] . . .

8 Spending in the Way of God

2 Cow 261–269

[261]The parable of those who spend their wealth in the way of God is that of a
grain that sprouts seven spikes, each spike with a hundred grains. And God
multiplies it for whomever He wishes; and God is Wide-Ranging, All-Knowing.
[262]Those who spend their wealth in the way of God and, then, do not follow
up what they have spent with favor-reminding or hurt, they shall have their reward
with their Lord; and no fear shall come upon them, and they shall not grieve. [263]A
kind word and forgiveness are better than charity followed by hurt; and God is
Opulent, Forbearing.
[264]O you who have believed, do not nullify your charities by favor-
reminding and hurt—like the one who spends his wealth to make a show before
people and does not believe in God and the Last Day. So his parable is that of a
smooth rock with soil on it; a torrent falls on it and leaves it barren. They will
have no power over any of what they have earned; and God will not guide the
ungrateful people.
[265]And the parable of those who spend their wealth, seeking the pleasure of
God and wishing to fortify themselves, is that of a garden on an elevation on which
falls a torrent and it brings forth double the amount of its produce. And if no torrent
falls on it, then a drizzle; and God observes what you do.
[266]Would any of you like it that he should have a garden of date-palms and
grapes, with streams flowing underneath, having, in it, fruits of all kinds, and age
overtakes him while he has offspring that are weak, and then a whirlwind, with fire
in it, hits it, and it is burned down? Thus does God elucidate His verses to you so
that you may reflect.
[267]O you who have believed, spend of the choice parts of what you have
earned and of what We have brought forth from the earth for you, and do not make
it your aim to spend out of what is of poor quality when you yourselves would not
take it unless you were to shut your eyes to it; and know that God is Opulent,
Worthy of Thankful Praise.
[268]Satan threatens you with poverty and bids you to commit glaring immorality,
whereas God promises you forgiveness from Him and bounty; and God is Wide-
Ranging, All-Knowing. [269]He gives wisdom to whomever He wishes; and he who is

given wisdom is given a great good. And none take remembrance except those possessed of understanding.

Sūrah 2 is Madīnan.

I. Introduction

This passage lays down what may be called the ethic of giving. The phrase "to spend in the way of God" is a Qur'ānic term meaning "to spend one's wealth for religiously approved and socially beneficial causes"—such as defense of the state, welfare of society, or assistance of the needy—with a view to winning the pleasure of God. The context will determine the particular cause in question. But, as is the Qur'ān's wont, once a topic is introduced, ancillary aspects come in for treatment, broadening the scope of the discussion. At about the middle of sūrah 2, the Qur'ān talks about the change of *qiblah*, the direction of prayer, from Jerusalem to Makkah (see chapter 5, "A Battle Between the Israelites and the Philistines"). The Kaʿbah, the newly designated *qiblah*, was under the Quraysh's control at that time, and, earlier in the sūrah, the Qur'ān dropped hints (see 2:190–195, 216–218, 243–251) that the Muslims might have to resort to war to retrieve that *qiblah* from the Quraysh's hands. The theme of war, in turn, led to the theme of financing the war, and this is where the spending of one's wealth in the way of God comes into the picture. In other words, the passage under discussion not only is general in import, but also has a specific referent—that of spending one's wealth to fight in the way of God. Especially relevant in this connection is a verse preceding this passage in the sūrah, namely, verse 245: "Who is the one who will give God a good loan, that He might multiply it manifold? And God diminishes and amplifies; and to Him you will be brought back." Occurring as it does between a verse that contains the command "fight in the way of God" (244) and a verse that speaks of the Israelites' determination to "fight in the way of God" (246)—in this particular instance, to fight against the Philistines—the injunction, in verse 245, to "give God a good loan" comes to mean: Spend your wealth to finance the fighting in the way of God. Verse 245, then, makes up the specific referent of this passage, which, as already indicated, also has the general meaning of spending one's wealth for a variety of religious and social causes.

II. Commentary

Verse 261: This verse speaks of the reward for spending one's wealth in the way of God—it is seven-hundredfold. In one place in the Qur'ān, the reward for a good act is said to be tenfold (6:160). "Tenfold" would appear to be the lower and "seven-hundredfold" the upper limit of such a reward, the difference between the two limits obviously being due to the circumstances under which wealth is spent and the quality of the act performed. But the statement "And God multiplies it for whomever He wishes" suggests that there is no fixed upper limit, that the reward may be greater than seven-hundredfold. And this should not be surprising, the verse seems to be saying, since nothing can take the measure of the bounty of God, who is "Wide-Ranging." Also, God is "All-Knowing," which, in this context, means that He has knowledge of all good acts performed, small or great, so people who spend their wealth for His sake should rest assured that they will receive adequate recompense for their good acts.

The phrase "for whomever He wishes" does not suggest arbitrariness on God's part. Since God's volition is in accord with His wisdom and justice, He will, following the principle of recompense, grant the aforementioned increase in reward only to those who are deserving of it.

Verse 262: It is not uncommon for people who spend wealth on others to expect the latter to dance attendance on them and adopt a groveling attitude toward them. If their expectations are not fulfilled, they try to humiliate the latter by reminding them of their favors to them and by hurting them in other ways. This verse says that spending in the way of God will fetch reward from God only if the act is not accompanied by favor-reminding or hurt, either one of which would rob one of any reward for the ostensibly good act of spending in the way of God and may, on that account, be called a major sin. Only those who fulfill this criterion of selflessness will deserve to enter heaven, where "no fear shall come upon them, and they shall not grieve."

Verse 263: This verse enjoins kind treatment of those in need of financial help. If one is unable to help such people, then one should at least speak kindly to them and show forbearance toward them, especially if such people have been rude or boorish either in asking for help or after having been told that they cannot be helped. Kind treatment of them is much better than giving charity that is followed by haughty, hurtful behavior.

"And God is Opulent, Forbearing." That is: God, possessing riches beyond measure, does not need people's wealth; if He asks them to spend their wealth on the poor, then it is only so that He may reward them for the good act. And He is Forbearing, so He is slow to punish those who follow up their charity with favor-reminding or hurt. But implicit in the word "Forbearing" is a threat also: God is Forbearing not in the sense that He will never punish those who are guilty of favor-reminding or of inflicting hurt, but in the sense that He is giving them another chance to change their attitude, and in the sense that He will take such people to task if they persist in their objectionable behavior.

Verse 264: The opening part of this verse restates the content of verse 262, with three differences. First, unlike verse 262, this verse has a strong admonitory tone. Second, verse 262 lays down a general principle; this verse addresses, in light of that principle, a specific group of people—the believers. Third, by likening one who hurtfully reminds a person of a favor that one has done him or who inflicts hurt on a recipient of a favor to one who lacks true belief in God and the hereafter, this verse underlines the heinousness of those two acts: one who follows up his spending with favor-reminding or infliction of hurt commits the great sin of hypocrisy, which is severely condemned in the Qur'ān.

The point of the parable cited in the verse is that people who follow up their spending of wealth with favor-reminding and infliction of hurt let their spending go to complete waste, for such spending lacks any basis in true faith and, consequently, is like a crop that has grown in a thin layer of soil covering a smooth rock and will be washed away along with the soil when a heavy rain falls. People who spend money with the hypocritical intention of creating an impression of generosity will, on the Day of Judgment, receive no reward for their selfish giving. "God will not guide the ungrateful people" here means: God will not guide such people to the right destination in the hereafter—that is, He will deny them entry into heaven.

Verse 265: This verse praises those who spend in the way of God in order to win God's pleasure and "to fortify themselves"—that is, to strengthen their commitment to their faith so that they are able to serve God even more diligently. The word used in the Arabic text, *tathbīt* ("fortification"), has connotations of standing firm or holding one's ground in the face of difficulties. In the present context, *tathbīt* would imply that one spends money in circumstances of hardship—for example, when one is poor, when there is a famine, or when one puts off satisfying one's own needs in order to help others—for it is such spending that produces *tathbīt*.

This verse likens the spending of those who spend only with the intention of pleasing God and fortifying their commitment to serve God to "a garden on an elevation." A garden located on a relatively high piece of land is safe against floods, receives the proper amount of sun and air, and, consequently, is dense and luxuriant and yields high-quality produce. The verse says that such a garden will, on receiving an adequate amount of rain, bring forth twice its usual produce but will yield a generous crop even if it were to receive a modest amount of rain. In other words, God will give abundant reward for the faith and sincerity with which one spends wealth in the way of God, though the amount of reward will vary in proportion to the degree of faith and sincerity involved.

"And God observes what you do" is meant to reassure those who spend their wealth with good intentions: they should have the confidence that God is aware of their good act and will reward them handsomely for it.

Verse 266: Verse 264 warned that an ostensibly charitable act of spending wealth will be nullified on Judgment Day if it is performed with hypocritical intentions or is followed by favor-reminding or hurt: "They will have no power over any of what they have earned"—that is, people who spend their wealth with less-than-sincere intentions might deceive themselves that they will earn reward for their act, but they will be deprived of all reward, and they will be powerless to reverse their fate. An analogy is now offered to illustrate the nullification of their seemingly good deed: Those who spend their wealth with impure intentions or hurt the feelings of those to whom they have given financial assistance in a time of need will see their charity go to waste, their case being similar to that of an owner of a garden who suddenly discovers that his garden, the economic mainstay of his life, has been overtaken by disaster. The elements of the analogy, as they are introduced one by one, incrementally heighten the effect of the misfortune that will befall the garden:

- The date-palms and vines make up the garden's main types of plants (both were highly prized by Arab garden owners).
- The constant supply of water ("streams flowing underneath") ensures that the garden will yield produce in all seasons.
- The garden brings forth not only dates and grapes but all kinds of other fruits as well.
- The owner is too old to tend the garden, and his children, who also depend for their sustenance on the income from the garden, are too young and weak to help their father in maintaining the garden in good shape.
- A hot sandstorm ("a whirlwind, with fire in it"—"fire" implying that the reference is to the so-called "simoom" [Arabic *samūm*]) hits the garden, burning it down.

As can be seen, the verse draws the picture of utter helplessness on the part of the hypocritical or selfish spender. The misfortune that befell the owner of the garden in the analogy will translate into a misfortune that will, on Judgment Day, befall the hypocritical spender, rendering null and void all his ostensibly good acts at a time when he is most in need of good acts for his salvation. Such analogies, the verse says, convey serious, profound ideas, but only thoughtful minds will draw appropriate lessons from them.

Verse 267: In spending in the way of God, one must spend of one's choice possessions rather than of what lacks worth. After all, whether one spends of one's money or of the produce obtained from the earth, one spends only of what one has received from God, and so it would only be appropriate to give back to God the best of one's possessions. It is only with extreme reluctance that one would accept, from someone else, a worthless offering, so how can one expect God to accept such an offering?

"And know that God is Opulent, Worthy of Thankful Praise." That is: God wants you to spend your wealth in His cause not because He is poor and needs your help, but only so that the wealth you spend may benefit your fellow human beings, and so that God may reward you for obeying His command to spend in His way. God's bountifulness toward the people of the world makes Him Worthy of Thankful Praise regardless of whether people actually offer Him such praise.

Verse 268: This verse bears a close connection to the preceding verses. It states Satan's twofold strategy to keep one from spending one's wealth in the way of God: On the one hand, Satan frightens one with impoverishment; on the other hand, he persuades one to spend lavishly for immoral pursuits, such that one is left with little money to spend in the way of God. God's twofold promise is to forgive one if one repents of immoral conduct and to give one His bountiful blessings if one turns toward Him. Being All-Knowing, God has complete knowledge of how much one has spent in His way and with what intentions, and, being Wide-Ranging, He will, both in this world and in the next, shower His bounty on those who spend their wealth in His way.

The little phrase "from Him" in "God promises you forgiveness from Him and bounty" suggests abundance of forgiveness: coming as it will *from God Himself*, forgiveness will be total and perfect. The same phrase can be taken as understood after "bounty" as well.

Verse 269: The statement made in the first half of the verse—"He [God] gives wisdom to whomever He wishes; and he who is given wisdom is given a great good"—has proverbial force. In the particular context of this passage, however, it carries a specific meaning: Those who spend their wealth in the way of God with the objective of pleasing God are possessed of wisdom—and, as such, of "a great good"—in that, ignoring Satan's threats and relying on God's promises (verse 268), they give of what they have received from God in the first place. Furthermore, in giving of their transient wealth, they can expect to receive an immense and lasting reward from God in the afterlife.

"He gives wisdom to whomever He wishes" means that God, since His will is not divorced from His wisdom, confers wisdom on those who, through spending of their wealth in His way, prove their worthiness to receive that wisdom. Not everyone is able to grasp this insight: only those possessed of deep understanding have the courage to forgo the cash of this world for the credit of the afterlife.

III. Literary Notes

1. Verse 263 contains an instance of significant omission. The preceding verse forbids favor-reminding and infliction of hurt, whereas this verse forbids only the latter. The omission of the former suggests that the two acts are two sides of the same coin—the one implying the other—that either one of them, if not kept in check, is likely to lead to the other, and that one must, therefore, fight the impulse to indulge in either one of them.

2. There is a shift of number in verse 264. The first part of the verse forbids the believers to be "like the one who spends his wealth to make a show before people and does not believe in God and the Last Day," whereas the latter part of that verse, referring to the same individual, says, "They will have no power over any of what they have earned." In the original text, the Arabic for "the one" is *alladhī*, which has been used in a generic sense and, as such, represents a class rather than a single individual. The use of "they" a little later in the verse, therefore, only spells out the multiplicity of individuals potentially present in *alladhī*. Furthermore, a parable, even if it is about a class of people, usually becomes more graphic when it deals in types, focusing the reader's attention on a single individual as typifying the whole class. The use of the plural pronoun "they" toward the end of the verse reminds the reader that what the verse is saying about such an individual is true of a large number of people. The use also paves the way for the verse's concluding comment, which also employs a plural: "And God will not guide the ungrateful people."

3. Verse 266 first talks of a garden with two kinds of fruits, "date-palms and grapes," and then speaks of "fruits of all kinds," even though the two kinds of fruits are included in the general category of fruits. "Date-palms and grapes" get lead billing in the verse because of their special importance to the Arab farmer. The reference to them represents the use of the literary device of stating the special before the general.

4. Verse 266 contains an instance of the nuanced use of language in the Qur'ān. It juxtaposes tree with fruit—"date-palms" (tree) and "grapes" (fruit)—rather than pairing off tree with tree (or plant) or fruit with fruit. The explanation lies in the fact that, to the Arabs, the most useful part of the vine was its fruit, grapes, whereas, in the case of the date-palm, not only its fruit, but all its other parts—its wood, its branches, its fiber, its leaves—also were considered highly useful. Thus, utility, rather than categorical equivalence, would seem to be the principle used for bracketing date-palms and grapes in the verse.

5. Verse 268 reads: "Satan threatens you with poverty and bids you to commit glaring immorality, whereas God promises you forgiveness from Him and bounty." Keeping the order of the verse in mind, *poverty* will be seen to be reversely parallel to *bounty* and *glaring immorality*, to *forgiveness*, the resulting structure being the chiasmus, or reverse parallelism, ABB'A'.

6. The nine-verse-long passage has no fewer than four parables (one each in verses 261, 264, 265, and 266), indicating the importance of parable as a literary device in the Qur'ān. Of the four parables, the one in verse 266 comes close to being an epic simile.

9 Making a Loan Transaction

2 Cow 282–283

282O you who believe, when you make a transaction of loan with one another for a stated term, write it down. And a scribe should write it down between you, in a just manner. And a scribe should not refuse to write the way God has taught him; so he should write. And he who incurs the obligation should be the one to dictate—and he should be fearful of God, his Lord—and he should not, in any way, understate it. So if the one who incurs the obligation happens to be weak-minded or weak-bodied, or is not capable of dictating himself, then his agent should dictate, in a just manner.

And take two witnesses from among your men, and if two men are not available, then one man and two women—from among witnesses that are acceptable to you—lest one of the two women should forget, in which case, the other would remind her. And the witnesses should not show reluctance, whenever they are summoned.

And do not be weary of writing it down, be it small or large, including its term—this is more equitable in the sight of God, more conducive to the rendering of correct testimony, and more likely to ensure that you will not entertain doubt—except if it be spot trading that you conduct between yourselves, in which case, you will not be at fault if you do not write it down. And take witnesses when you make a transaction.

And no harm may be inflicted upon a scribe or a witness. And if you do that, then it will be a transgression on your part.

And be fearful of God. And God instructs you. And God has full knowledge of all things.

283And if you are on a journey and do not find a scribe, then pledged articles that are taken in hand. Then, if you feel secure against one another, the one who has been charged with a trust should hand over his article that is held in trust; and he should be fearful of God, his Lord. And do not conceal testimony. And he who conceals it, his heart is sinful. And God has full knowledge of what you do.

Sūrah 2 is Madīnan.

I. Introduction

This passage is a typical example of the Qur'ān's treatment of legal matters. The Qur'ānic practice of situating a legal matter in a religious-ethical framework is evident here. Thus, the addressees— "O you who believe"—are told that, if their belief is true and sound, then they must carry out the injunctions they are about to receive. Likewise, the parties to the transaction here discussed are admonished to be fearful of God, who knows everything—the hidden intentions as well as the visible outward actions—and to conduct themselves with integrity.

The Qur'ān places great emphasis on the importance of writing or documentation (see General Introduction, section I). Q 2:282–283, which deals with certain procedural aspects of making loan transactions, is one instance of such emphasis.

The essential principles underlying the injunctions in this passage would seem to be valid even today.

II. Commentary

These verses make a series of stipulations, which may be stated and explained as follows:

1. Documentation. Transactions of loan, made for specified periods of time, should be documented. This commandment is in line with the above-noted Qur'ānic concern with reducing important matters, including business deals, to writing. Spot trading does not have to be documented—though, even here, witnesses should be taken if a deal of major proportions is involved. In all other cases, the loan, whether of small or large value, should be documented, for this practice will better fulfill the demands of justice, will be conducive to the bearing of true witness, and will help to eliminate doubt that either party may entertain about any details of the transaction.

Documenting loan transactions, especially when such transactions are made between relatives and friends, is sometimes considered improper because of the lack of mutual trust or confidence implied by the act. But such an attitude can often lead to complications at a later time. By urging documentation, the Qur'ān seeks to prevent such complications from arising.

The phrase "a stated term" in verse 282 does not mean that some loans are given for specified periods of time but some are not; all loans are supposed to be for specified periods of time. The opening part of the verse means: When you make a loan transaction—such a transaction being, by definition, for a stated term—then do so-and-so. In a sense, then, the phrase "a stated term" is a reminder that documentation of a loan transaction should include a statement of the period of time for which the loan is made—a point that is reinforced a little later in the verse when the addressees are urged to write down the amount of the loan, "be it small or large, including its term."

In "a scribe should write it down between you," the words "between you" imply that neither of the two parties to the transaction of loan should write the document, though the document should be prepared in the presence of the two parties so that neither party can accuse the other of falsification of the terms of the loan.

2. The Debtor. The debtor, rather than the creditor, should dictate the amount of the debt owed. The purpose of preparing a loan document is to guarantee the return of the loan, and this purpose is best served through the debtor's acknowledgment that a debt is owed. Also, the creditor, being in a stronger position, is more likely to manipulate the situation in his favor by dictating an inflated amount, so he is not allowed to dictate the amount owed. But the debtor, too, may be tempted to dictate a smaller amount than the one actually owed, so, while he is asked to dictate, he is reminded to be fearful of God and to dictate the correct amount. If the debtor is, for some reason, not in a position to give dictation—if, for example, he suffers from a mental or physical incapacity, such as dumbness, minority of age, decrepitude, or insanity; is a foreigner and speaks a language not understood by the scribe; or happens to be absent from the scene, then his representative may dictate on his behalf.

In the Arabic phrase here translated as "he who incurs the obligation," the key word is *ḥaqq*, which means "the obligation incurred." *Ḥaqq* literally means "truth," and, by using it, the Qur'ān warns the two parties, especially the debtor, that the transaction they are entering into has both a legal and a moral character.

3. Scribes and Witnesses. In the preliterate culture of Arabia, only a small number of people knew how to read and write. The Qur'ān enjoins these people to put their skills at the service of society. In the admonition "And a scribe should not refuse to write the way God has taught him," God is said to have taught the scribe how to write. This statement temporarily suppresses such intermediate causes as learning from a teacher, and it does so in the interest of highlighting the importance of the ultimate cause—God—for God is the ultimate cause of all things. To say that God has taught a scribe how to write is to say that God has blessed the scribe with the skill of writing, that the scribe must, therefore, show gratitude for the blessing, and that the scribe can show his gratitude by willingly putting his expertise at the disposal of society. A scribe, therefore, must not be reluctant to help in the preparation of a document of loan transaction when he is called upon to give such help. In preparing such a document, the scribe should act with complete impartiality, favoring neither the borrower nor the lender.

Two witnesses "from among your men" should be taken to the loan transaction or, if two men are not available, one man and two women; these individuals should possess qualities that make good, acceptable witnesses—that is, they should be honest and trustworthy. These qualifications suggest, on the one hand, that not everyone is fit to serve as a witness and, on the other, that care must be exercised in choosing witnesses. The Prophet Muḥammad said that the best witness is one who bears witness before he is asked to do so—that is, one who is willing, even enthusiastic, to play his role in serving the cause of justice and does not have to be implored by the aggrieved party to bear witness on its behalf.

The alternative stipulation of "one man and two women" does not mean that, in Islamic law, a woman's testimony is worth only half of a man's testimony. It only indicates that, at the time of the revelation of the Qur'ān, women, unlike men, were not deeply involved in business and commerce. Because of their relative inexperience in financial matters, their responsibility as witnesses is reduced in the Qur'ān, two female witnesses sharing the responsibility borne by one male witness. In matters in which women are thought of as more experienced, Islamic law may regard a single female's witness as decisive. For example, the witness of a single midwife who has assisted in a child's birth may have crucial value in a paternity suit. The Qur'ānic stipulation of "two women" is, therefore, constrained by situation rather than by gender.

Just as scribes should not be reluctant to offer their services at the time of need, so witnesses should not be reluctant to bear witness when they are called upon to do so. In other words, witnesses must be ready and willing to bear witness, must not conceal witness, and must not bear false witness.

Since both scribes and witnesses perform important social functions, neither party to the loan transaction should seek to harm the scribe or the witnesses with a view to furthering its own interests. The prohibition against harming scribes and witnesses would include the prohibition against causing them undue inconvenience, such as not paying the scribe for his services if he demands a fee or not covering the travel and accommodation expenses of the witnesses. In fact, even though scribes and witnesses are urged to provide their services for the benefit of society, the prohibition against harming them also means that they cannot be forced against their will to provide their services. Anyone who harms them, in any of the above-noted senses or in any other way, will be guilty of transgressing the commandment of God, according to this verse.

4. Transaction Made during Travel. If a loan transaction is made during travel and no scribe is available to record the transaction, no witnesses are available to vouch for the terms of the transaction, and the lender is unwilling to lend without some collateral, then the transaction may be made after the lender has been handed some valuable article as a pledge. The article is to be returned to the owner if conditions are created under which it becomes possible for the parties to trust each other and enter into a mutually acceptable arrangement. By using the word "trust" (Arabic: *amānah*) for the article held in pledge, the Qur'ān indicates that the lender can hold the article only as a guarantee of payback of the loan and that he does not have the right to draw any benefit from the article.

III. Literary Notes

As a rule quite terse, the language of the Qur'ān is, at times, marked by expatiation. In discussing legal matters—and the passage under discussion is an example—the Qur'ān often uses detail, adding riders, stating exceptions, and providing clarifications. In the course of such discussion, repetition may also occur, but such repetition, since it is meant to achieve precision, is purposeful. This will be borne out by a review of the portions of verses here given in italics:

(1) "when you make a transaction of loan . . . , *write it down*"

(2) "a scribe *should write it down* between you, *in a just manner*"

(3) "a scribe *should not refuse to write the way God has taught him*"

(4) "so *he should write*"

(5) "*he who incurs the obligation should be the one to dictate*"

(6) "he should be *fearful of God*, his Lord—and he should not . . . *understate* it"

(7) "*his agent should dictate, in a just manner*"

(8) "do not be weary of *writing it down, be it small or large*"

There are, strictly speaking, several repetitions here. For instance, (4)—"so he should write"—would seem to be repeating what has already been stated in positive terms in (2)—"A scribe should write it down"—and in negative terms in (3)—"a scribe should not refuse to write"; (8) "do not be weary of writing it down," makes the same point. (2) enjoins that documents be written "in a just manner"(or "impartially"; Arabic: *bi l-ḥaqq*). (3) would appear to be making the same point, for "the way God has taught him" has to mean the just way of preparing a document. The "he who incurs the obligation should be the one to dictate" of (5) and the "his agent should dictate" of (7), one thinks, might have been combined to yield a more terse statement, at the same time avoiding the repetition of "in a just manner." The first part of (6), which says that the dictating person "should be fearful of God," seems to be repeated in the second part of (6)—"should not . . . understate it"—for one who is fearful of God will not understate the amount owed. But we should remember that the Qurʾānic commandments assume a living context, one in which people, on hearing a commandment, are likely to react in some way—for example, by asking questions or expressing reservations—the phrasing of the commandment necessitating nuanced repetition. Thus, (1) lays down the general rule: loan transactions are to be documented: "write it down." (2) refers to the particular agency available for writing at that period—the scribe. Scribes, only a few at that time, were aware of the value of their skills and were liable to deny service to others out of self-conceit, so (3) reminds them that the skill they possess is a gift from God for which they can be properly grateful when they use it to serve others. After (3) has urged the scribes not to deny service to others, (4) reinforces that point in positive terms, taking away any lingering hesitation on the scribe's part. (3) implies that the commandment "to write the way God has taught" puts the Divine stamp of approval on the purely human virtue of acting "in a just manner," sanctifying that virtue. (8) has the character of a summary statement and receives its particular point from the phrase "be it small or large," for going through a formal process of documentation, especially in a case involving a small loan, is likely to be considered irksome.

IV. A Note on the Bible

In the Bible, the subject of advancing loans occurs in connection with the charging of interest: The Israelites were supposed to lend money to one another without charging interest, though they could charge interest on loans to non-Israelites (Deuteronomy 23:19–20). Q 2:282–283 does not deal with interest, but rather with the procedure for making a loan transaction. This discussion comes on the heels of the prohibition, stated in verses 275–281 of the same sūrah, against charging interest on loans. Thus, in both the Bible and the Qurʾān, the subject of loan transactions is somehow connected with the subject of dealing in interest. In the Bible, procedural elements, such as the taking of witnesses, the signing of deeds, and the taking of pledges, are found in a variety of contexts, some involving the making of loan transactions.

10 Creed and Commitment

2 Cow 285–286

285The Messenger believes in what has been sent down to him by his Lord, and
the believers do, too. All of them believe in God, His angels, His books, and His
messengers: "We do not discriminate between any of His messengers." And they
say, "We hear, and we obey. Your forgiveness, our Lord! And to You is the return."
286God does not impose any obligation on a being except to the extent of its
capacity; it shall have to its credit what it has earned, and against it shall be held
what it has striven to earn. "Our Lord, do not hold us accountable if we should
forget or make a mistake. And, our Lord, do not lay on us a burden the way you
laid it on those before us. And, our Lord, do not burden us with what we lack the
ability to bear. And overlook our failings, forgive us, and have mercy on us. You are
our Protector, so help us against the disbelieving people."

Sūrah 2 is Madīnan.

I. Introduction

This passage concludes sūrah 2. The sūrah invites the People of the Book, especially the Jews, to accept the Prophet Muḥammad and the revelation received by him, the Qurʾān. In the course of the sūrah, a critique is made of some aspects of Jewish religious conduct in history, and then a new religious community, that of Muslims, is charged with the responsibility of reviving the Abrahamic monotheistic faith. In the verses under discussion, a review of the essentials of the Islamic creed is followed by a statement of the commitment that, ideally, should be made by a community elected to perform the above-mentioned task.

II. Commentary

Verse 285: This verse begins by reporting that Muḥammad and his followers believe in the revelation sent down to Muḥammad. Taken in context, the report means that, if those invited to believe in the revelation—namely, the People of the Book—have refused to believe, then no matter, for the Prophet and his followers, at least, have reposed faith and, in doing so, have testified to the truth of the message of the Qurʾān.

Significantly, the Prophet is the first to be mentioned among those who believe. This underscores the point that a prophet, no less than any other believer, is obligated to believe in the revelation that comes from God and is, just like any other believer, subject to the commandments of the revelation. In terms of obedience owed to God, a prophet enjoys no special privileges. The primacy of a prophet's belief is both chronological and qualitative.

"All of them believe in God, His angels, His books, and His messengers." This accounts for four of the five articles of the Islamic faith (for a statement of the five articles, see Q 2:177, which is discussed in chapter 4, "True Piety"). The fifth one, belief in the afterlife, is not explicitly mentioned in this verse, but the passage under study clearly implies that belief forms part of the Islamic doctrine: in verses 285 and 286, the believers' earnest prayer to God to forgive them is made with the afterlife in mind, and it is with reference to the afterlife that verse 284 speaks of God holding human beings accountable and forgiving them or punishing them.

"We do not discriminate between any of His messengers." That is: We believe in all the prophets, without denying or rejecting anyone.

"And they say, 'We hear, and we obey.'" That is: We will not argue or question, look for loopholes, or offer excuses; the moment we hear a commandment, we will obey with all our hearts and minds. "We hear, and we obey" signifies that belief must be followed by action: it is not enough to hear and accept the message; it is necessary to give meaning to that message through acts of obedience.

"Your forgiveness, our Lord!" That is: We seek Your forgiveness if, in carrying out any of Your commandments, we have been guilty of neglect or slackness. In the original text, the omission of the verb—which would have translated as "We seek"—puts all the emphasis on "Your forgiveness," the omission serving to downplay the efficacy of the human act of asking for forgiveness and emphasizing the Divine act of granting forgiveness. It is as if those praying are saying to God: Although our sins are too many, Your kind forgiveness can wipe them off.

"And to You is the return." This part of the verse, too, contains a subtle emphasis. Like the preceding phrase, it removes the human petitioner from the scene. The verse does not say: We, the believers, will perform the right kinds of actions in this world, for we know that, in the afterlife, we will return to You, and You, our Lord, will pass judgment on us on the basis of our good actions performed in this world. Again, the phrase "And to You is the return" does not specify as to who will be returning, but the obvious implication of the generic expression "the return" is that all returns, or everybody's return, will be to God and, further, that it will be entirely up to God to decide on the fate of people on Judgment Day. If the final return of all human beings is to God and God alone will pass judgment on them, then, for the sake of their own salvation, human beings should live their lives on earth in submission to Him.

Verse 286: The verse opens with the statement—made by God using the third person—that God does not obligate any being beyond its capacity and that every being shall get the recompense it deserves. The statement appears to break the continuity of the prayer that the human speakers—the believers—have been making in the immediately preceding verse ("We do not discriminate between any of the messengers . . . ") and will continue to make after the Divine utterance ("Our Lord, do not hold us accountable if we should forget or make a mistake. . . ."). But, as we shall see (section III.4, below), the break in the human prayer is more apparent than real, for it serves a certain function, the continuity of thought in the passage remaining essentially intact.

"Our Lord, do not hold us accountable if we should forget or make a mistake." This prayerful request betokens humility on the speakers' part, for, as the religion of Islam teaches, God will pardon one for forgetting to carry out or for making a mistake in carrying out an obligation. The request that one be forgiven for something for which one is not accountable to begin with indicates modesty along with regret.

"And, our Lord, do not lay on us a burden the way you laid it on those before us." The reference here is to the severity of the commandments given to earlier nations, the verse saying: Do not impose on us the difficult obligations that you imposed on earlier nations—obligations that those nations failed to carry out. (On the indefiniteness of "burden," see section III.5, below.)

"And, our Lord, do not burden us with what we lack the ability to bear." This is not a repetition of the immediately preceding prayer. That prayer made reference to the objective severity of the obligations imposed on previous nations; this prayer now refers to the speakers' own weakness in fulfilling the obligations imposed.

"And overlook our failings, forgive us, and have mercy on us." These three short phrases make, each with a different slant, the same essential request for salvation. We may note the difference between "overlook our failings" and "forgive us." The first one (*uʿfu ʿannā*) is a request for forgiveness for acts of omission and means: Do not call us to account if we fall short or if we fail to carry out fully the commandments we are supposed to carry out. The second (*ighfir lanā*) is a request for forgiveness for acts of commission and means: Do not call us to account for any mistakes we make while carrying out the commandments.

"And have mercy on us." That is: Quite apart from the acts that we may perform or fail to perform, we appeal to Your mercy, for our salvation depends on Your showing us mercy since our actions are not worthy enough to entitle us to salvation.

"You are our Protector, so help us against the disbelieving people." This prayer is an expression of submission to God and a declaration of trust in Him: You alone can protect us against all dangers, and You alone can help us to overcome our opponents. At the same time, it represents a recognition on the part of the believers that, while they can and must put their trust in God and seek His help in their struggle against the disbelievers, they themselves must bear the brunt of action in historical context—that they have to act and fulfill their responsibilities in this connection.

III. Literary Notes

1. The Bifurcated Subject. In the opening part of verse 285, the subject is made up of "the Messenger" and "the believers." In its actual placement in the original text, however, the subject is bifurcated: "*The Messenger* believes in what has been sent down to him by his Lord, *and the believers do, too*"; it could have been, both in Arabic and in English: "*The Messenger and the believers believe* in what has been sent down to him by his Lord." But, in that case, the sentence would have lacked the particular nuance required by the context. As we have already noted, the thrust of verse 285 is that, if the People of the Book have refused to accept the message of Muḥammad, then, at least, others—now called the "believers"—have chosen to follow that message (see section II, verse 285, above). This being the case, the acceptance of Muḥammad's message by the "believers" deserves to be highlighted, and the bifurcation of the subject accomplishes that goal. The bifurcation also highlights a point already made—namely, that a prophet is the first one to submit to God and His authority (see section II, verse 285). (For a similar case of bifurcated subject, see chapter 3, "Abraham Builds the Kaʿbah and Prays for a Prophet," section IV.2.)

2. Shift of Person. In verse 285, there is a sudden shift from the third person to the first. Immediately after the report that the Prophet Muḥammad and the believers believe in God and in the angels, the scriptures, and the messengers, we encounter the following statement: "We do not discriminate between any of His messengers." The suddenness of the shift—made conspicuous by the omission of the prefatory words "They say" (it would be a single word in Arabic, such as *qālū*) between the third-person report and the first-person statement—represents the acknowledgment, made in direct and personal terms, by all the believers that they believe in all the prophets raised by God. The acknowledgment also reinforces the above-mentioned thesis—namely, that, if the People of the Book would not believe, then Muḥammad and his followers do believe.

3. Significant Variation. In the first part of verse 286, we read that a being shall be held responsible for its actions on earth: "it shall have to its credit what *it has earned*, and against it shall be held what *it has striven to earn*." The Arabic verbs for the two italicized phrases— *kasabat* and *iktasabat*, respectively—come from the same root, *k-s-b*—differing only in the form taken by that root in each case. Why does the Qurʾān employ two different verb forms from the same root? Actually, *iktasabat*, the longer word, is more emphatic than *kasabat* (the grammarians would say that *iktasabat* conveys the root's essential meaning, "to earn," with greater intensity), hence the translation "it has striven to earn." The semantic difference between the two words would seem to point to a certain irony. That a being ought to perform good deeds so that it may be rewarded in the hereafter is understandable and expected. But only a foolish person, the Qur'ān seems to be suggesting, would *strive to earn* bad deeds, that is, would make a special effort to perform deeds that will be held against it, for, to do so would be to dig one's own grave and to be responsible for one's own perdition. The irony is sharpened when we note that the reflexive nature of the verb *iktasabat* signifies that one is doing something for one's own sake—in this particular case, that one is eager, even greedy, to acquire bad deeds.

4. Hysteron Proteron. The opening statement of verse 286 reads: "God does not impose any obligation on a being except to the extent of its capacity; it shall have to its credit what it has earned, and against it shall be held what it has striven to earn." Being a Divine utterance, this seems to interrupt the human speakers' prayer which precedes it and will be continued after it, and one feels that it should have come at the end of the prayer, for it could be a fitting response to the prayer to God that He not burden the believers with what they lack the ability to bear. The insertion of this Divine utterance in the middle of the human prayer represents the use of the literary feature called hysteron proteron, which involves putting first what normally comes last and putting last what normally comes first. The particular positioning of the utterance signifies immediate acceptance of the prayer made: before the human speakers' prayer is finished, God grants the prayer, assuring the speakers that He will not place on them any burden they cannot bear. Thus, the apparent break in the prayer hides a deeper continuity of thought.

5. Indefiniteness of Magnification. In verse 286, the indefiniteness of "burden" signifies, grammatically, magnification, and it accomplishes three things:

- It represents, on the speakers' part, a recognition of the onerous nature of the task with which they are being charged.
- It reflects the humility of the speakers, who feel that they may not be up to the task in question.
- It reinforces the request being made—namely, that God not put too heavy a burden on the speakers.

11 Love of Desirable Things

3 Family of ʿImrān 14–17

14Made glamorous for people is the love of desirable things—women, sons,
gold and silver piled in heaps, branded horses, cattle, and tilled land. This is the
provision of worldly life, whereas with God lies the good return. 15Say: "Shall I
inform you of something better than that? For those who are godfearing, there are,
with their Lord, gardens with streams flowing underneath—in them, they will live
forever—chaste spouses, and God's pleasure—and God is watching His servants;
16those who say, 'Our Lord, we believe, so forgive us our sins, and save us from
the punishment of the fire'"—17the steadfast, the truthful, the obedient, the givers
of money, and the seekers of forgiveness at dawn.

Sūrah 3 is Madīnan.

I. Introduction

These verses occur in the context of the rejection of Muḥammad's message by his opponents. The opening verses of sūrah 3, saying that the Qur'ān has been revealed by the same God who revealed the Torah and the Evangel, threaten with punishment those who would reject the revelation sent down to Muḥammad. This passage now explains the motivation behind the disbelievers' rejection of the Qur'ānic message: love of worldly things. An anticipatory reference to such motivation is already made in a verse preceding the passage: "Indeed, those who disbelieve, their wealth and their children will not be of any avail to them against God" (verse 10). Verse 14 spells out that motivation in more detail, implying that only an irrational love of "desirable things," rather than an objective analysis of the content of the Divine message, lies behind the rejection of the Qur'ān by the opponents of Islam.

This passage presents two contrasting pictures—one, of those people whom worldly glamor has caused to forget or neglect the higher calling of serving God, and the other, of those who are godfearing and whose life is defined by a commitment to higher religious and moral values.

The primary addressees in the passage are Arabs—and Arab males at that. A tribal society is usually patriarchal—that is, the males are in charge of the family, the tribe, and the political and economic affairs—and that was the case in Arabia. In such a society, a message of change is targeted primarily, if not exclusively, at society's male leadership, and this is what happens in this Qur'ānic passage.

II. Commentary

Verse 14: The opening phrase, "Made glamorous"—only one word in the Arabic text, *zuyyina*—is in the passive voice. The verse says that "the love of desirable things" has been made glamorous, but it does not say by whom that love has been made glamorous. The question arises because elsewhere the Qur'ān employs the same verb in the active voice, *zayyana*, sometimes with God as its subject (for example, 6:108) and sometimes with Satan as its subject (for example, 8:48). Does God render "the love of desirable things" glamorous, or does Satan do so? We will examine the issue in some detail a little later (see section III.1, below). Here, it will suffice to note that the Qur'ān is not discussing "the love of desirable things" as such—for, in principle, such love is not objectionable in the Qur'ān's eyes—but the *glamorization* of "the love of desirable things," which, as the context of this passage makes quite clear, the Qur'ān does regard as objectionable. To invest a thing with glamor is to make it so utterly dear and attractive to one that one comes totally under its sway, loses all sense of proportion in regard to it, and sets it up as the sole criterion or yardstick for judging and evaluating everything else. It is this glamorization of which the Qur'ān is being critical.

The list of "desirable things" in the verse is representative, not exhaustive. At the top of the list is love of one's family—of one's wife and children (the verse is addressing males, as we noted above). "Sons," as opposed to "daughters," are mentioned because the Arabs attached greater value to male offspring. But, in view of the critical tone of the verse, the reference to sons, to the exclusion of daughters, contains an implicit critique of the Arabs' love of male offspring as constituting one of the elements of worldly glamor; this critique is made in more explicit terms elsewhere in the Qur'ān (for example, 37:149–154; 52:39). Horses, of great value in war, were prized property, and possession of "branded horses"—pedigree horses were often branded—was a mark of prestige. "Cattle" were important to the bedouin economy, whereas "tilled land" refers to settled, civilized life that follows the stage of bedouin living.

Depending on the context, the word "people" (*nās*) has different referents in the Qur'ān. Here, since the verse is critical of the excessive love of worldly things, the word refers to those opponents of Islam who are so engrossed in worldly pursuits that they give no thought to the higher values that the Qur'ān presents and invites them to accept.

Verse 15: This verse instructs Muḥammad to inform his opponents that, much better than the heedless enjoyment of the desirable things of a transient world is the reward that God will give to those who live their lives in mindful obedience to God.

The Arabic expression used in the text for those people is *alladhīna t-taqaw*, literally, "those who are godfearing." The word "Say" at the beginning of the verse means not only "tell," but also "proclaim." That is, Muḥammad is being told to announce to his opponents that their deep attachment to the "desirable things" of the world will cost them an enduring and far superior life in the hereafter.

By "the godfearing" are meant those who are mindful that, one day, they will have to stand in God's court and account for their actions in this world. The verse lists some of the rewards for such people. The first is "gardens," which is a translation of *jannāt* (sing. *jannah*). *Jannah* is the Qurʾānic term for heaven. The image of a garden as a place of beauty and comfort had great appeal for the Arabs, the people of the desert, who prized the oasis, a garden-like area. The heavenly garden, in which the deserving people will live forever, is here pictured as one that has streams of water running through it, the streams guaranteeing the garden's productiveness and luxuriance.

The second on the list is "chaste spouses." The Arabic word used for "chaste" is *muṭahharah*, which signifies not only physical purity, but purity of mind and soul as well.

"God's pleasure," or "God's approval," is mentioned last, but it is understood that it is the greatest of all rewards (see Q 9:72).

"And God is watching His servants" here means that God is watching the conduct of His good servants, who should rest assured that He will adequately recompense them for all their good actions.

Verses 16–17: These two verses list several other qualifications of the people whom verse 15 has called the "godfearing." In the first place, these people are acutely conscious of their failings: "Those who say, 'Our Lord, we believe, so forgive us our sins, and save us from the punishment of the fire.'" This suggests that they may have been enamored of the "desirable things" of the world but, after listening to the Qurʾān's message, repented and are now asking for forgiveness for the excesses they committed. Second, they are "the steadfast": they adhere to the path of faith and virtue against all odds and in difficult circumstances—in poverty and disease and in the face of temptation, opposition, and adversity—and they do so without complaining or despairing. (Note the definite article in "the steadfast": its use indicates that steadfastness is a permanent character trait of the people in question and has become part of their identity, such that they can be referred to as "*the* steadfast." The same is true of the qualities mentioned in the remaining part of the verse.) Third, they are "the truthful": they always speak the truth and always conduct themselves with integrity, there being complete harmony between their words and their deeds, and between their public lives and their private lives. Fourth, they are "the obedient"; that is, they are wont to making humble submission to God and never defy Him in arrogance. Fifth, they are "the givers of money": they regularly spend their wealth in the way of God, helping poor individuals and supporting charitable causes. Finally, they are "the seekers of forgiveness at dawn": they routinely wake up in the late hours of the night to seek God's forgiveness. The verse subtly suggests that the time of dawn, when one presents oneself before God in sincerity and without making any show of piety, is most conducive to praying for God's forgiveness and that a prayer made at that time stands a good chance of being granted.

III. Issues

1. Who Made the Worldly Things Glamorous—God or Satan? This question arises in connection with the use of the passive *zuyyina* in verse 14 (see section II, above). In answering it, we need to remember that Islam, far from looking down upon the world, wants its followers to take an active part in making this world a better place materially no less than spiritually. As such, Islam would regard the love of worldly things as perfectly legitimate and wholesome and would not make a blanket denunciation of it. On the other hand, Islam would not like its followers to be so deeply immersed in this world as to forget that there is another world to come. In other words, to the extent that love of worldly things is essential to our living of a fruitful, balanced, and responsible life in this world, God is the one who has imbued us with such love. But, to the extent that love of those things becomes all-engrossing, making us forget the next world, Islam would look at such love disapprovingly, and Satan is to be taken as the one who has created such love in us. In brief, this verse is critical of the excessive love of the "desirable things" of the world, not of the ordinary or normal love of those things.

The Islamic distinction between the approved, normal love of the world and the disapproved, excessive love of the world is effectively indicated by the word *matāʿ* in the latter part of verse 14. *Matāʿ* is "that which has utility" or "that which yields enjoyment": it signifies all sorts of goods and articles that carry utility for human beings or yield enjoyment, pleasure, and delight for them. In the present context, the word simultaneously means "that which lends itself to legitimate or profitable use by human beings" and "that which carries the potential of engrossing people so deeply as to make them neglectful of the afterlife." Both meanings are apparent in the following statement in the verse: "This is the provision of worldly life, whereas with God lies the good return." In other words, while one may legitimately make use of the transient worldly provision, one ought to make use of it in such a way as to earn for oneself the enduring blessings of the hereafter.

We said above that Satan is to be taken as the one who makes worldly things look exceedingly glamorous to human beings. But, in a certain sense, God, too, may be taken as the one who makes worldly things highly alluring to human beings. By investing worldly things with glamor, God intends to put human beings to the test; He wishes to determine who falls for the temptations of the world and who fights them successfully. Support for this view is furnished by Q 18:7, in which God says: "We have made what is on earth an adornment for it, that we may put them to the test." The

Arabic word for "adornment" in this verse has the same root as the verb *zuyyina* in our passage, both "adornment" and "glamor" falling within the semantic range of their common Arabic root—*z-y-n*.

It should be kept in mind that, while Satan may be said to have caused the excessive love of desirable things in human beings, Satan is not to be taken as an absolutely independent locus of power in opposition to an omnipotent God. In Qurʾānic theology, Satan has the ability to make the evil path glamorous to people, but he enjoys no coercive power over them and cannot force them to take the evil path; he can insinuate, but he cannot compel. In other words, if human beings choose the evil path, they will have to bear responsibility for making that choice.

We can now see that the use of the passive voice in verse 14 is quite strategic, and that both God and Satan can be taken, though each in a radically different sense, as the one who makes the love of worldly things glamorous to human beings.

2. Faith and Works. According to verse 16 of the passage, heaven belongs to those who say, "Our Lord, we believe, so forgive us our sins, and save us from the punishment of the fire." The speakers in this prayer cite only faith ("we believe"), to the exclusion of works, as the basis of their petition for forgiveness, and the context seems to approve of their prayer. That is not what the verse means, though. Just as silence can, at times, be more significant than speech, so omission, at times, can be more significant than statement. The speakers in the prayer are presented as very humble people. It would have been arrogant of them to say or imply that they not only believe but have performed so many good deeds that they deserve to be forgiven. Out of a profound sense of modesty, then, while they do mention their lapses ("so forgive us our sins"), they omit to mention their good deeds. Imagine them saying, to borrow the words of verse 17: "We are the steadfast, the truthful, the obedient, the givers of money, and the seekers of forgiveness at dawn!" Notably, the words of verse 17 are spoken by God, who, by spelling out the good deeds performed by the believers, supplies the aforementioned omission. To sum up, the reference to faith in Q 3:16 is to faith that is inclusive of works. Q 3:193 presents a very similar situation, involving the same omission by the speakers: "and so we believe, so forgive us our sins, our Lord." The response that the speakers receive two verses later (in 3:195) to their prayer is: "So their Lord granted their prayer, saying, 'I will not let the actions of anyone of you, male or female, go to waste.' " In this response, the use of the word "actions" clearly indicates that the speakers' faith was inclusive of deeds and that they had omitted to mention it only out of modesty.

IV. Literary Notes

1. A shift of person takes place in this passage. The third-person narration of verse 14 changes to second-person address in verse 15, with the directness of address in the present context adding to the prestige of what verse 14 calls "the good return," which the addressees are being invited to choose over worldly possessions.

2. Verse 14 lists several "desirable things" and then refers to all of them by means of the singular demonstrative "this." The shift of number—from the plural to the singular—implies a certain disdain, reinforcing the belittlement of the transient things of the world in comparison with the eternal blessings of the afterlife.

V. Some Comparative Verses from the Bible

The Qur'ānic passage may be compared to Psalm 19:9–10:

> [T]he fear of the Lord is pure, enduring forever;
> the ordinances of the Lord are true and righteous altogether.
> More to be desired are they than gold, even much fine gold;
> sweeter also than honey, and drippings of the honeycomb.

Some of the statements in the Qur'ānic passage under study will be found to resonate with other verses in the Bible. For example, Q 3:15 speaks of the reward of those who are fearful of God. This is comparable to Proverbs 22:4: "The reward for humility and fear of the Lord is riches and honor and life." The concluding phrase in the Qur'ānic passage, "the seekers of forgiveness at dawn," alludes to the state of solitude or privacy in which forgiveness is asked; this may be compared to Matthew 6:6: "But whenever you pray, go into your room and shut the door and pray to your Father who is in secret; and your Father who sees in secret will reward you."

12 Jesus: Birth, Miracles, and Mission

3 Family of ʿImrān 45–51

45When the angels said, "O Mary, God gives you the good news of a Word
from Him: his name is the Messiah Jesus son of Mary—eminent in the world and
the hereafter, and one of the intimates. 46And he will speak with people while he is
in the cradle and when advanced in years, and will be one of the virtuous."
47She said, "My Lord, how can I have a child when no man has touched me?"
He said, "Thus does God create what He wishes. When He decides on a matter, all
He says to it is 'Be!' and it comes to be. 48And He will teach him the Book and
wisdom, and the Torah and the Evangel. 49And a prophet to the Children of Israel!—
saying: 'I have come to you with a sign from your Lord: I create for you, from clay, a
bird-like form, then I breathe into it, and it becomes a bird, by God's will; and I cure
the born blind and the leper, and I revive the dead, by God's will; and I inform you of
what you eat and what you store up in your homes. In this, indeed, there is a sign for
you if you would be believers. 50And an actualizer of what has existed since before
me—the Torah—and so that I may make lawful for you some of what was made
unlawful to you. And I have come to you with a sign from your Lord, so fear God and
obey me. 51God is my Lord and your Lord, so serve Him. This is a Straight Path.'"

Sūrah 3 is Madīnan.

I. Introduction

In the passage preceding this one in the sūrah, Zachariah, a very old man whose wife is barren, prays to God for offspring and is told that God will grant his prayer by giving him a son by the name of John (verses 37–41). In this sūrah and elsewhere in the Qurʾān, the story of the birth of John the Baptist serves as a foil for the story of the birth of Jesus. Jesus' birth, like John's, was miraculous: John was born of a decrepit old man and a barren woman, and Jesus was born of only one parent. The point of the Qurʾānic narrative is that Jesus' miraculous birth is no proof of his divinity, any more than John's miraculous birth is proof of John's divinity. A similar argument is presented a little later in the same sūrah: "Indeed, the example of Jesus in God's eyes is like the example of Adam: He created him from earth and then said to him, 'Be!' and he comes into being" (verse 59). That is, if Jesus' birth without a father entitles him to deity, then Adam, who was born without any parents at all, would have a greater title to deity.

Besides referring to Jesus' birth, this passage talks about some of the miracles of Jesus and, most important, states the essential mission of Jesus.

II. Commentary

Verses 45–46: The angels inform Mary that she will bear a son—or, as the text says, a "Word" (Arabic: *kalimah*)—whose name will be the Messiah Jesus son of Mary. What does the Qur'ān mean by calling Jesus a *kalimah* from God? In light of verses 37–41 (the birth of John) and 59 (the birth of Adam) of the sūrah, to which reference has already been made, Jesus cannot be *kalimah* in the sense of being a deity. But he can be a *kalimah* in the sense that he came into being upon God's utterance of the word "Be!" Thus, Jesus is the *kalimah*, or word, "Be!" The identification of Jesus with the *kalimah* "Be!" represents, on the one hand, an honor bestowed on Jesus and, on the other, the power of God to bring anything into being by uttering a simple word, "Be!"

The angels' announcement to Mary may be briefly analyzed and explained as follows:

(1) Mary will bear a son. There is no mention here of Mary getting married or having relations with any man; the son's birth will be brought about by the *kalimah* of God, the son himself being known as *kalimah* in commemoration of the event.

(2) The son's name will be the Messiah Jesus son of Mary. That the angels tell Mary the name of the son she will bear implies that Jesus has the rare honor of being named by God Himself (this honor was also bestowed on John the Baptist, according to verse 39 of the sūrah). That Jesus will be called the "Messiah" means that Jesus will have great distinction in Israel. The literal meaning of "messiah"—from the Hebrew *māshīah*—is "anointed one." Israelite prophets anointed their successors; at a later time, Israelite kings, too, came to be anointed. The New Testament contains no reference to a ceremonial anointment of Jesus (Jesus' anointment at Bethany by a woman, as reported, for example, in Matthew 26:6–7, belongs in a different category). Islamic sources, however, present Jesus as one whose head appeared to have been rubbed with oil and who, therefore, was born anointed. This may have been the reason why the Qur'ān calls Jesus "Messiah," the title implying that Jesus had been anointed by God Himself (cf. Luke 4:18, in which Jesus says: "The Spirit of the Lord is upon me, because he has anointed me to bring good news to the poor. . . ."). It is equally possible that the Qur'ān uses the title "Messiah" for Jesus in the sense that God conferred messiahship on Jesus—that is, charged Jesus with a special set of responsibilities—even though no formal ceremony of anointment took place to designate Jesus as Messiah.

Since the angels are talking to Mary, one would expect them to tell her that her son will be called simply Jesus. Instead, they say that he will be known as "Jesus son of Mary." This naming of Jesus in the verse has fourfold significance:

(a) It asserts categorically that Jesus will be born of one parent only.
(b) It implies that, for a child to be known after its mother rather than after its father may, in ordinary circumstances, be considered a matter of shame, but in the case of Jesus, whose birth was brought about by the *kalimah* of "Be!" the matronymic constitutes a distinction.
(c) It signifies that Jesus being known after his mother is a distinction for his mother as well.
(d) Above all, it signifies that Jesus neither was the son of God nor had a human father, but was a human being born of a female human being.

(3) Jesus will enjoy a position of eminence both in this world and in the next. This means that, by special providence, Jesus' illustrious career has already been laid out and his exalted status already confirmed. The Arabic word *wajīh*, "eminent," signifies that Jesus occupied a distinguished position in Israel. But it also serves to correct a possible misunderstanding of the use of a matronymic for Jesus. It implies that Jesus is an exception to the so-called rule that a fatherless child does not attain honor in society.

(4) Jesus, while still an infant in his cradle, will have the distinction of speaking to people, and he will continue to speak to them when he is advanced in years. This means that performance of miracles will mark Jesus' life from the very start. As we learn from other verses in the Qurʾān, God gave the infant Jesus the ability to speak so that he may vindicate his mother against any accusations of unchastity; such accusations were leveled against her when, carrying the newborn child, she appeared before her community (Q 19:27–33). That Jesus will speak to people at an advanced age suggests that he will have a relatively long life. Also, the reference to Jesus speaking in infancy, since it occurs in conjunction with the reference to Jesus speaking at an advanced age, signifies that, even during his infancy, Jesus' speech will be marked by maturity and wisdom.

(5) That Jesus will be both "one of the intimates" and "one of the virtuous" is significant. The two phrases imply that Jesus, although he will be one of the "intimates" of God and although God will count him among the "virtuous," will yet not partake of divinity but will remain a human being. The Qurʾānic stress on Jesus' humanity is evident in this and other verses of the passage under discussion, as, indeed, it is in other places in the Qurʾān.

Verses 45–46, a succinct statement of the career of Jesus, underscore Mary's modesty—and, in doing so, give rise to mild irony. After hearing the initial part of the angels' announcement—that pertaining to the birth of a son—Mary, besides wondering how she could bear a child without having had any contact with a man, is extremely worried about her reputation in the community (see Q 19:20 in this connection). She, therefore, seems to pay no attention to the other details that the angels provide about Jesus. A little reflection by her on those details might have answered the questions in her mind and allayed her fears. A subtle but significant detail in the passage is worth noting. Mary receives from the angels the news of the birth of a son, but, being thoroughly perturbed, she addresses her question to God Himself, as if only God could answer such a question.

Verse 47: Upon learning the news of the birth of a son, a puzzled Mary addresses God, expressing her wonder that she will give birth to a child without having had any relations with a man. She gets the following response: "He [God or the angel visiting Mary (see section IV.1, below)] said, 'Thus does God create what He wishes'"—the word "create," incidentally, indicating that Jesus is a created being. The response signifies that God can bring something to pass even if the known system of causation makes the occurrence of an event seem unlikely or impossible. From a Qur'ānic standpoint, either the ordinary system of causation lacks absolute validity or, of the several systems of causation that may possibly exist, God may, on a certain occasion, decide to put one or another into operation. Philosophically, the Qur'ān would not negate the familiar system of causation, though it would challenge its absolute validity if such validity were claimed for it. For, in the ultimate analysis, the Qur'ān would say either that no such system exists in its own right or that it is contingent and subject to change or suspension at God's will.

Verses 48–50: These verses state the mission of Jesus and refer to some of the miracles that he will perform later in life. First, the miracles.

Verse 49 presents Jesus as telling the Israelites that he has come to them "with a sign." Although singular, the word "sign" here is generic in import and includes all the signs and miracles that Jesus presented in support of his prophecy. Verse 46 has already referred to the miracle of Jesus speaking in the cradle. Verse 49 mentions a few other miracles, stating twice that Jesus performed these miracles "by God's will":

- Jesus made clay birds and breathed into them, and they became living birds.
- He healed the born blind and the lepers—that is, people whose illnesses were believed to be incurable.
- He revived dead persons.
- He told people what they had eaten or stored up in their homes. That is, Jesus had knowledge of people's activities that would remain hidden to a stranger unless the latter acquired information about them through some source. The implication is that God was the source of Jesus' information about such activities of people.

By affirming that Jesus showed miracles "by God's will," the Qurʾān simultaneously negates the view that he was God and the view that he was a wonder-worker.

Coming now to the mission of Jesus. Verse 48 says that God has sent Jesus specifically to Israel and will teach him "the Book and wisdom, and the Torah and the Evangel." This phrase sums up the Qurʾānic understanding of the relationship between the Torah and the Evangel, the second half of the phrase explaining the first: the "Book" is the "Torah," and "wisdom" is the "Evangel" (see section III.2, below). That God will teach Jesus the Book, or the Torah, and wisdom, or the Evangel, signifies that Jesus will not only teach the words, or text, of the Torah, but also the wisdom that is necessary to get at the heart of the Torah. This, then, is the special mission of Jesus according to the Qurʾān. Israelite religious practice had reduced the Torah to a book of dry, mechanically understood and enforced laws, the spirit of those laws having suffered gross neglect, and Jesus, like many other prophets of Israel, was sent to restore the Torah to its rightful position in Israel's life. The ministry of Jesus is instructive in that it warns of the danger of a scripture's husk surviving at the expense of the scripture's kernel, of the danger of the letter of a law overpowering the spirit of the law. Having warned of that danger, Jesus' ministry would call for an effort to recover the integral and dynamic vision of life in obedience to God originally presented by the Torah.

In verse 50, Jesus calls himself an "actualizer" of the already existing Torah. The Arabic word used in the text, *muṣaddiq*, has two meanings: one, Jesus confirms the Torah—which is to say that Jesus had come not to repeal the Torah, but to establish—or rather, to reestablish—the primacy of the Torah in Israel's religious life (see section IV.3, below); second, in Jesus, the Torah's predictions about a new prophet, for whom the Israelites had been waiting at that time, were actualized (see section IV.2, below).

Verse 50 also states that part of Jesus' ministry consisted in making lawful for the Israelites what had been made unlawful to them. The words "what was made unlawful to you" in the verse refer to those severities that had come to be associated with the Torah but lacked foundation in the Law, being the product of the Israelite legal scholars' subjective interpretation of the Torah. An example would be the prohibition to heal the sick on the Sabbath, a prohibition which Jesus challenged by invoking the true meaning and purpose of the Sabbath: "Is it lawful to do good or to do harm on the sabbath, to save life or to kill?" (Mark 3:4; also 2:23–27, which concludes with Jesus remarking pungently: "The sabbath was made for humankind, and not humankind for the sabbath"). Seen in this light, Jesus' act of "making lawful" some of the things that were unlawful represented not an annulment of the Law but a restoration of the spirit of the Law that had been obscured from view on account of the Israelite scholars' overly rigid interpretations of the Law.

The last part of the verse is notable: "So fear God and obey me." This is the demand that every prophet makes: he asks his nation to obey him, but only in his capacity as God's representative and as the conveyer of His message. A prophet does not set himself up as the object of worship; he invites people to give their ultimate allegiance to God and to fear and worship only Him.

Verse 51: The concluding verse, while it sums up the teaching and ministry of every prophet, has special significance in the present context because it negates the idea of Jesus' Lordship: God is the Lord of Jesus just as He is the Lord of all other human beings.

III. Literary Notes

1. Verse 45 is highly proleptic. Anticipating Mary's surprise and consternation at the news that they are about to break to her, the angels make an elaborate preemptive attempt to lay her fears to rest. Their statement in the verse is intended not only to comfort her, but also to make her feel that, in giving birth to Jesus without having had contact with a man, she will earn a distinction that no other woman in history has ever had. The angels say that they bring "good news"; that Jesus will be a "Word" from God; that the boy's name, Jesus—as also his title, Messiah—has already been chosen by God Himself; that Jesus will occupy an especially high status in this world and in the next; that Jesus will, while still an infant, speak with people; and that he will survive his opponents' attempts to inflict harm on him and will reach an advanced age.

2. In verse 48, in the phrase "the Book and wisdom, and the Torah and the Evangel," the conjunction "and" (Arabic: *wāw*) occurs three times. The first and third *wāw*'s—the former joining "the Book" and "wisdom" and the latter joining "the Torah" and "the Evangel"—are simple conjunctions, but the second *wāw*, which divides the complete phrase into two equal parts, is explicatory or exegetical. On this construction, the phrase will be seen to have the parallel structure of ABA′B′.

3. While the passage emphasizes the importance of the Evangel for the purpose of revitalizing the Law, it does so without diminishing the importance of the Torah: the Evangel exists only in order to revitalize the Law represented by the Torah. The centrality of the Torah is underscored by the way the Torah and the Evangel are mentioned: Verse 48 speaks of both the Torah and the Evangel; then follows, in verse 49, a statement about Jesus' miracles; verse 50 comes back to the subject of scripture, but only the Torah is named this time.

4. Two instances of a significant use of the indefinite article may be noted. In verse 45, Jesus is called "*a* Word from Him [God]," the indefiniteness signifying that Jesus is only one of the many "words" of God and that, like many other events, the birth of Jesus was brought about by God's utterance of the simple command "Be!" In plain words, Jesus is not God. In verse 51, acceptance of God as the only Lord is termed "*a* Straight Path," the indefiniteness in this case representing the special kind of emphasis known in Arabic grammar as magnification. The phrase, thus, means: "This is *a superior and matchless* Straight Path."

IV. Jesus in the Bible and the Qurʾān

We cannot discuss at length the Biblical view of Jesus' birth, miracles, and mission. We will only consider how the Bible seems to help to elucidate some of the points made in the Qurʾānic passage under discussion and how the Biblical account is similar to or different from the Qurʾānic:

1. The birth of Jesus is described in the opening chapter of Luke:

> 26In the sixth month the angel Gabriel was sent by God to a town in Galilee called Nazareth, 27to a virgin engaged to a man whose name was Joseph, of the house of David. The virgin's name was Mary. 28And he came to her and said, "Greetings, favored one! The Lord is with you." 29But she was much perplexed by his words and pondered what sort of greeting this might be. 30The angel said to her, "Do not be afraid, Mary, for you have found favor with God. 31And now, you will conceive in your womb and bear a son, and you will name him Jesus. 32He will be great, and will be called the Son of the Most High, and the Lord God will give to him the throne of his ancestor David. 33He will reign over the house of Jacob forever, and of his kingdom there will be no end." 34Mary said to the angel, "How can this be, since I am a virgin?" 35The angel said to her, "The Holy Spirit will come upon you, and the power of the Most High will overshadow you; therefore the child to be born will be holy; he will be called Son of God. 36And now, your relative Elizabeth in her old age has also conceived a son; and this is the sixth month for her who was said to be barren. 37For nothing is impossible with God." Then Mary said, "Here am I, the servant of the Lord; let it be with me according to your word." Then the angel departed from her.

There are some obvious similarities between the Qurʾānic passage under discussion and the New Testament passage. In both scriptures, Jesus' birth is presented as a miraculous happening. In the Qurʾān as well as in the New Testament, Mary is visited by angels, who inform her that God will cause her to bear a son even though she is a virgin. That she is visited by one angel, Gabriel, in the New Testament but by a group of angels in the Qurʾān is not a major difference, especially since the Arabic plural *malāʾikah* used in the Qurʾān can, grammatically, be interpreted to mean that one member of the class of angels visited Mary—this angel then being identified as Gabriel. By referring to Elizabeth, Zachariah's wife, who is six months pregnant with John the Baptist, the New Testament passage establishes a connection between the birth of Jesus and the birth of John the Baptist. The Qurʾānic passage does not mention John the Baptist or his father or mother, but, as we noted at the beginning (see section I, above), in sūrah 3, in the passage immediately preceding the one we are discussing, Zachariah receives, from angels, the good news of the birth of a son, whose name will be John (a similar scenario is found in the first few passages of sūrah 19). In both scriptures, Mary, surprised at the news of the birth of a son, is told by the angels that God will bring about the birth of Jesus, for nothing is beyond God's power. The child is called Jesus in both scriptures.

There are also some obvious differences between the New Testament passage and the Qurʾānic passage. Unlike the Qurʾān, the New Testament provides more detail, giving names of specific persons and places. And, unlike the Qurʾānic passage, the New Testament passage acquires political overtones by predicting the ascendancy of the house of David over the house of Jacob. Most important, though, the New Testament passage, by calling Jesus "the Son of the Most High" and "Son of God," seems to divinize Jesus, whereas the Qurʾānic passage repeatedly emphasizes Jesus' humanity. From an Islamic standpoint, however, the word "son" in the New Testament expressions "the Son of the Most High" and "Son of God" ought to be understood in a figurative rather than in a literal sense. If so, then the word "son" or the expression "son of God" may be used of any human being, not exclusively of Jesus—just as God may be called the "Father" not only of Jesus but of any other human beings (see section IV.5, below).

2. Verse 49 calls Jesus a messenger to the Israelites. This suggests that Jesus was supposed to preach to the Israelites only. Matthew 10:5–6, referring to Jesus' twelve disciples, says:

> [5]These twelve Jesus sent out with the following instructions: "Go nowhere among the Gentiles, and enter no town of the Samaritans, [6]but go rather to the lost sheep of the house of Israel."

That the Israelites were expecting the rise of a prophet at the time of Jesus is attested in the New Testament. For example, the imprisoned John the Baptist, on receiving reports about the works of Jesus, sent two of his disciples to Jesus to determine whether he was the one awaited: "The disciples of John reported all these things to him. So John summoned two of his disciples and sent them to the Lord to ask, 'Are you the one who is to come, or are we to wait for another?'" (Luke 7:18–19). The following incident, too, indicates that the Israelites were expecting the rise of a prophet. While Jesus was at the house of the Pharisee Simeon, who had invited him to dinner, "a woman in the city, who was a sinner" came in and kissed Jesus' feet and anointed them, prompting Simeon to think: "If this man were a prophet, he would have known who and what kind of woman this is who is touching him—that she is a sinner" (Luke 7:36–39). Simeon's words "If this man were a prophet" indicate that the advent of a new prophet was expected by the Israelites at that time.

3. From a Qurʾānic standpoint, Jesus was sent to reinvest the Torah with the wisdom that the Israelites' formalistic religious practice had caused to disappear. The Evangel represents the wisdom complementing the Torah: it brings to the fore what had been consigned to the background. Without offering any new laws, the Evangel revives the forgotten insights of the Torah, thus fulfilling the Torah. As Jesus remarked: "Do not think that I have come to abolish the law or the prophets; I have come not to abolish but to fulfill" (Matthew 5:17). Jesus also said: "But it is easier for heaven and earth to pass away, than for one stroke of a letter in the law to be dropped" (Luke 16:17).

4. The New Testament, although it relates more than thirty-five miracles of Jesus, mentions only the second and third of the four miracles listed in verse 49 of the Qurʾānic passage (on the second miracle, see John 9:1–7; Matthew 8:1–3; Luke 17:11–14; on the third, see Matthew 9:18–25; Luke 7:11–16; John 12:11–44). And while it does not mention the miracle of Jesus speaking in the cradle, it does say that Jesus' learned conversation with the teachers at the temple of Jerusalem amazed his audiences when Jesus was only twelve years old (Luke 2:41–47). The important thing to note is that, in verse 49 of the Qurʾānic passage, the origination of Jesus' miracles is explicitly attributed to God: Jesus performed the miracles "by God's will." A Muslim reading of the New Testament will take "by God's will" as understood in the relevant texts in that scripture.

5. There is a clear resonance between Jesus' statement in verse 51 of the Qurʾānic passage, "God is my Lord and your Lord" (verse 51), and Jesus' statement in John 20:17, "I am ascending to my Father and your Father, to my God and your God."

13 God's Blessing upon the Arabs

3 Family of ʿImrān 102–105

102O you who believe, fear God as He ought to be feared; and you must not die
except that you be in submission. 103And hold firmly the Rope of God, all of you
together, and do not be divided. And recall the blessing of God upon you, when you
were enemies and God brought your hearts into concord, and you became brothers
by His blessing; and you were on the brink of a pit of fire, and He salvaged you from
it. Thus does God elucidate His signs to you so that you may be guided.
104And let there be, from among you, a group of people who would invite to
good, and would enjoin right and forbid wrong; and it is they who are the
successful ones. 105And do not be like those who became divided and developed
differences after manifest signs had come to them; and they are the ones for whom
there is a great punishment.

Sūrah 3 is Madīnan.

I. Introduction

This passage addresses the formerly pagan Arabs, reminding them of their life before their conversion to Islam: They were in a state of disunity, lacking as they did a unifying vision, a central political authority, and a cohesive social setup. As a result, they had become enemies of one another, wars among them had become endemic, and the strong among them brazenly exploited the weak. In a word, they lived in a state of near anarchy. They were about to be consumed by the fires of discord and oppression when God quenched those fires and salvaged them by raising among them a prophet who would unite them under the banner of Islam. Islam furnished the Arabs with the rationale for coming together and forming a well-knit group; it made them members of one large family, as it were—a great blessing of God upon them. The passage warns the Arabs, however, that the benefits that have accrued to them from their acceptance of Islam will not be secured automatically. Unity is not simply a function of conversion: the members of the new group must make a conscious and diligent effort to remain united; otherwise, they will relapse into their former state of disunity and anarchy. The passage also imposes an obligation upon the new Muslim community: There must arise, from within this community, a group of people who would undertake the ethical mission of promoting good and discouraging evil. And these people must, all the while, maintain unity among their ranks.

II. Commentary

Verse 102: The address of "O you who believe" establishes a connection between belief and the set of injunctions that follow. The fundamental point made is that belief must have a direct effect on one's life. It is not enough to believe in God; it is necessary to obey Him, carry out His commandments, and fear His wrath, which will overtake those who defy Him.

The phrase "fear God as He ought to be feared" distinguishes between fear of God and fear of people. Human beings have a limited ability to monitor and punish. God, being omniscient and omnipotent, has knowledge not only of one's actions but also of the secret motives lying behind one's actions. Furthermore, God's punishment for those who defy Him is extraordinarily severe. One should, therefore, fear God to a much greater degree than one might fear a human being.

"And you must not die except that you be in submission" does not, of course, mean that it does not matter how one lives one's life as long as one remembers to make submission to God just before breathing one's last. It means that fear of God and the desire to fulfill His commandments should characterize one's entire life. It implies that the course of life is, from beginning to end, marked by challenges, temptations, and pitfalls and that one must meet all challenges, overcome all temptations, and avoid all pitfalls, submitting to God to one's last breath. The need to do so becomes urgent when one keeps in mind that no one knows the hour of one's death and, accordingly, one must constantly watch one's step in life.

The last part of the verse may also be translated as "except that you be Muslims." But the word *muslimūn* (sing. *muslim*, literally, "submitter") in the original text puts the emphasis on the quality of submission rather than on a particular religious designation. In other words, the verse means not that one should die bearing a Muslim name, belonging to a Muslim household or community, and claiming to be a Muslim, but, rather, that one should die, being a *muslim* in the true sense of the word, offering complete and unqualified submission to God.

Verse 103: Verse 102, which says that the believers must not die except in a state of submission to God, was addressed individually to each member of the believing community. Verse 103 now instructs the members of that community to maintain unity among their ranks. The image used in this connection—that of the "Rope of God"—is significant in at least two ways.

First, the Arabic word used in the original for "rope" is *ḥabl*, which, in contexts like the present one, means "pact." When two Arab individuals or tribal chiefs made a pact with each other, each took a rope and joined it to the other's, symbolizing entry into an agreement or contract. To the Qur'ān's Arab audience, the novel phrase *ḥablu llāh*, the "Rope of God," must have signified God's covenant with human beings. In the case of Islam, this covenant may be described variously, without implying substantial difference between the several descriptions, as taking the form of the Qur'ān, the fundamental source of Divine guidance; of the Islamic code of conduct known as the Sharī'ah; or of the religion of Islam in general. In a *ḥadīth*, the Prophet Muḥammad calls the Qur'ān the "Rope of God" stretching down to earth from the heavens—with the believers expected to grasp that rope.

Second, the rope represents salvation, both in this world and in the next. One can picture a man who is about to drown in the sea or has slipped down a rock and has lost control: a rope is thrown to such a man, and he grasps it and is pulled up to safety.

Note that the verse says that the believers should, all of them together, grasp the "Rope of God." This means that not only the individual Muslims but the Muslims as a community must submit to God, for their unity and security will be guaranteed only if they hold that rope firmly both as individuals and as a collectivity.

"And do not be divided." This is a reinforcement, in negative terms, of the injunction to the Muslim community to seize the "Rope of God" together. The injunction now means that the Muslims' abandoning of the "Rope of God" will give rise to division and schism among them.

Further reinforcement of the same idea is provided in this verse through reference to the particular situation of the Arabs at the advent of Islam. As explained in section I, above, the lack both of a common outlook and of a durable political and social setup resulted in constant fighting among the Arabs, with the powerful elements of society oppressing the weak. Through Islam, "God brought your hearts into concord, and you became brothers by His blessing." In the verse's remark about God salvaging the Arabs from the brink of fire, the word "fire" has both a literal meaning—hellfire in the afterlife—and a metaphorical meaning—destructive discord in this life. The Arabs should, therefore, be grateful to God for His gift of Islam to them, for Islam serves as the basis of their unity in this world and will serve as a basis of their salvation in the next world.

In reminding the Arabs that God has blessed them with unity through Islam, the verse not only makes a comment that has general validity, but also alludes to a certain instance of conflict in Arabia. Before the rise of Islam, the two large tribes of the city of Madīnah, the Aws and the Khazraj, were locked in a deadly combat that had lasted for decades, taking a heavy toll on life and economy, on the one hand, and on peace and stability, on the other. In fact, one of the reasons why the Madīnans chose to become the followers of Muḥammad was that they saw in Muḥammad a man who possessed the leadership qualities necessary to bring back peace to the war-torn city. The Qur'ānic verse fits the particular situation of the Aws-Khazraj relationship before the Muslims' arrival in Madīnah (622) just as it fits the general situation of intertribal conflict in Arabia before the rise of Islam.

In view of its importance, the subject of unity and disunity has been treated in this Qurʾānic passage in some detail: "Thus does God elucidate His signs to you"—all with the aim "that you may be guided."

Verse 104: This is a statement of the new Islamic community's mandate: the community must ensure that it keeps producing—through institutionalized arrangement, the verse seems to be suggesting—"a group of people" who would uphold the Islamic ethical ideal of inviting others to good by commanding right and forbidding wrong; the implication, of course, is that these people must first live up to a high ethical standard themselves. The Arabic word used in the verse for the said "group of people" is *ummah*. Among the connotations of this word are largeness and centrality. The word's use in the verse implies, then, that the said group of people should be both significantly large in number and centrally important to the community. Since the larger—or rather, the worldwide—Muslim community, too, is known as an *ummah*, the use of the same word, in verse 104, for a certain group of people suggests that the larger *ummah* will become a true *ummah* only if it includes in its ranks another *ummah*, one epitomizing high ethical ideals and standards, for it is this latter *ummah* that will vindicate the larger *ummah* at the bar of history.

While the mandate with which the Muslim community is being charged is essentially ethical in character, that mandate, the verse states, can be fully implemented only when backed with political power. The verse does not merely say, "a group of people who would invite to good," but adds, "and would enjoin right and forbid wrong." Only a viable institutional setup possessing the necessary authority can serve to accomplish the goal of enjoining and forbidding mentioned in the verse. The establishment, in Islamic history, of the political institution known as the caliphate was in response to the imperative arising from the Qurʾānic mandate of enjoining good and forbidding evil.

"It is they who are the successful ones" makes reference not to the smaller group of people that, according to the verse, must exist to enjoin good and forbid evil, but to the entire community that will make an effort to hold fast to the "Rope of God."

Verse 105: Verse 103 urged the new Muslim community to unite and warned it against falling prey to schism. The concluding verse of the passage now urges the Muslims, who have received manifest guidance from God in the form of the Qurʾān, not to walk in the footsteps of those nations of the past that allowed themselves to suffer from schismatic division even though they were in possession of clear instructions from God to obey God and remain united. Those who fall prey to such schism while possessing Divine guidance commit an inexcusable sin and will face severe punishment in the hereafter.

14 One God, One Humanity

4 Women 1

O people, fear your Lord, who created you from a single being, and created, from it, its mate, and propagated, from the two, many men and women. And fear God—in whose name you petition one another—and the ties of kinship. God is keeping watch over you.

Sūrah 4 is Madīnan.

I. Introduction

This is one of the key verses of the Qur'ān. It states that, just as there is only one God, so, in the final analysis, there is one humanity. From these two statements, presented in the verse with almost axiomatic force, flow certain consequences, or certain rights and responsibilities, that human beings should be mindful of.

II. Commentary

The word "people" in the opening part of the verse is both specific and general. It is specific in that it stands for Muslims, who believe in the Qur'ān, by means of which they are being addressed; it is general in that the essential message contained in the verse is purported to appeal to all members of humankind.

In "fear your Lord," the word "fear" is a translation of the Arabic *ittaqū*, an imperative meaning "have *taqwā*." Often translated, as here, as "fear," *taqwā* does not mean "fear" in such phrases as "fear of darkness" or "fear of financial loss." As an elemental human feeling or emotion, fear does not have to be moral. A killer may have fear of being caught by the police, but such fear would not be called *taqwā*. *Taqwā* denotes fear that arises from one's conviction that overstepping the limits set by a righteous, just, merciful, and wise God is wrong and entails dire consequences. *Taqwā*, in this sense, is moral in character, so when the Qur'ān enjoins its followers to have *taqwā*, it asks them to cultivate a moral quality or attribute. From this, it is clear that one of the popular translations of *taqwā*, "God-consciousness," while not without merit, represents an overly intellectualized understanding of the concept. One might say, though, that *taqwā* is a religious virtue with both a cognitive and an actional aspect. The cognitive aspect has to do with the consciousness of the limits set by God; the actional aspect has to do with restraining oneself, in practice, from overstepping those limits.

The next part of the verse—"who created you from a single being, and created, from it, its mate, and propagated, from the two, many men and women"—is significant in several ways. The "single being" is, in light of other Qur'ānic verses, Adam. Adam's "mate," though not mentioned by name in the Qur'ān, is Eve, as we learn from the Bible. A comment on the use of the preposition "from" in the phrase "and [God] created, from it [the "single being"], its mate" is in order. The preposition (Arabic: *min*) denotes genus rather than source. That is, it denotes that Adam's mate was of the same class as Adam himself, the Qur'ān thus parting company with the view that Adam, the first human being to be created, served as the *physical source* from which his mate was extracted (see section V, below). After creating Adam, a male, and then Eve, a female, God "propagated, from the two, many men and women." All human beings, then, are descendants of Adam and Eve. Incidentally, the verse alludes to two different modes of creation: while the first human pair was brought into being through what appears to be a direct or special act of Divine creation—irrespective of whether such an act represented the culmination of a short or a long process—the rest of humanity came into being through procreation, in accordance with the laws of biology.

In the next part of the verse, "the ties of kinship" are elevated in status by being joined to "God" by conjunction. The addressees are instructed, on the one hand, to fear God, in whose name they ask one another for help and support in difficult situations, and, on the other hand, to fear severing the ties of kinship, for, on the maintenance and promotion of these ties depend the stability and harmony of both family and society. The particular construction of the sentence in the original Arabic text lends emphasis to "the ties of kinship" rather than to "God." This is probably fitting since the commandment to fear God has already been given in the earlier part of the verse. It is notable that, at the start of the verse, the commandment was to fear "your Lord" (*Rabbakum*) whereas the commandment in the middle of the verse is to fear "God" (*Allāh*). As a rule, *Rabb* ("Lord") denotes the Divine quality of providence, whereas *Allāh* denotes the Divine quality of majesty. As such, the opening of the verse reminds people that they will be held accountable for the blessings they have received from their provident Lord. Subsequently, though, the people are told that their failure to maintain the ties of kinship will bring them punishment from a powerful, majestic God.

Since the reference to "the ties of kinship" means that those ties must not be severed, the verse can be seen as saying: Fear God (that is, obey his commandments), and fear the bonds of kinship (that is, do not break or violate these bonds). But the phrase "in whose name you petition one another," which follows "God," may be taken as understood after "the ties of kinship" as well. The meaning now would be: Fear—that is, obey—God, in whose name you ask one another for help, and fear severing the ties of kinship, which, too, you invoke while seeking one another's help.

"God is keeping watch over you" is both a promise and a threat. God, who keeps constant watch over people, will reward those who keep his commandments but will punish those who violate those commandments.

III. Issues

1. Significance of *Taqwā* in the Sūrah's Context. The reference to *taqwā* in this opening verse of sūrah 4 has a special significance. Sūrah 4 contains a large number of commandments, many of which require one to act in strict accordance with rules in situations where one might be tempted to violate, or ignore, those commandments, and one needs to possess *taqwā* conscientiously to carry them out. For example, one of the sūrah's commandments is that one who is managing an orphan's property should hand over the property to the child when the latter becomes old enough to manage his own affairs. To forgo control of property, especially when it is substantial, requires a strong sense of responsibility and fairness, and only people with self-discipline, or *taqwā*, will be capable of it.

2. Humanity of Woman. The "single being" of whom the verse speaks is, in light of other Qur'ānic verses, Adam. Since, according to the verse, Adam's mate, Eve, was created "from" him—in the sense explained above—it follows that Eve, or woman, equally partakes of humanity and is not inferior to Adam in any respect. Thus, women can neither be reduced to a lower status in society nor deprived of the rights that belong to them in their capacity as human beings.

3. Kinship. The commandment to respect "the ties of kinship," though general in import, had a particular charge of meaning for the Qur'ān's first addressees (the dual aspect of generality and particularity is noticeable in many of the commandments found in sūrah 4—for example, in verses 2–5, which deal with management of orphans' property and, at the same time, comment on or allude to the relevant Arab attitudes toward orphans). Living as they did in a tribal setup, the Arabs regarded kinship as the cornerstone of their social existence. The Qur'ānic appeal to the Arabs to mind the ties of kinship, therefore, had a deep resonance for them. In the verse, the appeal serves as a subtle reminder to the Arabs that their attitude of hostility to Muḥammad and his message not only represents their lack of fear of God, but also violates the finest Arabian tradition of respecting the ties of kinship. At the same time, the Qur'ān, while retaining the *idea* of kinship as a unifying social force, is trying to substitute the *tribal basis* of kinship with a *religious one* by grounding kinship in a God-oriented worldview.

4. Adam and Eve as the First Ancestors of Humanity. Individual human beings seek their origins in their ancestors. Races, likewise, seek their origins in their ancestors of the ancient past or in events in which their first ancestors were actually or supposedly involved. But, as a rule, races, having identified one or more suitable ancestors, consider it unnecessary or inexpedient to push the inquiry farther back into history. In fact, it is only by stopping at some arbitrary point that races define themselves and give themselves an identity. This view of racial identity frequently is the cause of animosity, feud, even war between races. The Qur'ān rejects any such arbitrary point of origin of the human race, and it is in this vein that Q 4:1 remarks that the entire human race originated from a pair of human beings, the ancestors of all ancestors, implying that the unity of biological origins should lead human beings to consider themselves members of a single family.

By declaring that all of humanity has descended from one male and one female, the verse lays the groundwork for a broadly conceived human ethics, thus cutting the ground from under all racially based ethics. The verse seems to be saying that, in order for it to be suitable for all human beings, an ethics must be based on universally valid principles rather than on the consideration that the rights, privileges, or interests of one race are more sacred than those of others.

Closely allied to the ethical dimension—in fact, deriving from it—is the legal dimension of the Qur'ānic statement about Adam and Eve being the ancestors of all human beings, who must, therefore, regard one another as members of one universal family, discharge their obligations toward one another, refrain from usurping one another's rights, and, in general, treat one another with love, compassion, and fairness.

IV. Literary Notes

1. In its second occurrence in the verse, the imperative verb "fear" (Arabic: *ittaqū*) is used in a somewhat different sense with each of its two objects, "God" and "the ties of kinship." The verse means: fear the *punishment* of God and fear *severing* the ties of kinship. As such, the use of the word is an instance of zeugma.

2. The verse refers to the Divinity by using, first, the word "Lord" (*Rabb*) and, then, the word "God" (*Allāh*). The change in the vocabulary makes an oblique criticism of the division, made by the idolatrous Arabs of Muḥammad's times, between the Godhead and the Lordship of the Divinity. Rejecting the division, the Qur'ān is saying: the being who created the world—God—is the same being who is taking providential care of it—the Lord (see Chapter 1, "The Essence of the Qur'ān," section II, verse 1).

V. A Comparative Note on the Bible

The essential thesis of this verse—namely, that there is one God and one humanity—will be found abundantly attested in the Bible, and there is no need to discuss it here. A brief comparison between the Qur'ānic and Biblical accounts of the creation of Eve is, however, in order.

As stated previously, the preposition "from" (Arabic: *min*) in the phrase "And [God] created, from it [the very first human being created], its mate" denotes genus rather than source, the Qur'ān differing with the view that the first being created by

God, Adam, served as the *source* from which Adam's mate, Eve, was brought forth. In the Bible, the creation of Eve is described in these words:

> So the Lord God caused a deep sleep to fall upon the man, and he slept; then he took one of his ribs and closed up its place with flesh. And the rib that the Lord God had taken from the man he made into a woman and brought her to the man. Then the man said,
>
> "This at last is bone of my bones and flesh of my flesh;
> this one shall be called Woman, for out of Man this one was taken." (Genesis 2:21–23)

In the passage in the Hebrew Bible, the preposition *min* occurs no fewer than five times:

- in "one of his ribs"—the construction in the Hebrew original being "*from* his ribs, one"
- in "the rib that the Lord God had taken *from* the man"
- in "bone of my bones," which, in a literal translation of the Hebrew original, would be "bone *from* my bones"
- in "flesh of my flesh," which, literally, would be "flesh *from* my flesh"
- in "out of Man," which, again, literally, would be "*from* Man"

A perusal of these occurrences of the preposition suggests that, in the Bible, the preposition *min* denotes, primarily, source, and, secondarily and derivatively, genus: Adam was the physical source from which Eve was brought forth, and, later, Eve was considered to be of the same genus as Adam.

15 Orphans, Justice, and Polygamy

4 Women 2–4

[2]And give the orphans their wealth. And do not exchange the unwholesome for the wholesome, and do not devour their wealth by joining it to your wealth; this, indeed, is a very great sin. [3]And if you suspect that you will not act equitably in regard to the orphans, then marry any of the women that are good for you—two each, three each, four each. But if you suspect that you will not act justly, then one—or what you possess in your hands; this will make it more likely that you will not deviate. [4]And give the women their dowers, graciously. Then, if they willingly relinquish a part of it in your favor, consume it with pleasure and relish.

Sūrah 4 is Madīnan.

I. Introduction

These verses were part of the Qur'ānic program to reform Arabia's social system. Early Qur'ānic revelations criticized the rich people of Makkah for ill-treating orphans and usurping property that the latter may have inherited. Other revelations faulted society as a whole for allowing unfair treatment of women. This passage addresses men who were guardians of orphans, instructing them to serve as responsible caretakers of the orphans and their property and permitting them to marry the orphans' mothers if that would help them to discharge better their obligations toward the orphans. The permission to marry more than one wife is made conditional upon treating the wives with justice.

A brief note on translation: The Arabic word for "women," *nisā'*, occurs twice in this passage, once each in verse 3 and in verse 4. Since, in both verses, I take it to refer to particular women—the mothers of orphans—I have translated it in both cases with the definite article: "the women."

Q 4:127–130, the subject of chapter 17 ("Matrimony: Some Issues"), is closely related to the present passage since, revealed at a later time, it addresses some of the questions that arose in the minds of Muslims upon the revelation of the present passage.

II. Commentary

Verse 2: This verse addresses the guardians of orphans, reminding them that they have been put in charge of the orphans' wealth only temporarily and that, eventually, they must return the wealth to its rightful owners without embezzling or mismanaging it. (Verses 5–6 of the sūrah, coming immediately after this passage, enjoin that the property of the orphans be turned over to them when they reach adulthood and are able to handle financial matters.) Two unlawful ways of taking the orphans' wealth are mentioned: replacing an orphan's valuable article of wealth with one's own that is worthless or defective ("And do not exchange the unwholesome for the wholesome") and combining an orphan's wealth with one's own with the intention of usurping the orphan's wealth under the pretext of joint management ("And do not devour their wealth by joining it to your wealth"). The demonstrative *this* in "this, indeed, is a very great sin" refers to each of the two acts.

Significantly, this verse occurs right after the sūrah's opening verse (discussed in the previous chapter), in which the believers are advised to "fear God—in whose name you petition one another—and the ties of kinship." The move from that admonition to one about responsible caretaking of orphans' property underscores the importance attached by the Qur'ān to the rights of orphans.

Verse 3: If the guardians of orphans are afraid that they cannot by themselves fulfill their responsibility toward the orphans and would need the help of the orphans' mothers to carry out the responsibility and, to that end, wish to marry the orphans' mothers, then they are allowed to do so—provided, first, that the number of a man's wives does not exceed four and, second, that a man is able to treat all his wives equally. If, however, a man suspects that he will not be able to treat his wives equally, then he must marry only one woman or a female slave, for this is likely to keep him from violating the principle of justice, which principle he risks violating if he were to marry more than one woman. Since the verse distinguishes "female slave(s)" from "women," it follows that, here, "women" means "free women."

The phrase "that are good for you" (*mā ṭāba lakum*) can be interpreted in several, but not necessarily incompatible, senses: (1) who are lawful to you—that is, whom the law allows you to marry; (2) who are willing to marry you; and (3) marriage with whom will bring harmony to your life.

The next part of the verse permits marriage with two, three, or four women, but not with more than four.

"What you possess in your hands" means "female slave(s)" (see section III, below). The image behind the phrase "what you possess in your hands"—a slave "held" in one's hand—is found in other languages, too. For example, the English verb *manumit*, which is of Latin origin and means "to release from slavery" (n. *manumission*), is composed of *manus*, "hand," and *mittere*—literally, "to send from one's hand." *Emancipate*, a synonym of *manumit*, has a similar etymology.

Verse 4: Men who have orphan wards and wish to marry their mothers might think that they are already doing those women a favor and, therefore, do not have to give the women a bridal gift. This verse disabuses them of any such thought, commanding them to give the dower.

In the original text, the Arabic word used for "dowers," *ṣaduqāt*, comes from a root (*ṣ-d-q*) that denotes truthfulness and sincerity. The use of this word in the verse implies that it is important for the man to pay the dower as a token of his serious and sincere commitment to the marital relationship.

The phrase "And give the women their dowers, graciously" carries multiple points of emphasis, and stressing different words will bring out the full implications of the statement:

- Stressing the word *give* would imply that the bridal gift must be given and cannot be withheld.
- Stressing the word *women* would imply that the recipient of the bridal gift is the woman herself and not her family, that the gift is not a "bride-price" that is to be handed over to the woman's parents or guardian, and that no pressure must be put on the woman by others, not even by her husband, to relinquish the right to the bridal gift in whole or in part.
- Stressing the word *graciously* would imply that a man who wishes to marry an orphan's mother must not be a grudging giver of a dower.

The last part of the verse forbids the man to force his bride either to forgo, in whole or in part, her right to the dower or to return the dower, in whole or in part, to him. The dower belongs to the woman, and it is her exclusive privilege to make use of it the way she decides. If, however, the woman gives all or part of the dower back to her husband of her own free will, then, and only then, the dower lawfully belongs to the husband, who may use it "with pleasure and relish"—that is, without fear of accountability in this world or in the next and without any qualms or reservations.

It was said above that the Arabic word *nisā'* ("women"), which occurs in verses 3 and 4, refers to particular women—to the mothers of orphans. It goes without saying that the prescribed conduct toward such women is the prescribed treatment toward women in general as well.

III. Issues

1. Polygamy. Verse 3 of this passage permits polygamy (strictly, polygyny) but puts restrictions on it. In pre-Islamic Arabia, there was no upper limit to the number of women a man could marry. This verse limits the number to four.

In the verse, the permission to marry more than one wife occurs in the context of the need to protect the rights of orphans and, as such, can rightly be said to be ancillary to that theme. But the view that protection of the orphans' rights is the sole basis of the Islamic permission of polygamy is clearly apologetic and is at odds both with the Prophet Muḥammad's practice and with the historical Muslim practice and understanding. Besides, one might argue that the real basis for the Qur'ānic permission to marry more than one woman is social need and that protection of orphans' rights represents only one of the many possible types of social need. On the other hand, it is obvious that the text does not regard marrying more than one woman as a preferred option. It is no less clear that the verse considers equal treatment of wives to be of such paramount importance that it forbids polygamy where such treatment is not possible, raising the question whether such a consideration can become the basis of legislation or policy formation in a Muslim society. Finally, a distinction needs to be made between command and permission. The strong insistence, in Islam, on getting married suggests that, barring impediments to it, marriage—that is, marriage in its elemental form, monogamy—is mandatory in Islam. Marrying more than one woman is, however, at best, a permission, and, arguably, the overall thrust of verse 3 is to discourage—perhaps, even to prohibit—polygamy.

2. Slavery. The injunction, in verse 3, about marriage with female slaves calls for a brief discussion of the Islamic view of slavery.

Slavery, though not part of the Islamic religion itself, was, nevertheless, part of the social system inherited by Islam in seventh-century Arabia. The class-based Arabian society made a sharp distinction between free persons and slaves. In keeping with its philosophy of introducing graduated change, Islam, over the years, took several steps to abolish slavery and integrate slaves into society as the equals of free persons: it called the freeing of slaves a good act that brought great reward; it prescribed the freeing of slaves as an act of atonement for certain violations of the law or lapses of conduct; it designated the freeing of slaves as one of the objectives for which the funds collected under the scheme of mandatory giving called *zakāh* could be spent (see chapter 22, "Charity Offerings"); and it obligated slave owners to accept the offer made by their slaves to win their freedom on payment of an agreed-upon sum of money or on performance of certain services. Before the measures outlined above could produce the desired result, certain other measures, for the interim, were needed. One such measure was the prohibition to force female slaves into prostitution, a practice common at the time of the rise of Islam. The injunction about marrying female slaves, given in verse 3 of this passage, constituted another such measure. The injunction, since it is presented as an alternative to the injunction about marrying a free woman, is meant to raise the status of female slaves.

In ancient Arabia, slaves were acquired in three ways: (1) raids were launched with the specific aim of capturing booty, including slaves; (2) children born of female slaves remained slaves, which made slavery a self-perpetuating institution; and (3) in a war fought between two tribes, the captives, men and women, were made slaves. Islam outlawed the first two of the three ways, allowing only the third one, and that as a provisional measure that would be used reactively—in modern terminology, as leverage or as a bargaining chip—in a situation where the enemy, having taken Muslim prisoners of war, enslaves them, refusing to exchange them for its own troops taken prisoner by Muslims. Today, with the evolution of international laws concerning prisoners of war—such laws favoring exchange of prisoners of war and rejecting the notion of enslavement—the last of the above-mentioned three ways of acquiring slaves would also seem to have become irrelevant, making slavery a nonissue in Islam.

IV. Literary Notes

1. In explaining verse 2 (see section II, above), attention was drawn to the significance of verse 2 following verse 1, the latter verse being the subject of discussion in the previous chapter. That significance is further underscored by the conjunction "and," with which verse 2 opens. The use of the conjunction indicates that the commandment in this verse to hand over the orphans' wealth to them is, in substance and spirit, based on the same principles that were laid down in verse 1. Thus, the conjunction not only establishes a grammatical connection between the two verses, but links up the verses on a conceptual level as well—one reason why, as stated in the General Introduction (section VII.2), it is advisable to retain the translation of the conjunction in English.

2. In verse 3, the phrase "that are good for you" is an example of the Qur'ān's use of words and expressions with multiple meanings, all allowable and simultaneously applicable (see section II, verse 3, above).

V. A Comparative Note on the Bible

The subjects dealt with in this Qur'ānic passage are dealt with in the Bible as well.

1. Orphans. While both the Qur'ān and the Bible contain a number of general injunctions about treating orphans with kindness and justice, the spirit informing the prohibition in the Qur'ānic passage against devouring the orphans' wealth is very much present in the Biblical criticism of the wicked, who "drive away the donkey of the orphans" (Job 24:3).

2. Polygamy. Polygamy is an acceptable form of marriage in the Bible, and, in principle, no limit is set to the number of women a man can marry. Many of the major Biblical figures were simultaneously married to more than one woman—for example, Abraham, who had two wives, Sarah and Hagar (Genesis 16:3), and, either before or after Sarah's death, took the concubine Keturah as his wife (25:1); Jacob, who was married to Leah (29:23), Rachel (29:28), Bilhah (30:4), and Zilpah (30:9); and Solomon, among whose wives were "seven hundred princesses and three hundred concubines" (1 Kings 11:3).

While, unlike the Qur'ān, the Bible appears to allow a man to marry as many wives as he wishes, the overall thrust of the Bible, as that of the Qur'ān, seems to be in the direction of monogamy. Polygamy, especially in later Biblical times, was practiced largely in royal households. Like the Qur'ān, the Bible urges a man with more than one wife to treat his wives with justice, as is attested by Exodus 21:10: "If he takes another wife to himself, he shall not diminish the food, clothing, or marital rights of the first wife."

3. Slavery. The Bible permits men to marry women captured in war (Deuteronomy 21:11–13), and marriage with female slaves, whether captured in war or purchased, was practiced in Biblical times. Hagar, given to Abraham by his wife Sarah, was a slave-girl (Genesis 16:3); two of Jacob's wives, Bilhah and Zilpah, were the handmaids of, respectively, Leah (Genesis 29:24) and Rachel (Genesis 29:29), also Jacob's wives; and Solomon's three hundred concubines are counted among his wives (1 Kings 11:3).

Slavery was not invented by Judaism any more than it was invented by Islam. Like Islam, Judaism had to reckon with an already existing slavery-based social system, and, like Islam, it took a series of measures to mitigate the negative effects of slavery.

4. Dower. That offering the dower was an accepted practice in Judaism is evident from Genesis 34:12, in which Shechem expresses his desire to marry Jacob's daughter Dinah ("Put the marriage present and gift as high as you like"), and from 1 Samuel 18:25, in which Saul sends a message to David, offering to make the latter his son-in-law ("The king desires no marriage present except a hundred foreskins of the Philistines"). The Hebrew word for "dower," *mōhar*, is sometimes translated as "bride-price" (as in Exodus 22:16–17). Unlike the Qur'ānic dower, which is to be given to the bride herself, the Biblical dower, it seems, was supposed to be given to the bride's parents.

16 Structure of Authority in Islam

4 Women 59

O you who believe, obey God, and obey the Messenger and the authorities from among yourselves. Then, if you dispute with one another about a matter, refer it back to God and the Messenger if you believe in God and the Last Day. This is better, and more excellent in respect of outcome.

Sūrah 4 is Madīnan.

I. Introduction

This is, perhaps, the most compact statement in the Qur'ān about the structure of authority in Islam. According to the verse, the members of the Muslim community owe allegiance, primarily, to God and Muḥammad and, secondarily, to "the authorities" (see section II, below). The verse lays down a principle for the resolution of conflicts, saying that Muslims, if they truly believe in God and the afterlife, must abide by that principle.

II. Commentary

Reflection on the injunction about obeying God, the Messenger, and "the authorities" yields a number of points:

First, Muslims must obey God, Muḥammad the Messenger, and "the authorities" (the Arabic phrase *ulū l-amr* literally means "those in charge of the matter"). The three objects of obedience represent, in the order given, the hierarchy of authority in Islam. "The authorities" must be "from among yourselves," that is, they must be Muslims.

Second, the authority of God is original in that it is not derived from any source external to God but is intrinsic to Him, whereas the authority of Muḥammad and that of the *ulū l-amr* are derived from God. A messenger is obeyed, as Q 4:64 says, only "by God's will," and, as Q 4:80 says, "He who obeys the Messenger in fact obeys God." If the Messenger's authority receives its warrant from God, then the *ulū l-amr*'s authority is legitimate only insofar as it receives the approval of God and the Messenger and only insofar as it is exercised subject to the limits imposed by God and the Messenger.

Third, while the authority of both Muḥammad and the *ulū l-amr* is derived, the authority of Muḥammad is qualitatively different from that of the *ulū l-amr*. Of the three objects of obedience mentioned in the verse, the first two ("God" and "the Messenger") are preceded by the imperative "obey," but the third ("the authorities") is not. This means that Muḥammad's authority, necessarily less than God's but greater than the *ulū l-amr*'s, would be bracketed, in terms of importance, with the former rather than with the latter.

Fourth, to obey God means to abide by the commands and prohibitions found in the Qur'ān, the Word of God, and to obey the Messenger means to obey Muḥammad in his lifetime and to emulate his Sunnah, or normative conduct, after his death. The Prophet's Sunnah is available in the form of *Ḥadīth*, which is a record of his sayings and actions.

Fifth, the commandment that Muslims must refer a disputed matter back to God and the Messenger implies that God and the Messenger—or the Qur'ān and the Sunnah—are the only authorities that may not be defied or differed with. Even the authority of the *ulū l-amr*, that is to say, is subject to challenge. It can also be inferred from the commandment that the *ulū l-amr* can be denied obedience if orders issued by them are at variance with a commandment found in the Qur'ān or the Sunnah. In fact, the commandment to refer a matter *back* to God and the Messenger implies that all matters are to be referred to the Qur'ān and the Sunnah in the first place, and that if, in the absence of an explicit and definitive injunction in the Qur'ān and the Sunnah, a dispute arises—between the *ulū l-amr* and ordinary people, among the *ulū l-amr*, or among the people—then the matter should be referred back to the Qur'ān and the Sunnah, in the sense that an attempt should be made to resolve the matter in light of the general principles and guidelines enshrined in the Qur'ān and the Sunnah. The verse, thus, sets up the Qur'ān and the Sunnah as the two permanent and most fundamental sources of Islam, making them the first as well as the last courts of appeal in all matters.

Sixth, since the verse does not limit the injunction about obedience to God and the Prophet to a certain area, it follows that the injunction has general application—that it is relevant to all departments of life, especially to the religious and political spheres, in which the issue of obedience to authority typically arises. Thus, the term *ulū l-amr* would include such people as statesmen, administrative officials, military commanders, religious scholars, and jurists. Furthermore, the *ulū l-amr* can be individuals or groups of people, and they can be individuals representing institutions—or, for that matter, institutions as such. Q 4:83 defines the *ulū l-amr* as those who have the ability "to fathom the truth" of a matter.

"If you believe in God and the Last Day" means that true belief in God will lead one to behave in the manner prescribed in the verse. The phrase also contains an implicit threat: violation of the prescription is liable to result in punishment in the afterlife.

"This is better, and more excellent in respect of outcome" means that the prescribed method of resolving disputes is a better way of arriving at the correct, right decision. A decision reached in this manner is more likely to be in accord with the spirit of the religion and is also better in respect of outcome both in this world (in the sense of providing a resolution of disputes) and in the next (in the sense of earning salvation and reward).

III. A General Note

By denying the *ulū l-amr*, "the authorities," absolute power and, at the same time, by enjoining the parties to a dispute to have recourse to God and the Messenger, or to the Qur᾽ān and the Sunnah, the verse seems to mandate a distribution of power in society. Exactly how power should be distributed the verse does not say. The ambiguity is probably deliberate since a definitive delimitation by the Qur᾽ān of the powers enjoyed by two individuals or agencies holding authority in a given situation at a certain time would create unnecessary complications in different setups, places, times.

There is no doubt that, in order effectively to mediate disputes with reference to the Qur᾽ān and the Sunnah, there must exist a body of scholars who have the necessary competence to interpret the Qur᾽ān and the Sunnah in such a way as to provide solutions to issues arising from the conduct of the *ulū l-amr* in society. Implicit in the verse, therefore, is a reference to the need for society to make institutional arrangements to produce such scholars.

17 Matrimony: Some Issues

4 Women 127–130

[127]And they ask you for a ruling concerning women. Say: God Himself gives you a ruling about them; about what is being recited to you in the Book concerning the orphans of those women whom you would not give what has been prescribed for them but whom you desire to marry; and about the helpless from among children—and that you should treat orphans justly. And whatever you do in the way of good, God has full knowledge of it. [128]And if a woman suspects oppression or neglect on her husband's part, then no blame will rest upon the two if they reach a compromise between themselves. And compromise is better. And souls are confronted with greed. And if you do good and cultivate piety, then God is aware of what you do. [129]And you will never be able to act justly between women, even if you so desire, so do not incline away so completely as to leave her like one dangling. And if you rectify things and cultivate piety, then God is Very Forgiving, Very Merciful. [130]And if the two break up, God will make each self-sufficient out of His bounty; and God is Wide-Ranging, Wise.

Sūrah 4 is Madīnan.

I. Introduction

Previous Qur'ānic revelations dealing with the proper treatment of women, especially Q 4:2–4 (for details, see chapter 15, "Orphans, Justice, and Polygamy"), gave rise to certain questions, which are addressed in the present passage. This relationship between Qur'ānic revelations given at different times points up the intratextual nature of the Qur'ān. Revealed in an evolving context, the Qur'ānic texts—verses, passages, sūrahs—often bear reference to one another, underscoring one of the interpretive principles stated in the General Introduction (section V.2)—namely, that some parts of the Qur'ān explain others—and this passage, taken in conjunction with Q 4:2–4, provides an illustration of that principle.

II. Commentary

Verse 127: The opening words, "And they ask you for a ruling about women," do not specify what question was presented by people to the Prophet Muḥammad. The rest of the verse, together with the other verses of the passage, gives details of that question: the

Prophet was asked, first, a general question about proper treatment of women and, second, a particular question about marriage with the mothers of the orphans in a man's care. To these issues, the Qur'ān adds a third, already implied in the statement about the second issue—namely, that of proper treatment of orphans. Accordingly, the pronoun "them" in "God Himself gives you a ruling about them" refers to the first issue; the phrase "what is being recited to you in the Book concerning the orphans of those women whom you would not give what has been prescribed for them but whom you desire to marry" refers, primarily, to the second issue; and the phrase "the helpless from among children" refers to the third issue.

How does the Qur'ān respond to the aforementioned three issues? The key to the answer is found in the phrase "and that you should treat orphans justly." This short phrase seems to have a bearing only on the last of the three issues. But the conjunction "and" (Arabic: *wāw*) at its beginning indicates that the phrase is joined by conjunction to an implied statement—namely: treat women justly (response to the first issue), and, in particular, those women who are mothers of your orphan wards and whom you wish to marry (response to the second issue). In light of Q 4:3, verse 127's prescribed treatment of women would include giving—both women in general and women with orphan children—the dowers due to them and, in a polygamous situation, treating all the wives equally.

The phrase "those women whom you would not give what has been prescribed for them but whom you desire to marry" is critical of a certain mindset. It alludes to the reservations entertained by some men about the need to give dowers to women who were mothers of orphans and whom those men wished to marry. Thinking that, by offering to marry such women, they were already doing them a favor, those men felt that they were not under a strict obligation to pay the women a dower or, in a polygamous situation, to treat them equally. The words "what has been prescribed for them" (the Arabic, *mā kutiba lahunna*, has the sense of "what is being laid down as the law") are a strong reminder that payment of the dower and equal treatment of wives are legally binding upon a man.

The verse begins with "And they ask you for a ruling concerning women." The next part of the verse reads: "God Himself gives you a ruling about them." This translation reflects the emphasis present in the original Arabic construction (*Allāhu yuftīkum fīhinna*), the verse, thus, saying: People want you, O Prophet, to give them a ruling, but, on this important matter, God Himself will provide a ruling on your behalf.

Verse 128: The legal rigorism of verse 127 is, in this verse, tempered with considerations of reality. From a legal standpoint, it is a woman's right to receive the dower from the man and to be treated justly by him. Sometimes, however, a woman may have reasons to suspect that her husband will deny her her rights or neglect her completely and, possibly, abandon or divorce her. In such a case, the woman may offer to give up some of her rights if, in her view, making such a concession will salvage the situation, and the man is allowed to accept the offer, no blame resting on either spouse for reaching such an agreement. It is much better to make such a compromise and maintain the bond of marriage than to take inflexible positions and either bring the marriage to an end or make marital life insufferable.

On the face of it, the verse calls upon both marriage partners to compromise ("no blame will rest upon *the two* if *they* reach a compromise"), but, in fact, it is the woman who is being urged to compromise ("And if *a woman* suspects oppression or neglect on her husband's part"). The point being made is that, while ideally, both marriage partners should exhibit a flexible attitude in order to maintain the important bond of marriage, at least one of them should give ground if the other proves to be stubborn, and that, in a situation like this one, the woman should show accommodation.

The Arabic for "And souls are confronted with greed" is *wa-uḥḍirati l-anfusu sh-shuḥḥa*, which literally means "Souls are brought into the presence of greed." That is, human beings—since they never leave the presence of greed, as it were—are disposed toward greed, the implication being that they will need to make an effort to resist the temptations of greed.

Apparently general in import, the statement "And souls are confronted with greed" is, actually, aimed at the husband, whom it implicitly criticizes as being greedy in expecting to receive a compensation for agreeing to a compromise.

The appeal made to the woman to act altruistically to save the marriage is balanced in the verse with an appeal to the man: "And if you do good and cultivate piety, then God is aware of what you do." This part of the verse, following as it does the statement about human vulnerability to greed, explicitly mentions only the possibility of doing good, for it seeks to steer its addressees in the direction of good and away from greed.

"And if you do good . . . what you do" also appears to be a general statement, but it, too, is directed at the husband, who is being exhorted to act with generosity (the Arabic for "if you do good" is *wa-in tuḥsinū*, the word *tuḥsinū* in a context like the present one implying the need to act more charitably than is required by the law) and to be motivated by piety. The phrase "then God is aware of what you do," thus, puts the men on the spot, telling them that God is fully aware of what they do—and that He will reward them well if, instead of making greed-driven demands on their wives, they act magnanimously toward them and do their part to save the marriage.

Verse 129: A key idea in the last two verses was that of treating wives equally and justly. Verse 127, as explained above, makes reference to verses 2–4 in the same sūrah, verse 3 in this latter passage urging a man to marry only one woman if he is unable to treat more than one wife equally and justly. (Verse 128, too, approaching the same issue of justice from the wife's viewpoint, implies that it is the husband's likely departure from the principle of justice that might force the wife to accept a compromise and that it is greed that would make the husband violate the principle of justice.) Verse 129 now adds that it is impossible for a man to treat all his wives equally, in the sense of apportioning his love equally among them. A man is certainly responsible for treating his wives equally in respect of providing maintenance to them and looking after their daily needs, but, in respect of love and affection, a man, even if he tries, may not be able to help being inclined more toward one of his wives than to the others. But even if this happens, a man must not show such disinclination toward one of the wives as to leave her "like one dangling"—that is, as if she were neither married nor divorced—the word "dangling" drawing the picture of something that is hanging in midair between the sky and the earth. As long as a man makes an effort to maintain a balance in his relationship with his wives, tries to rectify any lapses that he might have committed in this connection, and is motivated in his conduct by piety, God, who is "Very Forgiving, Very Merciful," will look kindly upon his failings.

Verse 130: Up to this point, the passage has talked about measures that may be taken to maintain the integrity of the matrimonial relationship in the face of problems. Verse 130 now says that, if none of those measures work, or if the woman, being well within her right, refuses to make what she regards unreasonable concessions, and the couple must break up, then they may do so, putting their trust in God. God, whose bounty is, for these two individuals as for other people, unconstrained and whose dictates, in this matter as in others, are wise, will make each member of the couple self-sufficient—that is, will enable each to survive independently of the other and, perhaps, to find a better, more compatible mate as well.

This verse seems to address both marriage partners, but it is primarily aimed at the wife, who is being told that, if her altruistic behavior fails to influence the husband's behavior, then she should stand on her dignity and refuse to put up with the husband's unfair treatment of her beyond a certain point, and that she should have the confidence that God will help her overcome her difficulties.

III. Maintaining the Matrimonial Bond: The Woman's Role

This passage is notable for the advice it gives to women for maintaining the bond of marriage when that bond comes under stress. Given against a background of a husband's possible unjust treatment of his wife, the advice is pragmatic rather than philosophical in nature, urging the woman to yield ground in certain situations and agree to a give-and-take arrangement in the interest of preserving the matrimonial relationship. The passage implies that, compared with man, woman is, by nature, more accommodating and can show a greater flexibility of attitude to ensure the continuity or stability of a marriage. At the same time, the passage urges the husband to analyze the motives of his conduct toward his wife, to show largeheartedness in dealing with his marriage partner, and to be as heavily invested in the marriage as his wife is. But notwithstanding the practical nature of the advice it gives to the woman, the verse does make the suggestion that it is important for the woman to preserve her self-esteem and, to that end, if necessary, to consider the possibility of divorce, putting her trust in God. Thus, a synoptic view of the several injunctions in the verse brings out the nuanced nature of the advice given to women.

IV. Literary Notes

1. In a number of places, the Qurʾān quotes and replies to questions presented to Muḥammad by his Companions. Typically, the questions are brief, and details of them can be inferred only by looking at the answers provided. Verse 127 provides an example of this special aspect of Qurʾānic verbal economy. Its opening words, "And they ask you for a ruling concerning women," do not tell us anything about the content of the request. On reading the next part of the verse, however, we can determine what the request was about.

2. In verse 127, immediately following the opening conjunction *wāw* ("and") in the Arabic text is the word *yastaftūnaka*, "they ask you for a ruling." The root of the word—*f-t-w*—has connotations of clarification and definitiveness. Keeping in mind that this passage harks back, in thought, to Q 4:2–4 (see section I, above), the use of the word *yastaftūnaka* in the verse provides an insight into the minds of those people who are asking for the ruling: it is people who, in spite of the transparent nature of the statements in Q 4:2–4, have allowed themselves to believe that, on marrying the mothers of their orphan wards, they would not have to pay them the dower or treat them equally as wives (see section II, verse 127, above). Entertaining these—at least in some cases, self-induced—doubts about the imperative nature of the injunctions in Q 4:2–4, those people ask the Prophet for a definitive or categorical statement on the matter. By employing the word *yastaftūnaka*, verse 127 is saying: It is a little odd that these people still feel the need for a clear, definitive ruling, but if they do, then here is the ruling. It is in light of this understanding of the word *yastaftūnaka* that one can appreciate the mild irony of the following phrase in the next part of the verse: "those women whom you would not give what has been prescribed for them but whom you desire to marry."

3. Often, the Qurʾān speaks in generalized terms even when it is referring to a particular individual or party. More than one example of such language was noted in the commentary on the verses. In verse 128, both marriage partners are asked to avoid a break-up by reaching a compromise, though the primary addressee is the wife, for her interests may be under greater threat. The seemingly general statement in the same verse, "And souls are confronted with greed," is mainly aimed at the husband, for, earlier, the verse spoke of his possible oppression or neglect of his wife and also suggested that the advice to the wife to reach an agreement with her husband is premised on the husband's possibly materialistic motivation. Likewise, verse 130, apparently, tells both marriage partners that, should they decide to get a divorce, God will make each one of them self-sufficient, but, primarily, it is the woman who is being consoled and reassured in the verse.

4. Q 4:2–4 (see chapter 15, "Orphans, Justice, Polygamy") opens with a statement about orphans and ends with a statement about women and marriage. The present passage opens with a statement about women and marriage and ends with a statement about orphans. Thus, taken together, the two passages present a case of reverse parallelism.

5. The expression "no blame will rest upon the two" in verse 128 is an instance of litotes, or understatement. It means, literally, "you will not be doing anything wrong," but, actually, "you will be doing the right thing."

18 Prophets and Revelation

4 Women 163–165

[163]We have sent revelation to you just as We sent revelation to Noah and the prophets after him. And We sent revelation to Abraham, Ishmael, Isaac, Jacob and his descendants, Jesus, Job, Jonah, Aaron, and Solomon; and We gave David Psalms. [164]And to messengers whose stories We have already related to you, and to messengers whose stories We have not related to you—and God actually spoke with Moses—[165]messengers giving good news and giving warnings, so that people may have no argument against God after the messengers. And God is Mighty, All-Wise.

Sūrah 4 is Madīnan.

I. Introduction

A few verses before this passage, in verse 153 of the sūrah, we are told of the People of the Book's demand that Muḥammad provide a certain proof of his prophecy: "The People of the Book demand that you cause to descend upon them a scripture from the heavens." The present passage responds to that demand by saying that even the fulfillment of such a demand would not satisfy the critics and objecters, for, after all, the Israelites, knowing full well that "God actually spoke with Moses" (verse 164), told Moses that they would believe him only if he presented God before their eyes (Q 2:55; 4:153). In other words, the demand for miracles is misplaced and is, in fact, made by those who, unwilling to believe, invent excuses for withholding belief.

Taken in context, then, this passage refers to and responds to the People of the Book's rejection of the prophecy of Muḥammad and the revelatory status of the Qur'ān. It argues that the People of the Book, both Jews and Christians, being familiar with the phenomena of prophecy and revelation, should not find it difficult to accept Muḥammad's prophecy as valid and the Qur'ānic revelation as true. In other words, Muḥammad belongs to the same prophetic-revelatory tradition that started with Noah and included many other illustrious names familiar to the People of the Book.

II. Commentary

The passage declares that God has sent down to Muḥammad the same revelation that He had previously sent down to other prophets. Thus, Muḥammad is a member of a group of prophets that includes such well-known and respected figures as Noah, Abraham, Moses, and Jesus. The words "just as" in verse 163 refer to both the mode and the content of the revelation: Muḥammad has received revelation in the same way in which other prophets before him received revelation (Q 42:53 mentions the several ways in which God "speaks" to prophets, all of those ways being equally authentic), and the content of the revelation received by him is essentially similar to the content of the revelation received by other prophets. These facts, the Qur'ān implies, are sufficient to validate Muḥammad's prophecy, which is no different from the prophecy of earlier individuals elected by God to convey His message to their nations. As Q 46:9 instructs Muḥammad to announce: "Say: I am no innovator among the messengers." In other words, those who believe in the previous prophets have no grounds for rejecting Muḥammad as a bearer of revelation from God.

Verse 163 concludes with a reference to the Psalms that were given by God to David, and verse 164 ends with the statement that God actually conversed with Moses. The point of both statements is that God revealed His message to different prophets in different ways, there being nothing out of the ordinary in the way He is sending down revelation to Muḥammad.

The list of the prophets in the passage is not exhaustive. As verse 164 says, Muḥammad has been told, by means of the Qur'ān, about some of the prophets, but not about others. In fact, the tone of the verse implies that the prophets whose stories have not been told far outnumber those whose stories have been told. But the verse seems to be saying that an exhaustive list of prophets is not crucial to substantiating the claims of Muḥammad's prophecy; the important thing is that his teachings are in conformity with the teachings of the prophets known to the People of the Book. The primary function of prophets is to give good tidings and issue warnings. To neglect those good tidings and warnings and, instead, demand that a prophet present miracles in support of his prophetic claims is to miss the point of prophecy and revelation both.

"So that people may have no argument against God after the messengers" (verse 165) means that God's purpose in sending prophets to various nations is to convey Divine guidance to those nations, thus taking away their alibi that they never knew the truth since no messenger ever came to help them to tell the right path from the wrong one.

The two Divine attributes of might and wisdom cited at the end of the passage have a bearing on the main theme of the passage. An all-powerful God could, theoretically, punish people without raising any prophets among them, holding them accountable on the flimsiest of grounds. Since, however, the all-powerful God is also wise, He has not only imbued human beings with a rational sense and an instinctual feel for the truth, but has also raised prophets among the peoples of the world to enable the latter to draw a clear and unmistakable distinction between truth and falsehood. If, however, people still defiantly reject the truth, then the all-powerful God will take them to task.

III. Consolation to Muḥammad

If, as stated above, this passage responds to the People of the Book's rejection of Muḥammad's prophecy and of the Qurʾān, then it seems that it should have been addressed to the People of the Book, whereas it is addressed to Muḥammad. Why is this so? The answer is that the passage seeks to console Muḥammad, who wondered whether his opponents withheld belief in his message because of any fault on his part in presenting the Divine message. The passage says that, while the identity of his message with the message of the previous prophets is proof enough that he is a prophet, there always will be people who would refuse to accept evidence regardless of how compelling it might be and would demand to see miracles as a precondition of reposing belief. To the Qurʾān, the test of the authenticity of a prophet or a scripture consists not in the existence of some supporting miracle, but in the character of the teachings of the prophet or the scripture. And this test, the verse implies, can be applied at all times. For, even if the skeptics and objecters had been shown the miracle of a Qurʾān actually descending from the heavens, there is no guarantee that all of them would have believed in Muḥammad. Such a miracle might have convinced some of those who had witnessed it, but it may not have carried conviction with people of later generations. The only proof that can, theoretically, satisfy all people, whether of the Prophet's times or of later ages, is the agreement of that message, in structure and spirit, with the message of the earlier prophets. In other words, the Qurʾān invites its addressees to make an analytical study of its message by placing that message in the context of the long-standing tradition of prophecy and Divine revelation.

IV. Literary Notes

The passage begins by addressing Muḥammad ("We have sent revelation to you") and then identifies twelve prophets by name: Noah, Abraham, Ishmael, Isaac, Jacob, Jesus, Job, Jonah, Aaron, Solomon, David, and Moses (this list excludes Muḥammad, who is being addressed in the passage). From Noah to Jacob and his descendants, the prophets are mentioned in chronological order, but then the order becomes qualificative. Jesus, Job, Jonah, and Aaron are grouped together on account of the severity of the ordeals they went through and the special Divine support that each one received (see below). David and his son, Solomon, are prophet-kings in the Qurʾān and, therefore, are mentioned together. The reversal of the chronological order in citing these two figures focuses attention on the Psalms, the revelation received by David. The last to be mentioned is Moses, who serves as the counterpart of Muḥammad, who is addressed at the beginning of the passage. The resemblance between Moses and Muḥammad—in respect of founding a law-based community—is highlighted both in the Qurʾān and in *Ḥadīth*.

It will be helpful to explain briefly, with reference to the Qurʾān, the ordeals of Jesus, Job, Jonah, and Aaron and the ways in which all four prophets received special Divine help:

(1) *Jesus.* Jesus' birth was a trial for his mother, who was accused of giving birth to a child out of wedlock, but God vindicated her through the infant Jesus, who spoke up in her defense (Q 19:27–33; see chapter 12, "Jesus: Birth, Miracles, and Mission," section II, verses 45–46). Also, Jesus' opponents and persecutors tried to kill him but did not succeed in their attempt (Q 4:157).

(2) *Job.* He suffered the loss of family and experienced pain and sorrow in other ways, but when he showed extraordinary patience, God compensated him for his loss and suffering (Q 21:83–84; 38:41–44).

(3) *Jonah.* Disappointed in their response to his preaching, he left his people and was swallowed by a large fish during a sea voyage, but, upon making repentance, was disgorged by the fish; he returned to his people, preaching to them successfully (Q 10:98; 37:140–148; 68:48–50).

(4) *Aaron.* Serving as Moses' deputy during the latter's forty-day visit to Mount Sinai, Aaron was unable to prevent the Israelites from being tricked by the Samaritan who had made them a golden calf for worship. Aaron was exonerated by God, with Moses punishing the Samaritan and destroying the calf (Q 20:85–97).

V. The Bible on Prophets and Revelation

The Bible seems to have a much broader definition of prophecy and revelation than the Qurʾān. In the Bible, the wise Miriam, sister of Moses and Aaron, is called a prophet (Exodus 15:20), as are certain bands of people who spoke in a state of frenzy or ecstasy (1 Samuel 10:10; 19:20), but such individuals or groups would hardly qualify as prophets in the Qurʾān. On the one hand, the Biblical concern with the distinction between true and false prophecy is not very conspicuous in the Qurʾān. The Qurʾān does distinguish a prophet from such figures as soothsayers, poets, and possessed individuals (Q 52:29; 69:41–42), but the Qurʾānic observations in this connection are of the nature of footnotes to an otherwise focused treatment of what the Bible would call true prophecy. On the other hand, the great Biblical prophet Moses would perfectly fit the Qurʾānic profile of a prophet. One might say that the Biblical definition of a prophet in its strict form—an individual chosen by God to convey a definite religious and moral message from God to humanity, a message that bears on and has implications for human life and human destiny—is in complete agreement with the

Qur'ānic definition. This would still leave open the question of whether certain Biblical figures are to be designated as prophets from a Qur'ānic standpoint. For example, Abraham is a prophet in the Qur'ān, but he is a patriarch in Judaism and Christianity, though Genesis 20:7 calls him a prophet, raising the issue of the relationship between patriarch and prophet.

The Biblical definition of revelation, similarly, is more general than the Qur'ānic, for the Qur'ān would appear to be distinguishing revelation from inspiration much more strictly than does the Bible. In both the Bible and the Qur'ān, revelation may take the form of scripture, but it does not have to, the name "revelation" being equally applicable to a message that a prophet receives from God and then delivers to his people orally. In its essential formulation, the idea of revelation would be found to be fairly identical in the Bible and the Qur'ān.

19 Torah, Evangel, and Qur᾽ān

5 Feast 44–48

44Indeed, We sent down the Torah, which contained guidance and light: the prophets, who had submitted, rendered judgment in accordance with it, for those who had become Jews, and so did the rabbis and the judges, on account of the fact that they had been given custody of the Book of God—and they were witnesses over it. So, do not fear people, but fear Me, and do not take a small price for My verses. And those who do not judge in accordance with what God has sent down, they are the disbelievers.

45And We wrote down in it: "A life for a life, an eye for an eye, a nose for a nose, an ear for an ear, a tooth for a tooth; and, for injuries, retribution. So he who forgoes it charitably, it shall be an atonement for him." And those who do not judge in accordance with what God has sent down, they are the wrongdoers.

46And We sent, in their wake, Jesus son of Mary, being an actualizer of what
already existed before him, of the Torah; and We gave him the Evangel, which
contained guidance and light, being an actualizer of what already existed before it,
of the Torah, and as guidance and admonition for the pious. 47And let the People
of the Evangel judge in accordance with what God has sent down in it. And those
who do not judge in accordance with what God has sent down, they are the
transgressors.

48And We have sent down to you the Book with truth, being an actualizer of what already existed before it, of the Book, and a keeper over it. So judge between them in accordance with what God has sent down, and do not follow their whims in deviation from what has come to you of the truth.

For each, We have laid down a law and a path. And had God desired, He would have made you a single people, but so that He may put you to the test in respect of what He has given you. So, compete in respect of good deeds. To God you are going to return, all of you, then He will apprise you of what you were disputing about.

Sūrah 5 is Madīnan.

I. Introduction

This passage speaks of three scriptures—the Torah, the Evangel, and the Qur'ān—sent to three religious communities—Jews, Christians, and Muslims, respectively. It presents the Qur'ān's understanding of (1) the Torah and the Evangel, (2) the relationship of these two scriptures, and (3) its own relationship to the two. Leaving details to the commentary, we will briefly note here that, in this passage, all three scriptures are called revelations from God. Furthermore, the Evangel is called a book that actualized, or fulfilled, the Torah, and the Qur'ān is called a book that actualizes, or fulfills, both the Torah and the Evangel.

II. Commentary

Verse 44: The Torah was meant to be a guide to the right course of conduct and to bring people out of the darkness of ignorance into the well-lit realm of knowledge. It served as the principal source of law for the Jews, and it was in accordance with the Torah that the Israelite prophets, and also the rabbis and judges of Israel, rendered judgment. Rendering judgment in light of the Torah signifies that the Divine scripture is meant to serve as the chief source of guidance and direction in social, political, and legal matters and as the arbiter of differences and adjudicator of disputes. The phrases "who had submitted" and "on account of the fact that they had been given custody of the Book of God" are notable. The prophets not only judged others in light of the Torah, they lived their own lives in accordance with the Torah; before commanding others to submit to God, they themselves made submission to God. Following in the footsteps of the prophets were rabbis and judges, who were acutely conscious that they had been charged by God and by the prophets with the responsibility of safeguarding the integrity of the Torah in letter and spirit, of implementing the Torah honestly and impartially, and of witnessing to its truth through word and action. The Qur'ān means to draw a contrast: There was a time when the religious leaders of the Jews truly believed in the Torah and conscientiously adhered to its teachings in practice, but the Jewish religious leaders of the times of the Qur'ān are a far cry from their illustrious role models of the past.

The statement "So, do not fear people, but fear Me, and do not take a small price for My verses" can be taken as a commandment addressed to the prophets, judges, and rabbis at the time they were made custodians of the Torah. In other words, those leaders of Israel were reminded that they must uphold the Torah by passing judgments on its basis, without being influenced by vested interests and without selling the verses—namely, commandments—of the Torah short. But the real addressees of the injunction are the Jewish scholars of Qur'ānic times, who are being told that they, too, were made custodians of the Torah and made witnesses over their vocation but that, unlike the great leaders of early Israelite history, they have not lived up to their titles: they fear people more than they fear God, for they interpret the Torah to suit the needs and demands of influential people and to make paltry worldly gains—paltry because, even when considerable, they are inconsequential when compared with the great reward that faithful adherence to the Torah would bring in the hereafter.

The verse concludes with a trenchant comment (this comment, too is part of the statement that opened with the commandment "So do not fear people"): In a sense, the real disbelievers are those who, even though they may have accepted the authority of Divine scripture in principle, deny the authority of that scripture in practice by refusing or failing to make the scripture the basis of their judgments.

Verse 45: "And We wrote down in it" means that the injunction that is about to follow was laid down by God and by no one else, its authority, therefore, being unchallengeable. The principle underlying the injunction is that punishment must be proportionate to the crime. The objective of the injunction is establishment of justice. But if the offending party is pardoned by the injured party (or by the agent of the wronged party in case of a murder), then the pardon will serve as atonement for the criminal, who will be spared punishment by the state (the pronoun "him" in "it shall be an atonement for him" is here taken as referring to the one who gives the pardon). The connotation of charity present in the Arabic verb used in the verse for the act of pardon (*taṣaddaqa*) subtly suggests that the injured party should, if possible, consider pardoning the offender.

At the end of this verse, too, those who fail to abide by the law of God are criticized: they are wrongdoers.

Verse 46: The word "their" in "in their wake" refers to the above-mentioned prophets, making Jesus also a prophet. Affirming Jesus' status as a prophet, this verse parts company both with the Jewish view, which denies Jesus prophetic status, and with the Christian view, which elevates Jesus to the level of deity. Jesus son of Mary, this verse says, was a prophet—no more, no less—and he came in the wake of other Israelite prophets, he himself being one of them. Also, the phrase "in their wake" (Arabic: *ʿalā āthārihim*) denotes not only subsequence—Jesus came *after* those prophets—but also the identity of the message presented by Jesus and those prophets: Jesus walked in the footsteps of the earlier prophets and did not present a new religion.

Jesus is spoken of as one who actualized the Torah—that is, by objectifying or fulfilling the prophecies made in the Torah about him. He, too, was given a scripture, the Evangel, which also (1) contained guidance and light; (2) like Jesus, actualized the Torah; (3) and, especially for those among the believers who wished to walk in the path of piety, furnished guidance and served admonition.

The Qurʾānic text uses the same Arabic word to describe both Jesus and the Evangel—*muṣaddiq* ("actualizer")—implying that prophets and scriptures are, in a sense, two names of the same reality since a prophet is a living embodiment of the scripture he presents.

Verse 47: The Arabic imperative translated as "And let the People of the Evangel judge in accordance with what God has revealed in it" is, in respect of its timing, analogous to the imperative in verse 44. That is, like the Israelites, who were commanded to fear God rather than people in interpreting the Torah, the Christians were commanded to judge in accordance with the Evangel. The last part of this verse once again makes, with a minor variation, a comment that has already been made twice: Those who do not judge in accordance with Divine revelation are the real transgressors.

Verse 48: God has revealed to Muḥammad (the addressee in this verse) the Qur'ān, which performs two functions: first, it actualizes "the Book"—primarily, the Torah, and, secondarily, other scriptures, like the Evangel; and second, it serves as a keeper over the Book. The Arabic word used in the text for the second function is *muhaymin*, which literally means "one that protects," "one that guards," or "one that keeps watch." To say that the Qur'ān is a *muhaymin* over "the Book" is to claim hermeneutical privilege: it is to say that the Qur'ān watches over the meanings of the other scriptures—that those scriptures ought to be interpreted in light of the Qur'ān. Muḥammad is, therefore, instructed to "judge between them"—that is, to pass judgment on matters that Jews and Christians present before him in his capacity as the chief leader and judge of Madīnah. It is implied that failure to judge in accordance with the Qur'ān would constitute a wrong.

"Do not follow their whims" means: Do not be led, as those who believed in other scriptures were led, to interpret scripture to suit your interests, for, if you do so, then—as the next part of the verse states—you will violate the truth that has come to you in the form of the Qur'ān.

"For each" means "for each of the three above-mentioned groups"—namely, Jews, Christians, and Muslims.

"A law and a path." The "law" is the set of commandments conveyed by God to a people; the "path" represents the injunctions emanating from a prophet in his capacity as the spokesman of God. The law and the path together make up the structure of a revealed religion. Since, in Qur'ānic perspective, the *essence* or *inner spirit* of all revealed religions has always been the same, the law and the path—which, this verse says, have varied in different ages—must be interpreted to mean the *form* or *outer structure* of a given revealed religion.

"And had God desired, He would have made you a single people, but so that He may put you to the test in respect of what He has given you." That is, it would not have been difficult for God to eliminate all differences among the various peoples of the world and to unite all of humanity on a single system of belief and conduct, but He chose not to do so because He wished to test people "in respect of what He has given you"—that is, in respect of the gifts of reason, freedom of the will, and revealed guidance. According to the Qur'ān, God sometimes alters the outer form of religion in order to put people to the test—to distinguish those who would accept the truth irrespective of the form in which it is presented from those who become so attached to a particular form of the truth that they would refuse to accept the truth in any form other than the one to which they have become accustomed. By varying the law and the path—that is, by altering the form or outer structure of the essential religious truth—for different communities, God intends to distinguish those who would make the right use of the above-mentioned gifts of reason, free will, and prophetic guidance from those who would misuse those gifts. And that objective would have been defeated if God had forced all of humanity to follow a single, predetermined course of thinking and action. It would not have been fitting that God should deprive human beings of the ability to make independent choices, even if those choices were to turn out to be wrong or mistaken and even if they were to lead to disagreement and conflict.

Addressing Muslims at the end, this verse says: Regardless of other people's acceptance or rejection of the guidance that has come to you in the form of the Qur'ān, you should be earnest in performing good deeds. As for the differences between peoples in respect of belief and practice, God will pass judgment on them in the hereafter, for, in the end, all human beings will return to God.

III. Issues

1. Those Who Do not Judge by Revealed Scripture. Two points need to be made about the Qur'ānic statement that those who do not judge in accordance with God's revelation are disbelievers (verse 44), wrongdoers (verse 45), and transgressors (verse 47). First, the statement, although ostensibly aimed at the historical Jewish and Christian communities, is general in its import and applies with equal force to all those religious communities—the Muslim community not excluded—that claim to be the recipients of prophetic revelation. Second, it is addressed especially to those individuals in those religious communities who occupy a position of religious, legal, or intellectual authority but abuse that position, rendering judgments and adjudicating between people in violation of the clear scriptural injunctions and principles to which they profess allegiance but whose authority they reject in practice.

2. Theological Relativism? Verse 48 is sometimes interpreted to mean that the Qur'ānic declaration "For each, We have laid down a law and a path" sanctions the equal validity of several religions, asking the adherents of Judaism, Christianity, and Islam each to abide by their own scriptures and render judgment in accordance with whatever revelatory guidance they happen to accept. Indeed, there do exist, within the Qur'ān and in the larger framework of Islamic religion, grounds for interreligious tolerance, conversation, and harmony, but, in the passage under discussion, the Qur'ān is not preaching relativism; it is presenting a certain aspect of its theology and, like any other scripture, the Qur'ān takes its theology seriously. For one thing, the tone of the entire passage—and also the context in which this passage occurs (see, especially, verses 41–42, which precede, and verses 49–51, which follow, the passage under study)—indicates that the Qur'ān is here asserting the merit of its theology vis-à-vis other theologies. For another, a relativistic understanding of Qur'ānic theology would render irrelevant all criticism—sometimes quite severe—to which the Qur'ān subjects other religious outlooks, doctrines, and philosophies.

IV. Literary Notes

1. The Bifurcated Subject. In verse 44, which is quoted below in full, the italicized portions indicate a bifurcation of the subject:

> Indeed, We revealed the Torah, which contained guidance and light: *the prophets*, who had submitted, rendered judgment in accordance with it, for those who had become Jews, *and* so did *the rabbis and the judges*, on account of the fact that they had been given custody of the Book of God—and they were witnesses over it.

The subject for the verb "rendered judgment" is made up of "the prophets" and "the rabbis and the judges." By spacing "the rabbis and the judges" apart from "the prophets," the Qur'ān confers honor both on the prophets and on the rabbis and the judges: on the prophets because, being divinely appointed, they were the direct heirs to the prophet Moses and the continuators of the religious and legal tradition based on the Torah; and on the rabbis and the judges because, although not divinely appointed, they served as important agents in the mission of implementing the Torah at several levels in the larger society. Furthermore, since the verse's direct addressees are the Jewish religious leaders—such as the rabbis and judges—of the times of the Qur'ān, the bifurcation of the subject puts an independent spotlight on the Jewish religious leaders of earlier Israelite history whom the Qur'ān lauds, sharpening, as a result, the contrast between the highly praiseworthy rabbis and judges of earlier times and the not-so-praiseworthy rabbis and judges of Qur'ānic times.

2. Repetition with Variation. Verses 44, 45, and 47 each conclude with a refrain-like statement. Verse 44 reads: "And those who do not judge in accordance with what God has revealed—they are the disbelievers." For "the disbelievers" in this verse, verse 45 substitutes "the wrongdoers," and verse 47, "the transgressors." Such variant repetition serves to put special emphasis on the statement in question. In the present context, it underscores the enormity of professing belief in scripture while refusing to allow scripture to serve as adjudicator in real-life situations.

3. Omission. Part of verse 48 reads: "And had God desired, He would have made you a single people, but so that He may put you to the test in respect of what He has given you." There is an omission of thought after the conjunction "but." The complete construction would be something like this: "but *He has chosen not to make you a single people*, so that He may put you to the test in respect of what He has given you," the italicized portion representing the omission.

4. Wordplay. In referring to "those who had become Jews" (verse 44), the Arabic text uses the verb *hāda*, which literally meant "to turn in repentance," but which later came to have the technical meaning of "to become a Jew." By playing on the two meanings of the verb, the Qur'ān implies that the essence of Judaism consists in turning toward God in repentance—a truth that the Jews remembered for some time but later forgot. The use of the phrase "who had become Jews" also makes possible a contrast with another phrase—"who had submitted," used of the prophets. The prophets possessed the universal, nonsectarian characteristic of being *submitters*, whereas their followers in later ages became, in a sectarian sense, *Jews*, the word "Jews" having a narrower range of meaning than the word "submitters."

V. Retribution in the Torah, the Evangel, and the Qur'ān

Verse 45 refers to the Torah's commandment about retribution. The commandment is found in the following verses of the Torah:

> If any harm follows, then you shall give life for life, eye for eye, tooth for tooth, hand for hand, foot for foot, burn for burn, wound for wound, stripe for stripe. (Exodus 21:23)
>
> Anyone who maims another shall suffer the same injury in return: fracture for fracture, eye for eye, tooth for tooth; the injury inflicted is the injury to be suffered. (Leviticus 24:20)
>
> Show no pity: life for life, eye for eye, tooth for tooth, hand for hand, foot for foot. (Deuteronomy 19:21)

While the Qur'ānic reference to the Torah's commandment seems to have been made in a historical context, there is every reason to believe that the Qur'ān is here quoting the commandment approvingly and, as such, appropriating it. The commandment, in fact, forms part of the Islamic criminal law. The manner of the Qur'ānic citation of the Biblical commandment is evidence that the Qur'ān regards itself as part of the same scriptural tradition to which the Torah and the Evangel belong. From an Islamic theological perspective, the Qur'ān's appropriation of the commandment represents one way in which the Qur'ān—to use its own term—"actualizes" the Torah. And, from the general perspective adopted in the present work, it is proof of the Qur'ān's engagement with the Bible in a substantive way.

Matthew 5:38–39, which is part of the Sermon on the Mount, reads: "You have heard that it was said, 'An eye for an eye and a tooth for a tooth.' But I say to you, 'Do not resist the evildoer. But if anyone strikes you on the right cheek, turn the other also.'" These verses (and a few others in Matthew 5) are sometimes interpreted to mean that Jesus is being critical of the Torah's above-cited commandment about retribution. But, in view of Matthew 5:17—"Do not think that I have come to abolish the law or the prophets; I have come not to abolish but to fulfill"—it is probably best to interpret Matthew 5:38–39 as an exhortation to go beyond a strict construction of the Torah's commandment but without nullifying that commandment. In other words,

Matthew 5:38–39 may be taken as strongly recommending forgiveness as a response to infliction of injury without necessarily rejecting the idea of retribution altogether. This view, if correct, would be significant in the present context in two ways. First, it would make the Evangel, at least in respect of the commandment under discussion, a "fulfillment" of the Torah. Of course, the notion of forgiveness is not foreign to the Torah, and, in emphasizing it, Jesus would not be importing into the framework of Torah teaching something unprecedented or unheard of. A strict construction of the Torah's commandment about retribution, however, may be said to have consigned the notion of forgiveness to the background in the actual Jewish practice of the law. As such, in verses like Matthew 5:38–39, Jesus would only be bringing back to the forefront the teaching that was very much part of the spirit of the Torah but had suffered neglect in actual practice. This, then, would be the Qur'ānic understanding of the "actualization" of the Torah by Jesus and by the Evangel. Second, the view would establish a link between the Evangel and the Qur'ān. The connotations of charity present in the phrase "So he who forgoes it charitably" in verse 45 of the Qur'ānic passage (see section II, above) serve to raise the act of pardon to the level of forgiveness recommended in Matthew 5:38–39. As such, the Qur'ānic verse would appear to combine the Torah's commandment of retribution with the Evangel's recommendation of forgiveness, and, in doing so, to "actualize" both the Torah and the Evangel.

20 Nature as a Repository of Signs

6 Cattle 95–99

95Indeed, it is God who splits open the grain and the fruit pit; He brings forth
the living from the dead, and He is going to bring forth the dead from the living.
This is God! So where are you straying off to?
96One who rips out the morning! And He has made the night a source of rest,
and the sun and the moon a reckoning. This is the planning of the Almighty, the
All-Knowing.
97And He is the one who has installed the stars for you, that you may be
guided by them in the darknesses of the land and the sea. We have set forth the
signs in detail for people who would learn.
98And He is the one who has raised you from a single being, and so there is a
dwelling place and a depository. We have set forth the signs in detail for people
who would understand.
99And He is the one who sent down from the sky water, by means of which,
then, We brought forth shoots of all things, from which, then, We brought forth green
branches, bringing forth from them grain layer upon layer—and from the date-palm,
from its spathe, clusters hanging low—and gardens of vines, the olive tree, and
the pomegranate tree, alike and different; observe its fruit when it blossoms, and
its ripening. In this, indeed, there are signs for people who would believe.

Sūrah 6 is Makkan.

I. Introduction

This passage occurs in the context of an argument for monotheism. It cites a number of phenomena that point to the existence of one God. By repeatedly referring to God as "He is the one who" does such and such things, the passage negates that any other beings share in the power of God. The passage emphasizes the harmonious relationship characterizing the phenomena of the universe, citing this relationship as a proof of monotheism (see section III, below). Of the five verses of the passage, the fourth (verse 98) is about human beings. But it presents God's creation of the human race "from a single being" as one of the signs of God and, as such, fits in with the overall theme of the passage, namely, that nature is a repository of signs pointing to the existence of the one and only God.

II. Commentary

Verse 95: God "splits open the grain and the fruit pit" means that God causes seeds to grow into plants and trees that become a source of a variety of foods for human beings. Proper intonation of the Arabic construction would put the emphasis on the word for "God"—*Allāh*—implying that God alone has the power to perform the act described. As such, the verse would be critical of those who set up peers to God or believe in other deities besides Him.

"He brings forth the living from the dead"; that is, God causes inexistent life to come into existence—inexistence being a kind of death. Conversely, "He is going to bring forth the dead from the living"; that is, God is going to cause living beings to die. In other words, the law of life and death is inexorable, and every created living entity—animal or human, individual or nation—is subject to it.

"This is God! So where are you straying off to?" means that only God controls life and death, as noted above. Since no one else enjoys such control or power, no one else can be deity, and, therefore, people who worship beings besides God or set up peers or associates to Him are drifting about in error.

Verse 96: "One who rips out the morning!" God brings forth the morning by splitting open the shell of the darkness, as it were. The Arabic for "One who rips out" is *fāliq*, which is also used in the preceding verse to refer to God as one "who splits open the grain and the fruit pit." The range of the phenomena covered between the two verses—from the minuscule and the hidden (the grain and the fruit pit inside the ground) to the cosmic and the spectacular (daybreak)—implies that the same God rules over the heavens and the earth.

"And He has made the night a source of rest." Sleep during the night provides rest from fatigue and anxiety and renews one's vigor for the next day's activities.

"And the sun and the moon a reckoning." The Arabic construction admits of two simultaneously valid interpretations: (1) God has made the sun and the moon by, or in accordance with, a certain reckoning, such that the two heavenly bodies follow designated paths and move or behave in accordance with certain fixed laws. (2) God has made the sun and the moon instruments for telling time so that people may know by means of them the division of time into days, months, and years, the two heavenly bodies, thus, serving certain practical needs of human beings. The two interpretations would appear to be related, the movement or behavior of the sun and the moon (1) making it possible for people to reckon time (2).

"This is the planning of the Almighty, the All-Knowing"—that is, as opposed to the planning, or the lack thereof, of the alleged deities, who are either deficient in or lack both power and knowledge. Observation of and reflection on the conduct of the heavenly bodies will indicate that these heavenly bodies, both in respect of their behavior and in respect of the benefits they yield for human beings, owe their existence to an outside power—a being that is almighty and all-knowing. Being *Almighty*, God has reduced the sun and the moon to subjection, and, being *All-Knowing*, He knows how best to manage them and employ them to certain ends. God's power thus complements His knowledge to bring the best into being.

The demonstrative "this" in the quoted part of the verse can refer (1) to God's act of making the sun and the moon a reckoning; (2) to both God's act of splitting open the morning and His act of making the sun and the moon a reckoning; or (3) to all the acts of God enumerated from the start of the verse to this point. It is, perhaps, best to take (3) as the referent.

Verse 97: The same God who has installed the sun and the moon in the skies (verse 96) has also installed therein stars, harnessing them into service for human beings: the stars provide guidance by helping travelers to determine the time at night and to find their way through land and sea.

"We have set forth the signs in detail for people who would learn." God has set forth in detail these and other signs, but only those who have a sincere wish to learn the truth will be able to draw the appropriate lessons from them.

Verse 98: In spite of the many differences that mark the human race, all human beings descend from a single being, Adam, created by God (see chapter 14, "One God, One Humanity"). They also have a common nature in respect of their feelings, instincts, wishes, hopes, and aspirations. Their common origin and their common nature indicate that all human beings have one creator—God. The same conclusion is reinforced by another fact: Every person lives and moves about in a certain part of the earth—this verse calls it a "dwelling place" (Arabic: *mustaqarr*)—and will be buried, upon death, in a certain place—the verse calls it a "depository" (Arabic: *mustawdaʿ*). Q 11:6, using those two Arabic words, says that God, who provides sustenance to all, knows every person's "dwelling place" and "depository." Like 11:6, then, 6:98 implies that, since one lives out one's whole earthly career, from birth to death, under God's watchful eye, there is no point in relying on any being or power other than God.

Two words in this verse need attention. The first, "raised," is a rendering of the Arabic *anshaʾa*, which not only means "to create," but also signifies "to bring up" and "to cultivate." In other words, God not only brings into existence, but also brings up, sustains, provides, and nurtures. The second word we have encountered already—"depository," a translation of *mustawdaʿ*, which, in this context, means "burial place," but which literally means "a place where something is deposited for safekeeping." The use of the word *mustawdaʿ* to denote "burial place" suggests that the person buried in a place has been placed there only "for safekeeping" and will, one day, be taken out and presented before God for judgment.

"We have set forth the signs in detail for people who would understand." The signs that establish the oneness of God and other realities have been elucidated in the

Qur'ān in detail, but only those people who wish to understand the truth and, having understood it, are willing to accept it will benefit from these signs.

Verse 99: God is the one who, by means of the rainwater he sends down from the heavens, causes crops to yield rich grain and trees to bear fruits of various kinds. The munificent God, that is to say, has not only provided human beings with basic foods obtained from grains, such as wheat and rice, but has also supplied them with delicacies, such as fruits. The vegetation produced by rainwater also includes plants that yield fodder for animals.

This verse mentions, by way of example, some of the fruits with which the people of Arabia were familiar. These fruits are "alike and different"; that is, each fruit has many varieties, which, even though they look alike, are different in respect of taste, color, shape, and other properties, thus giving evidence of purpose and design in creation.

"Hanging low," used of "clusters," means that these are within easy reach.

"Observe its fruit when it blossoms, and its ripening" means: Observe the fruit as it goes through the different phases of its growth, from the time it blossoms into existence to the time it becomes ripe for consumption, and you will conclude that a certain being is tending it and directing its growth.

The verse concludes with the statement: "In this, indeed, are signs for people who would believe." One of these signs is that to which reference is made in the beginning of the verse—namely, that a single cause, water, produces a variety of vegetation, of which fruit trees alone are of numerous types.

III. Universal Harmony as Evidence of Monotheism

The passage presents an argument from universal harmony in support of monotheism. According to the argument, the diverse phenomena of the universe cooperate with each other to produce a single result, in which, it seems, the entire universe has a stake. For example, the heat of the sun and the rainwater from the sky are directly involved in causing the underground seeds and fruit stones to grow into crops and fruit trees; the night provides the much-needed rest to human beings fatigued from the day's work so that they may engage in various kinds of activity during the day; and the stars shine down on earth, providing guidance to travelers in untraversed lands and uncharted waters. The remarkable coordination and harmony witnessed all over the universe would have been completely missing, this passage argues, if the different regions of the universe had been created and ruled by different deities.

IV. Invitation to Reflection on the Universe

Besides citing universal harmony as evidence of the existence of only one God, this passage—along with many others in the Qur'ān—constitutes a general invitation to human beings to make a reflective study of the universe. It is no exaggeration to say that it was in response to this Qur'ānic invitation that Muslims took keen interest in the objective study of nature, cultivating such sciences as astronomy, mathematics, chemistry, and medicine and, more important, developed the inductive method. Conquest of nature seems to have been a strong motif in the intellectual history of early Islamic centuries. In Qur'ānic perspective, however, all achievements, scientific or other, acquire true worth only when imbued with spiritual meaning—when, that is to say, they lead back to God as the source and originator of the universe and as the only being deserving of human submission and loyalty. It may also be noted that the Arabic word for "signs" in this passage is *āyāt* (sing. *āyah*). A high-frequency word in the Qur'ān, *āyah* means both a "sign" of nature (as in the present passage) and a "verse" of the Qur'ān. That the word has both these meanings signifies that, from an Islamic viewpoint, nature points to the same realities that the Qur'ān speaks of, and that a study of the Qur'ān and a study of the universe would lead to essentially similar conclusions.

V. Literary Notes

1. Sequence of Citation of the Signs. In referring to the phenomena of nature, the passage employs an interesting sequence: an upward movement from the terrestrial level to the celestial and a downward movement from the celestial level to the terrestrial are detectable. The passage refers, first, to the grain and fruit pit that germinate underground and, then, to the cycle of life and death that marks life on earth (verse 95). Next, it refers to phenomena that fill the earthly atmosphere—namely, day and night—and, then, pointing further up, refers to the sun, the moon, and the stars (verses 96–97). The reference, first, to the creation of humanity from a single soul and, then, to every human being's dwelling place and burial place (verse 98) seems to be a kind of footnote to that part of verse 95 which talks about bringing forth life from lifelessness and causing the living to lose life. At this point, the downward movement starts, with the rainwater descending from the sky to irrigate land and grow crops and trees.

2. Order of Words Signifying Progression of Thought. The last three verses of the passage each conclude with the statement that God has furnished signs "for people who would learn" (verse 97), "for people who would understand" (verse 98), and "for people who would believe" (verse 99). The three verses are similar in construction, especially verses 97 and 98, but each concludes with a different word. The particular order of occurrence of these three words—"learn," "understand," and "believe"—signifies a certain movement of thought: those who would *learn* will, if they make the right use of what they have learned, come to *understand*, and will, if they put their understanding to the right use, eventually come to *believe*. The idea of progression from learning, through understanding, to believing acquires literary force through the use of rhyming words in the original text: *ya'lamūn*, *yafqahūn*, *yu'minūn*.

3. Omission. Three instances of omission may be noted. In verse 95, the "grain and the fruit pit" are split open and, it is understood, spikes and blossoms are brought forth; thus, the source (grain and fruit pit) is mentioned, but the product (spikes and blossoms) remains unstated. In verse 96, it is the—implied—darkness of the night that is split open and the morning brought forth from it; thus, the product (morning) is mentioned, but the source (night) remains unstated. In verse 99, the complete construction behind the phrase "observe its fruit when it blossoms, and its ripening" is "observe its fruit when it blossoms, and its ripening *when it ripens*." "When it ripens" is omitted since it can be inferred from the analogous "when it blossoms."

4. Significant Variation. Verse 95 reads, in part: "He brings forth the living from the dead, and He is going to bring forth the dead from the living." Note the difference between *He brings forth* in the first clause and *He is going to bring forth* in the second. In the Arabic text of the Qur'ān, a verb, *yukhriju*, is used for the first phase, whereas a participle, *mukhrij*, is used for the second—the difference between a verb and a participle in Arabic rhetoric accounting for the following explanation: *He brings forth* is simple description, whereas *He is going to bring forth* connotes strong resolve. After having come into existence, no living organism voluntarily resigns itself to the fate of extinction. God, however, does not confer immortality on anyone: It is His firm decision to bring forth the dead from the living. The change from the verb to the participle indicates this Divine resolve.

5. Brevity and Detail, Repetition, and Envelope. The passage contains an example of the Qur'ān's practice of stating something briefly and then amplifying it. The last verse of the passage, verse 99, is an explication of the opening verse: the grain and the fruit pit briefly mentioned in verse 95 generate the more fully described rich, grain-laden plants and fruit gardens of verse 99. Seen in this light, verse 99 repeats the idea presented in verse 95, but, obviously, it is no mechanical repetition. Furthermore, the passage begins and ends by stating, if with considerable variation, the same idea—an example of the literary feature called envelope.

6. Shifts of Person and Number. Several times in this passage—in verses 97, 98, and 99—shifts of person and number take place: God is first referred to by means of the third person singular "He" and then by means of the first person plural "We." Such shifts, quite common in the Qur'ān, yield the full range of their meaning only when studied in context. As a rule, the use of the third person signifies distance and, accordingly, in the present case, Divine transcendence and majesty—which are reinforced by the use of the singular. The use of the first person, on the other hand, signifies closeness and, accordingly, in the present case, Divine immanence and providence—which are reinforced by the use of the plural. As such, the shifts of person and number provide subtle literary support to the philosophical thesis advanced in the passage—namely, that the entire universe is ruled by the same God, that the transcendent and majestic God of the heavens is also the immanent and provident God of the earth.

21 The Primordial Covenant

7 Heights 172–173

[172]And when your Lord took from the children of Adam, from out of their loins, their progeny and made them bear witness over themselves: "Am I not your Lord?" They said, "But yes, we bear witness!"—lest you should say, on the Day of Resurrection, "Indeed, we were ignorant of this"; [173]or lest you should say, "It was our ancestors who set up copartners earlier, and we were just descendants after them. Will You, then, destroy us on account of what the practicers of falsehood did?"

Sūrah 7 is Makkan.

I. Introduction

Addressing the idolatrous Quraysh, the rulers of Makkah, sūrah 7 narrates Arabian and Israelite prophetic history to warn the Quraysh that their rejection of the Prophet Muḥammad will earn them the same punishment that was meted out to the rebellious nations of the past. This passage now says that monotheistic doctrine, which is composed of the twin beliefs of God as the only deity and God as the only provident being, is vindicated not only by the aforementioned prophetic history, but also by the covenant that God made with all members of humanity in a primordial state of existence. Exactly how the event described in this passage took place is not explained, though the main point is clear: all human beings have a native ability to recognize monotheistic truth and are, consequently, responsible for accepting that truth.

II. Commentary

In the opening part of the verse, grammatically, a single individual is addressed, "your" in "your Lord" being singular. But the use of the singular can be interpreted to mean that many people are being addressed, one at a time, and that seems to be the case here. The addressees are asked to recall the time in the past when a certain event, about to be described, took place. Since, as indicated in section I, above, the event took place in a primordial or prehistorical setting, one might wonder whether any human being could have memory of that event. This question will be taken up shortly (see section III.1, below). Here, we will only note that, according to this passage, on a certain occasion before the start of humanity's earthly tenure, God made all human beings bear witness to His providence, the act including the bearing of witness to His oneness. The purpose of the witnessing was to take away any excuse that human beings might present on the Day of Resurrection—namely, (1) that they were ignorant of the truth about the existence of a unique and provident God or (2) that their ancestors were the ones responsible for falsely setting up copartners with God and that they themselves, therefore, should not be punished for the idol worship of their ancestors, whom they simply emulated.

The phrase "from out of their loins" serves to specify that the act of witnessing to God's oneness was performed not by some but by all human beings—that is, by all human beings who were ever to be born, one generation of human beings coming out of the loins of the preceding generation, as would later happen in the normal course of procreation on earth. The phrase, in other words, underscores the universal nature of the witness borne.

III. Issues

1. Memory of the Event. Do human beings remember or have any consciousness of the event described in this passage? An analogy may help to answer the question. The citizens of a country, called upon to defend their country against a foreign invasion, may not plead ignorance of a certain ceremony held in the past at which they were obligated to give their lives for their country, for their legal obligation to defend their country derives from the moral commitment they are presumed to have made as beneficiaries of the citizenship of that country. In the same vein, the Qur'ānic passage suggests that human beings, by virtue of their particular position in the scheme of things, must declare God to be their only Lord—that is, their only provider—since they are the beneficiaries of God's providential care. Thus, the passage under discussion can be interpreted to mean that human beings have a natural and intuitive knowledge of God's oneness and providence, and that this knowledge is sufficiently well entrenched in human nature to elicit from human beings the acknowledgment that God, indeed, is their Lord. It is this inherent knowledge of human beings that is triggered, so to speak, by the external stimulus of prophetic message, which explains why the Islamic Scripture calls itself a "reminder" (for example, Q 3:58; 12:104; 21:50)—that is, a reminder of the verities of which, at some level and in some form, human beings are already aware.

2. Basis of Accountability in the Hereafter. Since, deep down, all human beings possess an awareness of God as Lord, that awareness, this passage implies, will serve as a basis for holding them accountable in the hereafter. In other words, even if some people never received prophetic guidance during their lifetime, they will be held accountable, at least in a broad or general way, since they naturally possess a consciousness of God as their Lord. Prophetic message makes accountability specific and detailed, but the absence of such a message does not, in principle, render all accountability null and void.

3. God as Lord. In this passage, the question asked by God of human beings is not, "Am I not your *God*?" but "Am I not your *Lord*?" According to the Qur'ān, the Arabs believed in God as the supreme deity and as the maker of the universe (Q 29:61, 63), but their belief in other deities had compromised God's position as the only Lord, or as the only provident being. Thus, this passage holds up a mirror to Muḥammad's opponents, telling them that they have violated the very terms of the covenant that they, along with other human beings, made with God.

IV. Literary Notes

In verse 173 of the passage, the Qur'ān explains to the Quraysh why it has cited the Primordial Covenant to them: lest, on the Day of Judgment, they should argue that they were unaware of any such covenant or should plead that idol worship was invented by their ancestors, of whom they just happened to be the descendants. In presenting the second of the two putative arguments, the Quraysh say, after referring to their ancestors' polytheism, "and we were just descendants after them." The word "descendants" is a translation of the Arabic *dhurriyyah*, which, significantly, is indefinite. The Arabic word could have been definite, that is, *dhurriyyatahum*, "their descendants," which, actually, would have made good sense. By opting to use the indefinite *dhurriyyah* instead of the definite *dhurriyyatahum*, the Quraysh try to distance themselves from their polytheistic ancestors: they wish to be known only as "descendants," not as "*their* descendants," as if they had no direct and intimate relationship with their ancestors. Their verbal dissociation from their ancestors reflects the Quraysh's indifference, to be shown by them on the Day of Judgment, to their ancestors and stands in sharp contrast to the Quraysh's attempt, made in earthly life, to set themselves up as the proud defenders of their ancestral polytheistic faith, as reported in the Qur'ān (for example, 2:170; 5:104).

Incidentally, it is to bring out the full force of the indefiniteness of *dhurriyyah* that I have translated this word as "just descendants" ("only descendants" is another possibility). As the grammarians would say, the indefiniteness here signifies abasement or minification.

22 Charity Offerings

9 Repentance 60

The charity offerings are but for the poor and the needy, those administering them and those whose hearts are to be won over, in the cause of slaves and debtors, and in the cause of God and of the traveler—an obligation from God! And God is All-Knowing, All-Wise.

Sūrah 9 is Madīnan.

I. Introduction

In the verses immediately preceding this passage in the sūrah, reference is made to certain people who, not being very well off, had been drawn to Islam mainly by their hopes of making financial gains upon conversion. Called, along with certain other groups of people, hypocrites in the Qur'ān, these people expected to be regular recipients of a share of the charity offerings made by the members of the Muslim community. Pleased when they received a share of the offerings, they were quick to carp and complain if they did not get a share. In the passage under study, the Qur'ān says that the charity offerings are meant not for the hypocrites, but, rather, for certain designated people.

II. Commentary

"Charity offerings" is a translation of *ṣadaqāt* (sing. *ṣadaqah*), which includes all kinds of offerings, whether given to fulfill a religious obligation (in which case they are called *zakāh*) or given of one's free will. The Arabic word comes from a root meaning "truth," and the use of that word in the verse signifies that, by making charity offerings, one performs a concrete act of sacrifice, giving proof of the truth of one's convictions.

The tone of the opening phrase, "The charity offerings are but for . . . ," should be noted. Being greedy, the hypocrites expect to receive a sizable share of the charity offerings, irrespective of whether they are deserving of it. This verse tells the hypocrites that only people falling into certain categories are legitimate recipients of charity offerings. The verse lists eight heads of disbursement of the charity offerings:

(1) "The poor" are those who lack adequate means to satisfy their basic needs.

(2) "The needy" are those who, for some reason, find it difficult to engage in the struggle to earn a livelihood and, consequently, live in destitution. As such, they are worse off than the poor.

(3) Those who administer the charity offerings are to be paid out of the revenues made up of those offerings. In other words, the charity offerings are to be managed, at least partly, through a self-financing system.

(4) The charity offerings may be used to win the hearts of people who are unfavorably disposed toward Islam or the Muslim community or who need support and encouragement to enter the fold of Islam or to stay neutral in Islam's struggle against its opponents. Even Muslims with a lukewarm commitment to their religion may receive funds under this head.

(5) "In the cause of slaves" means "for the purpose of liberating slaves."

(6) "In the cause of . . . debtors" means "for the purpose of helping those who have incurred debts that they are unable to pay." It is assumed that the debts are due to some genuine cause—for example, a natural disaster or a severe and unexpected business loss—and are not due to the debtor's having indulged in religiously forbidden or morally reprehensible acts.

(7) "In the cause of God" has both a restricted meaning and a general meaning. The restricted meaning is "for the purpose of fighting in the way of God"; the general meaning is "for the purpose of promoting the religion of Islam." Promotion of the religion of Islam may take a variety of forms, such as educating people in the religion and establishing institutions that cater to the welfare of common people.

(8) Travelers, irrespective of their economic or financial status, might need help because simply being away from home can make fulfillment of even ordinary needs difficult.

The concluding part of this verse—"An obligation from God! And God is All-Knowing, All-Wise"—means that the injunction laid down in this verse must be observed by the believers since it comes from God, who knows what the best use of the charity offerings is since He is possessed of knowledge and since His decisions and actions are wise.

III. Issues

1. Classification of the Heads of Disbursement. The eight heads of disbursement can be divided into four groups (the translation of the verse provided above reflects the division). The first two—the poor and the needy—form two segments of a single group. By bracketing the two together, the verse means to say that poverty is to be eradicated at whatever level it exists, whether at an ordinary level (the poor) or at an extraordinary level (the needy).

The second group is made up of the administrators and "those whose hearts are to be won over." The administrators of the charity offerings are to be paid for their services and not on account of any financial need they might have. "Those whose hearts are to be won over" makes up a head of disbursement that is political in character, and disbursement of monies under this head is, therefore, subject to the discretion of the government. Like the previous head of disbursement, which has an instrumental character—because it makes possible the operation of the system of collection and distribution of the charity offerings—this one serves to protect the Muslim body politic against schism or against subversion by disaffected elements. These two heads of disbursement are also alike in that the recipients of charity offerings under them—the administrators and "those whose hearts are to be won over"—may receive charity offerings regardless of their financial standing.

The next two heads, which make up the third group, are aimed at removing a certain kind of handicap: The slave, even if able-bodied, suffers from the constraint of subjection to his master. And the person who is deep in debt on account of circumstances beyond his control may find himself at the mercy of his creditors.

The fourth group consists of the last two heads. Going out "in the cause of God"—in its restricted sense of setting out to fight in the way of God—and going on a journey both have an element of uncertainty or adventure about them since those who go out to fight and those who travel (one should keep in mind the often dangerous conditions of travel in seventh-century Arabia) are away from their home or base, where they would feel more secure.

While the verse limits the disbursement of the charity offerings to the above-mentioned eight heads, it does not stipulate that the charity offerings must be divided equally among the eight heads, or even that at least some amount must be allocated under each head.

2. Responsibility of the State. The commandment laid down in this verse presupposes the existence of a state. The third head of disbursement—namely, the officials responsible for administering the charity offerings—clearly implies that institutional arrangements are to be made for the collection and disbursement of the charity offerings. Likewise, the fourth head of expenditure—"those whose hearts are to be won over"—refers to the possibility of spending money by a state-like institution to neutralize, placate, or win the goodwill of powerful individuals or groups, whether Muslim or non-Muslim, whose hostility may pose a danger to Islam or the Muslim community.

Once it is seen that the verse assumes the existence of a state, it will follow that both the collection and disbursement of the charity offerings should be the responsibility of an Islamic state, which should undertake to manage the charity offering on a relatively large scale and in a systematic manner with a view to making optimum use of the available resources. It will also be clear that an Islamic state can use the revenues made up of the charity offerings to initiate and implement schemes to create a welfare-oriented socioeconomic system. For example, it can use the resources generated by the charity offerings (1) to set up an indemnity fund to help debtors; (2) to provide support to new converts to Islam with a view to helping them to find a footing in the new religious and social environment; and (3) to build facilities like inns, rest houses, and eating places along highways to serve the needs of travelers.

23 Joseph Interprets the Dreams of His Prison-Mates

12 Joseph 36–42

[36]Two young men entered prison along with him. One of them said, "I see myself in a dream pressing wine." And the other said, "I see myself in a dream carrying bread over my head, with birds eating of it." "Tell us its interpretation; we regard you as one of those of good conduct."

[37]He said, "No food that is served to you shall come to you except that I shall have told you its interpretation before it comes to you. This is of what my Lord has taught me. I have abandoned the way of people who do not believe in God; and they are the ones who deny the hereafter. [38]And I have followed the way of my ancestors—Abraham, Isaac, and Jacob. It does not behoove us to associate anything with God. This is of God's bounty upon us and upon people, but most people do not offer gratitude. [39]My fellow-prisoners, are various masters better or God, the One, the Dominant? [40]You do not worship any other than Him except names that you and your ancestors have named: God has sent down no sanction for them. Rule belongs to none but God. He has commanded that you worship none but Him. This is the right religion, but most people do not know. [41]My fellow-prisoners, as for one of you, he will serve wine to his master; and as for the other one, he will be crucified, and birds will eat of his head. The matter about which you are seeking my opinion is decided." [42]And he said to the one who, of the two, he thought, was going to be saved, "Mention me to your master." But Satan caused him to forget to mention him to his master, and so he remained in prison for several years.

Sūrah 12 is Makkan.

I. Introduction

This passage relates an incident from the story of Joseph, one of the sons of Jacob and—in Islam—a prophet. According to the Qurʾānic story, narrated in detail in sūrah 12, the jealous half-brothers of young Joseph drop him in a well, from which he is recovered by a group of caravaneers and sold in Egypt to a person called, in Q 12:30, *ʿAzīz* (literally, "one possessed of power"; that is, one occupying a position of power) and, in the Bible, "an officer of Pharaoh, the captain of the guard" (Genesis 39:1). The exceptionally handsome Joseph is pursued by the captain's wife, but he repulses her advances, and she, becoming vengeful, has him imprisoned. Two young men enter prison along with Joseph. In the prison, the Qurʾānic passage suggests, Joseph becomes known for his excellent character and acquires the reputation of a wise man. The two prisoners each have a dream and request Joseph to interpret it. Joseph interprets the dreams, but not before he has presented to the two prisoners the essential tenet of the creed he follows—the tenet of monotheism.

II. Commentary

Verse 36: "Two young men" is a translation of the Arabic *fatayān*. The same word, in the singular—*fatā*—is used for Joseph a few verses before the passage, implying that Joseph is about the same age as the two other prisoners. That the two prisoners are impressed with Joseph means, then, that Joseph had, at a young age, earned a solid reputation for being a good, wise individual.

"Pressing wine" means "obtaining wine by pressing grapes."

Verses 37–40: Asked by the two prisoners to interpret their dreams, Joseph senses that he has a perfect opportunity to acquaint them with his faith and either get them to accept it or create a soft spot for it in their hearts. But he is intelligent enough to put them at ease first since he knows that they are eager to find out the meaning of their dreams and would have little interest in hearing a lengthy disquisition on serious religious or philosophical issues. He also realizes that his presentation to them cannot encroach on the meal time, which offered one of the few breaks in the dull prison routine and was something the prisoners looked forward to. It seems that the time for the next meal was approaching, and so, after reassuring the two prison-mates that he will interpret their dreams before the next meal arrives, Joseph makes his case.

The sequence in which Joseph lays out the elements of his argument is notable. To begin with, he disclaims, very modestly, any credit for his ability to interpret dreams: he owes this ability to God, he says. The disclaimer also indicates that, in Joseph's view, the knowledge of the interpretation of dreams is speculative in character—except in those cases in which such knowledge has a revelatory base. In other words, Joseph is distinguishing between soothsaying and revelation. Next, Joseph dissociates himself from the people who deny God—that is, who deny the oneness of God or set up peers to God—adding that people who do so lack belief in the hereafter as well, the implication being that the right belief in God necessarily includes belief in God as judge in an afterlife. Having rejected belief in setting up copartners to God, Joseph declares, in positive terms, that he follows the monotheistic religion of his ancestors—Abraham, Isaac, and Jacob. The manner in which Joseph refers to Abraham, Isaac, and Jacob suggests that the names of these personages were not unknown in Egypt, or even in the larger region of which Egypt was a part. The reference to the ancestors also implies that Joseph is not following some newfangled religion but a major and well-known religion with which respected persons like Abraham, Isaac, and Jacob are associated.

"It does not behoove us to associate anything with God" means that it is unbecoming of human beings to set up copartners to God, for God has given human beings enough sense and furnished them with enough evidence in nature and in their own lives for them to realize that nothing is fit to be God's peer or equal.

"This is of God's bounty upon us and upon people, but most people do not offer gratitude." Joseph is saying that, although a bountiful God has put enough resources at the disposal of all human beings to reach the truth about God, most people, out of willful ignorance, fail to reach that truth and, as a result, do not offer to God the gratitude they owe Him. Joseph makes a subtle distinction, though. By "us" in "upon us" he means the followers of Abraham; by "people" in "upon people" he means humankind, or the people of Egypt, to whom his two fellow prisoners belong. The distinction implies that, unlike Abraham and his family and followers, who are monotheists and are grateful to God for guiding them to the truth, most people do not have the right belief about God and show little appreciation of the guidance that God has furnished to them. Joseph strengthens his case by asking the two prisoners a pointed question, one that they could answer from their own experience: Is it better to serve one master or several different masters? Building on the expected, though unstated, answer—namely, that it is better to serve a single master—Joseph asks whether it is right to serve anyone other than "God, the One, the Dominant." Having presented his main argument, Joseph can now afford to be blunt, and so he declares that all beings other than God whom their devotees call upon for help are mere names without substance for which no Divine sanction exists. And rounding out his statement about monotheism, he adds that God is the only ruler there is and the only being worthy of worship. "Rule belongs to none but God" means that God alone has the right and privilege to give commandments and pass judgment. The statement—which, Joseph comments, represents the essence of "the right religion"—probably carries political as well as religious implications.

Verse 41: Having argued for monotheism, Joseph now interprets his prison-mates' dreams: one of the two prisoners will be released from prison and reinstated in his position of serving wine to the king, while the other will be crucified. In offering his interpretation, Joseph avoids specifying which of the two individuals is meant in the case of each interpretation and, instead, uses ambiguous language: "As for one of you . . . and as for the other one." By not identifying the prisoner who is destined to be crucified, he is, possibly, trying to avoiding hurting that prisoner's feelings too much, even though it is obvious which prisoner will meet that fate.

Verse 42: Joseph requests the prisoner who is to be released to mention him to the king upon his release. The Qur'ān says that Satan caused that prisoner to forget to mention Joseph to the king, and that Joseph, consequently, remained in prison for quite a few years.

What is the meaning of Satan's causing of the prisoner to forget to mention Joseph to the king? The meaning seems to be that reinstatement in his former position at the king's court made the prisoner forget about his life in prison and, consequently, he neglected to mention Joseph to the king. The prisoner's heedlessness, being unvirtuous in character, is attributed to Satan.

III. Issues

1. Joseph's Character. Joseph's speech to his prison-mates sheds light on certain aspects of his character. That he was quite young at the time of his imprisonment suggests, as already noted, Joseph's precocity: at a very young age, he had fully imbibed the Abrahamic monotheistic teaching that he must have received in his father Jacob's house before being forcibly separated from him. That he remains devoted to the Abrahamic faith of monotheism through his prison ordeal—which, according to the sūrah, is only one of the several ordeals he goes through—shows his maturity and perseverance. We have already remarked about Joseph's intelligence, evidenced by his seizing of the right moment to preach to the two prison-mates. We may add that, in the short amount of time available to him, Joseph does an excellent job of presenting the essence of his religion to his fellow prisoners; he focuses on the kernel of the Abrahamic faith, presenting both a critique of polytheism and a strong statement in support of monotheism, speaking, throughout, in an idiom that the two prison-mates would find quite easy to understand (note, especially, the contrast drawn by Joseph between serving one master and serving many masters). And the prefatory statement he makes before presenting his faith to the two prison-mates—namely, that he owes to God his ability to interpret dreams—serves to reinforce his preaching to the prison-mates since he is clearly implying that the accuracy of his interpretation of dreams derives from the truth of the monotheistic creed which he has inherited from his forefathers, the creed which he is about to invite his fellow prisoners to accept.

The passage underscores Joseph's modesty. In referring to his illustrious ancestors, he makes no attempt to win respect or honor for himself by claiming association with the Abrahamic line, but only stresses that he follows the way of Abraham, Isaac, and Jacob (verse 38). Also, he takes no credit for his ability to interpret dreams but calls that ability a gift from God (verse 37).

2. Egyptian Society. From Joseph's speech, one gathers that the two prisoners who enter prison along with Joseph hold beliefs that are typically held by the larger, polytheistic Egyptian society. The passage indicates, though, that Egyptian society was not entirely unfamiliar with monotheistic ideas, and that Abraham, Isaac, and Jacob were known figures among the Egyptians. It is against this setting that Joseph expresses his loyalty to "the way of my ancestors—Abraham, Isaac, and Jacob," explaining, in the same breath, that this way consists in rejecting polytheism and espousing monotheism (verse 38).

Verse 36 suggests that, according to popular Egyptian belief, at least some types of dreams were considered significant and that individuals known for piety and wisdom were believed to have the ability to interpret them.

IV. Literary Notes

1. Who are the two prisoners who enter prison along with Joseph? The Qur'ān, following its general practice about the depiction of characters, does not provide much detail about their identity or background. According to the Bible, one was the king's chief butler, while the other was the king's chief baker. Why were they sent to prison? Again, the Qur'ān is silent on the matter; the Bible, too, does not give the reason for their imprisonment. According to the Talmud, however, the king was angry with both because, on one occasion, the bread was found to be gritty, and the wine served to the king was found with an insect in it. Muslim commentators on the Qur'ān speculate that the two were accused of conspiring to kill the king by poisoning his food. From the Qur'ānic standpoint, however, it is not crucial to determine the cause of the king's indignation. At this point, a certain stylistic feature of the Qur'ān may be noted.

Qur'ānic narrative usually focuses on the essence of the matter at hand, skipping details. In fact, it defines the essence of the matter sometimes by leaving out details that it considers redundant or of secondary importance and sometimes by implying such details in its description. This often results in what may be called time jumps, an example of which occurs at the beginning of this passage: Immediately after Joseph and the two youths enter prison, the latter request Joseph to interpret their dreams. A review of verse 36 gives us an idea of the amount of information that is implied rather than explicitly stated in the story, furnishing an example of Qur'ānic verbal economy:

- Joseph and two other youths enter prison.
- All three remain in prison for a sufficiently long time for Joseph's fellow prisoners to form an estimate of his character.
- Joseph's fellow prisoners each see a dream (the use of the imperfect tense *arā* in each prisoner's statement suggests that each saw his dream repeatedly but failed to arrive at a satisfactory interpretation of it, such that he is sufficiently perturbed about the dream to ask Joseph—who has, in the meantime, earned the trust of both of them and impressed them with his wisdom and good character—to interpret the dream).

2. In verse 36, the second prison-mate relates his dream in these words: "I see myself in a dream carrying bread *over* my head." Here, the use of the preposition "over" (*fawqa*) as against the expected "on" (*'alā*) is quite significant. It is only when you are walking at a fast pace or are almost running that you carry, say, a basket, *over* your head, holding it aloft, your vertically outstretched arms not allowing the basket to touch your head. The baker, in other words, saw himself rushing along in his dream. Joseph interprets the baker's dream to mean that the baker will be crucified. Little did the baker know that he was only rushing to his death!

3. In verse 37, Joseph's statement that he has "abandoned the way of people who do not believe in God" does not necessarily mean that Joseph himself was once a disbeliever. The word "abandoned" in the verse means "rejected," but its use in preference to "rejected" has twofold significance. First, Joseph is implying that he follows the monotheistic creed of his forefathers not because he is partial to that creed but because he has found merit in it after having examined it objectively. In other words, Joseph is no mere imitator; he has *consciously adopted* his ancestral religion and *consciously given up* or *abandoned* idolatry. Second, Joseph is subtly suggesting to the prison-mates how they should act now that they have been informed about the true religion: they should *abandon* their ancestral religion.

4. After interpreting their dreams, Joseph says to his prison-mates: "The matter about which you are seeking my opinion is decided" (verse 41). The impersonal character of the passive voice—"is decided" (Arabic: *quḍiya*)—here denotes the finality of the interpretations: the matter in question has been decided and is not subject to change. Furthermore, the use of the passive voice signifies that the source of the interpretations lies outside Joseph—God, obviously, being the source alluded to. And there is the added suggestion that God will necessarily cause the interpretations to materialize.

V. The Biblical Account

The Biblical story of Joseph is much more detailed than the Qur'ānic, but we will make only three points about it, keeping in mind the Qur'ānic passage under study. First, the Biblical detail helps to make specific what is left unspecified in the Qur'ān; for example, as already noted, the two prisoners are given identities in the Biblical stories—one is the king's butler, and the other, the king's baker. Qur'ānic commentators, in fact, borrow this and other information from the Bible or Jewish sources (without necessarily naming the sources). Second, the Qur'ānic narration of the anecdote of Joseph preaching to his prison-mates does not find an analogue in the Bible, or even in the Talmud. Third, the passage under study would, in view of the above, draw a picture of Joseph that is, in some respects, different from the Biblical picture. The passage gives the Qur'ānic story of Joseph a very sharp religious and ethical focus.

24 Inviting People to the Faith

16 Bee 125–128

[125]Invite to the path of your Lord with wisdom and good counsel, and argue
with them in the best manner; your Lord—He knows full well who has gone astray
from His path, and He knows full well those who would be guided. [126]And if you
should retaliate, then retaliate to the extent to which you have been wronged. But if
you are patient, then it is much better for those who are patient. [127]And be patient.
And it is not possible for you to have patience except with God's help. And do not
grieve over them, and do not be in distress on account of their scheming.
[128]Indeed, God is with those who are godfearing and who perform good works.

Sūrah 16 is Makkan.

I. Introduction

At the time of the revelation of sūrah 16, as verses 126–127 of this passage indicate, the Muslims, still in Makkah, were being fiercely opposed, were even being persecuted by the Quraysh, the ruling tribe of Makkah, there being a possibility that the Muslims would react sharply and angrily against their oppressors. In these circumstances, the sūrah advised the Muslims to act with patience; to retaliate, if they must, proportionately to the wrong committed against them; and, above all, to continue their mission of inviting people—"with wisdom and good counsel"—to the faith of Islam. This passage may be compared with Q 22:38–41 (see chapter 27, "War in Self-Defense").

II. Commentary

Verse 125: Addressing the Prophet and, through him, the Muslims, the verse lays down the basic guidelines for inviting nonbelievers to enter the fold of Islam. The invitation must be characterized by (1) wisdom, which here stands for sound argument and reasoning, and (2) good counsel, which signifies sincere advice or admonition tendered with gentleness and affection.

The verse permits Muslims to "argue" with their opponents, but it stresses that they must argue "in the best manner"—that is, in a calm and dignified manner and without becoming offensive or contentious. Their responsibility, the verse tells the Muslims, is to convey the message to those outside the faith and not to compel conversion, for God knows full well who has strayed from the path of guidance and will not return to it, just as He knows full well who has a genuine interest in obtaining guidance and will hasten to accept guidance even upon making cursory acquaintance with it.

Verses 126–128: If, in a particular situation, the Muslims decide to retaliate against oppression or persecution, they must not overretaliate. And, of course, they must not, under any circumstances, cross the limits set down by the Islamic ethical code for dealing with others. Showing patience is, at any rate, better than exacting retribution, for, in exacting retribution, one is not only likely to commit excesses, but is also liable to hurt the cause of inviting others to the faith. Being patient under provocation is difficult, so one must seek God's help and pray to Him to grant one patience.

As for those who would not believe in the truth, the Prophet and his followers must neither lose any sleep over them nor worry about the plots such people are hatching against Islam and Muslims, for God is with those who are godfearing—that is, who refrain from committing prohibited acts and who actively perform good actions—and will protect them against their opponents and will also ensure their eventual success.

25 Commandments

17 Night Journey 22–39

[22]Do not set up another deity along with God, lest you end up as one
censured, forsaken. [23]And your Lord has decreed that you shall not worship
anyone except Him. And that you shall treat your parents well. Should one of
them, or both, happen to reach old age while they are with you, do not say *Uff!*
to them; and do not rebuke them; and speak to them in kind words. [24]And lower
the wing of humility, out of mercy, for them, and say: "My Lord, have mercy on
them, just as they brought me up when I was little." [25]Your Lord has full
knowledge of what is in your hearts. If you are virtuous, then He is very forgiving
to those who come back.

[26]And give the kinsman his due, and the one in need, and the traveler, and
do not be extravagant in spending; [27]the extravagant spenders are the brothers
of satans; and Satan is very ungrateful to his Lord. [28]And if you must draw away
from them, while seeking your Lord's mercy, which you are expecting, then
speak to them in gentle words. [29]And do not tie up your hands to your neck,
and do not spread them out all the way, lest you end up as one reproached,
without resource. [30]Your Lord amplifies sustenance for whomever He wishes,
and curtails it; He is One Well-Informed about His people, One Watching over
them.

[31]And do not kill your children for fear of poverty: We give sustenance to them as well as to you; killing them is a great sin.

[32]And do not come close to illicit sex; it is a glaring immorality, and it is an evil path.

[33]And do not kill a being whom God has declared inviolate, except for just cause; and one who is killed wrongfully, We have given his next of kin authority, but let him not exceed the limits in killing; he is going to be helped.

[34]And do not come close to the orphan's wealth, except in a manner that is most fitting, until he reaches maturity. And fulfill commitments; commitments are going to be questioned about.

[35]And fill up the measure when you give measure, and weigh with an even balance; this is better, and is more excellent in respect of outcome.

[36]And do not follow what you have no knowledge of; the ears, the eyes, the heart—each of these shall be questioned about it.

[37]And do not walk on earth with a swagger: you will never tear up the earth, and you will never reach the mountains in height. [38]All of that, the evil thereof, is displeasing to your Lord.

[39]This is of what your Lord has revealed to you of wisdom. And do not set up another deity along with God, lest you are thrown into hell as one reproached, repelled.

Sūrah 17 is Makkan.

I. Introduction

This passage is a compact statement of Islamic commandments. The focus of the commandments—no fewer than twenty-five—is social conduct, ranging from discharging one's obligations to one's parents to refraining from cheating in selling merchandise. The commandments are related to and derived from the matrix of monotheistic belief, which is stated in the opening verse (22) and is repeated in the exact same words in the last verse (39). The passage is punctuated with exhortations to adopt an attitude marked by gentleness, humility, moderation, and conscientiousness.

II. Commentary

Verse 22: After stating the most fundamental commandment of Islam—"Do not set up another deity along with God"—the verse warns that violation of the commandment will reduce one, in the afterlife, to the state of "one censured, forsaken." "Censured" means condemned by God, and "forsaken" means betrayed by erstwhile friends and supporters, including Satan, called the "Great Forsaker" in Q 25:29. Since one who sets up deities besides God will be censured and forsaken, the monotheist, one can infer, will earn praise and receive Divine support.

This verse is apparently addressed to the Prophet (the "you" in the Arabic text is singular), but the real addressee is the entire Muslim community, the Prophet having been addressed as the leader or representative of that community. The commandment, in other words, is general.

Verse 23: The prohibition against worshipping anyone other than God is here repeated, and the commandment to treat one's parents well is given next. There is a connection between the two injunctions: In this world, after God, one's parents are the ones to whom one is most beholden. But while the parents must be treated with the utmost respect and kindness, they may not be raised to the level of deity. If this is true of parents, then with much stronger reason must it be true of all other human beings.

Notably, the commandment about being kind to parents is joined by conjunction to that of worshipping only one God. By bracketing the two commandments together, the Qur'ān elevates the status of parents.

One's parents deserve one's care and affection at any age and not only when they reach old age. The reference to old age in the verse underscores the point that it is especially when they get old, become weak or disabled, and, perhaps, develop eccentricities of attitude that the parents might become difficult to deal with and care for. It is at this time that their children, who, quite possibly, are in the prime of their youth and are living their own lives and pursuing their own interests, need to remember that their parents took care of them and put up with them when they were helpless little kids and must realize that it is time for the children to repay some of the kindness they received from their parents at an earlier time. Accordingly, the Qur'ān says that, in dealing with their parents in the latter's old age, the children must make a special effort to be kind to their parents: they must not even utter the word *Uff!*—an Arabic interjection signifying impatience and frustration—and they must not chide or scold them for anything they do. The prohibition against uttering *Uff!* to one's parents would apply, of course, to the word's counterpart in any other language. It goes without saying, too, that the prohibition would apply with stronger reason to inflicting greater hurt on the parents.

"While they are with you" means: If they are living with you or if you are responsible for taking care of them. The phrase is meant to alert the children to the fact that taking care of the old, weak, and possibly disabled parents, who are either living with their children or for whom their children are the primary caregivers, may, at times, become too demanding a task and that the children will, therefore, need to be especially patient and forbearing. The phrase also suggests that old parents living with their children or children being directly involved in the caretaking of their parents should be a norm in Muslim society. And there is the implied reminder—reinforcing a point already made—that there was a time when, as dependents, the children lived with their parents, who took care of their children and put up with their at times difficult or odd behavior.

There is a certain poignancy in the words "Should one of them, or both, happen to reach old age while they are with you." If one of the parents dies, the surviving parent feels lonelier and is in greater need of support and consolation; if both parents reach old age, caregiving may present great difficulties. It is this challenging nature of the task to which the verse is referring.

Verse 24: The idiom "to lower the wing of humility for somebody" means "to obey *or* submit to somebody." The image is that of a parent bird protecting its young ones by covering them under its wings, and the Qur'ān uses it to point out to the children that it may be time to reverse roles: Their parents spread out their wings of nurturing love for their children when the latter were weak infants, and now the children must cover the parents, so to speak, under the wings of dutiful obedience and love. The phrase "out of mercy" signifies that submission or obedience to the parents must be offered out of true love and compassion.

Verse 25: Verse 24 enjoined the children to adopt an attitude of love and submission to their parents during their old age. Verse 25 now says that such an attitude toward one's parents must arise out of genuine sentiment, for God knows whether, in treating one's parents in a certain way, one is abiding by the injunction in spirit as well as in letter or whether one is putting up a show ("Your Lord has full knowledge of what is in your hearts"), and He will reward one, or withhold reward from one, depending on the quality of one's faith and actions. Those who are remiss in carrying out their obligations to their parents will, if they repent, be forgiven by God, for God forgives "those who come back"—that is, those who seek forgiveness for their lapses.

Verses 26–28: Verse 26 does not say, "And help the kinsman, the one in need, and the traveler," but "And give the kinsman his due, and the one in need, and the traveler." The word "due" is a translation of *ḥaqq*, which denotes the obligation of giving one the right that belongs to one. One's poor kinsmen are the first on the list of those who deserve help. "One in need"—*miskīn* in the original—is one who is destitute and, therefore, worse off than an ordinary poor person. A kinsman who is also destitute would, of course, be doubly deserving of help. As for travelers, they are entitled to help regardless of their financial status if, being away from home, they find themselves resourceless at some point. Addressing those who are well-off, the verse says that the people belonging to the above-listed categories—poor kinsmen, needy individuals, travelers—are deserving of help and that, in coming to their aid, one must not think that one is doing them a favor, for to help them is only to discharge one's obligation toward them and to give them the *ḥaqq* that rightfully belongs to them.

The prohibition, in the second part of verse 26, against extravagant spending is closely connected in thought to the commandment, given in the first part of the verse, to help those in need: Since it is one's obligation to help the less fortunate, one cannot be allowed to squander one's wealth. Verse 27 reinforces that idea. Underlying the verse is the argument that the proper way to offer gratitude for wealth, a gift from God, is to spend it responsibly. Extravagance keeps one from carrying out one's obligations to people in need and is, for that reason, the way of Satan, who, being ungrateful to God, would also like human beings to be ungrateful to God. Verse 28 adds the rider that, if one lacks the resources to help people in need but expects to come by some money in the near future and, therefore, wishes to "draw away" from such people—that is, avoid them so as not to have to refuse them bluntly—then one should, at least, speak to them gently and not hurt their feelings. The words "seeking your Lord's mercy, which you are expecting" suggest that if one does not have the means to provide financial assistance to those who have petitioned for such assistance, then, instead of completely disappointing them, one might promise to help them on achieving a degree of prosperity.

Verse 29: "To tie up one's hands to one's neck" means "to be tightfisted"; the idiom draws the picture of one who is unable to "spread" one's hand—that is, to spend one's money—when asked to give financial help. "To spread out one's hands," by contrast, means "to be extravagant." Verses 26–27 prohibited extravagant spending. Verse 29, anticipating a possible reaction, says that the prohibition against such spending is not meant to keep one from meeting one's own needs. The right thing to do is to take the middle ground—to be neither a skinflint nor a squandermaniac. Only moderation in spending will enable one to meet one's own needs and, at the same time, to help others. Reckless spending on oneself will incur people's reproach—for one will not be able to assist those who ask for assistance—and render one incapable of fulfilling one's obligations toward others—for one will be left with no resources with which to meet those obligations.

Verse 30: The first part of verse 29 urged the believers not to be miserly. Miserliness is actuated by the thought that one's effort is the sole and exclusive determinant of one's financial position in the world, and that one can avoid poverty only by keeping one's resources to oneself. Verse 30 criticizes that thought, saying that the ultimate source of both riches and poverty is God, who is watchfully aware of people's circumstances and who decides, in his wisdom, whom to give how much. The right attitude for people, then, is to spend moderately, satisfying one's own needs and discharging one's financial obligations to others.

Verse 31: The same attitude that underlies miserliness underlay the ancient Arab practice of female infanticide. Thinking that girls, incapable of making a significant contribution to their families' or tribes' wealth, were a liability, some Arabs buried their female children alive, prompting the Qur'ān to make a comment similar to the one made in verse 30—namely, that God is the ultimate source of both abundance and indigence. God sustains all—children no less than their parents. It is, therefore, a great sin to commit infanticide for fear of impoverishment.

Verse 32: The prohibition against getting close to illicit sex means that one must not only stay away from it, but must also refrain from doing anything that might, directly or indirectly, lead to it. Illicit sex is "a glaring immorality" in the sense that the generality of human beings regard it as such and that no proof is required to establish it as an immoral act. It is "an evil path" in the sense that society's acceptance and practice of sexual promiscuity will undermine the family system, thus compromising the stability and health of society.

Verse 33: Human life has sanctity. Taking someone's life is, therefore, forbidden, except when some just cause exists—for example, when one kills someone wantonly and, in doing so, forfeits one's own life. The near relatives of one wrongfully killed have the right to demand punishment for the killer or to receive compensation from him in the form of blood money. But the relatives should realize that, since the law is on their side, giving them the support of the penal and judicial system, they must not go overboard in exacting revenge—for example, by killing a man of distinction from the aggressor party in place of the real killer if the latter happens to be an ordinary individual or by killing more people from the aggressor party in return for a single individual killed. Such excesses in taking revenge were commonly committed in pre-Islamic Arabia, and this verse orders a departure from those practices.

According to this verse, the real plaintiff in a case of homicide is not the state but the heir or survivor of the person killed; the function of the state is only to enforce the will of the heir or survivor.

Verse 34: One in charge of an orphan's property must manage it with the utmost care and responsibility, handing over the property to the orphan when the orphan reaches maturity. One who takes charge of an orphan's property makes a commitment—not only to the orphan but also to God—to manage the property with integrity and will, on Judgment Day, be held responsible for this as well as all other commitments.

Verse 35: One who sells merchandise must give full measure and weigh accurately. Such practices constitute sound economic policy in this world and will ensure a better outcome—that is, salvation—in the afterlife.

Verse 36: This is a prohibition against indulging in slander and rumormongering. "What you have no knowledge of" means "what you lack definite knowledge about" and, hence, "what lacks basis in truth and certitude." One who is disposed to engaging in the aforementioned acts would do well to remember that, on the Day of Judgment, God will hold people accountable not only for the things they hear with their ears and see with their eyes, but also for the thoughts they secretly entertain in their hearts.

In "the ears, the eyes, the heart—each of these shall be questioned about it," the pronoun "it" refers to "what you have no knowledge of" in the first part of the verse. In other words, the ears, the eyes, and the heart each will be asked: Why did you get involved in untruths?

Verses 37–38: These verses enjoin modesty of behavior: Do not walk about arrogantly on God's earth, for you will not tear up the earth if you stomp around on the ground, and you will not be able to rival the mountains in height if you tried. In other words: It behooves you to be humble before God, whose limitless power is attested by the phenomena He has created, such as the vast earth and the lofty mountains.

In "All of that, the evil thereof, is displeasing to your Lord," the words "All of that" refer to the prohibitions stated in the preceding verses. The complete phrase implies that those who violate the prohibitions will earn God's displeasure.

Verse 39: The demonstrative "this" refers to all the good qualities or characteristics that have been cited in this passage. Referring to all of them, this verse says that the instructions given in the preceding verses represent part of the wisdom that has been revealed by God to the Prophet Muḥammad. The passage ends with a repetition of a commandment of fundamental importance, the one given at the beginning of the passage—the real addressee, again, being the believing community at large: Do not associate anyone with God, for those who do so will be cast into hell—having earned disgrace and having been driven away from God's mercy on account of their sins.

III. Literary Notes

1. This passage opens (verse 22) and ends (verse 39) with the prohibition of idolatry, thus employing the literary device of envelope to underscore the importance of monotheism as the ground of all belief and conduct. More specifically, the envelope stresses that monotheism should be, so to speak, the alpha and omega of all thought and action and that monotheism serves as a wall that encloses and guards the teachings of the passage, these teachings enduring only for as long as the wall stands in its place.

2. The Arabic text of the passage contains several instances of shift of number. We will note a few of them. Verse 22, employing the second person singular form, seems to address the Prophet Muḥammad. Obviously, the commandment, "Do not set up another deity along with God" (verse 22) or "[Y]ou shall not worship anyone except Him" (verse 23) does not imply that there was a danger that Muḥammad would start worshipping idols. The use of the second person singular in this verse is, therefore, meant to address Muḥammad as a representative of the larger Muslim community, and it is the community that is being enjoined, through Muḥammad, to guard against relapsing into idol worship. This interpretation of the use of the second person singular in verse 22 is confirmed in the next verse, in which the second person singular (Muḥammad is the addressee) is quickly followed by the second person plural (the community is the addressee), thus: "And your [Muḥammad's] Lord has decreed that you [the community] shall not worship anyone except Him."

In verse 23, again, the second person singular, ostensibly used to address Muḥammad, is actually meant to address the members of the Muslim community at large: "And that you shall treat your parents well. Should one of them, or both, happen to reach old age while they are with you, do not say *Uff!* to them; and do not rebuke them; and speak to them in kind words." Muḥammad, as an individual, could not have been the addressee in the verse since neither of his parents was then alive: he was born after his father's death and his mother had died while he was a little child.

3. This passage illustrates some of the patterns used by the Qurʾān in presenting its material. Thus, in the Qurʾān, the injunction to treat one's parents with kindness often comes on the heels of the injunction to worship the one and only true God; verses

22–23 of the passage exemplify that pattern. Also, a statement of the imperative to respect the life of others is often followed in the Qur'ān by a statement of the imperative to respect the property of others. In this passage, the injunction, in verse 33, against taking someone's life is preceded by a reference to a certain type of killing, that of female infanticide, practiced by some tribes in Arabia, whereas the injunction, in verse 34, against mismanaging orphans' property is followed by a certain type of commercial malpractice, that of giving short measure—thus yielding a subpassage consisting of verses 33–35.

IV. Biblical Parallels

An obvious Biblical parallel to the Qur'ānic passage is the Decalogue, or the Ten Commandments, in Exodus 20:1–17 (and Deuteronomy 5:6–21). The Decalogue, too, begins with the prohibition against idol worship and lists several of the other commandments contained in the Qur'ānic passage:

> [1]Then God spoke all these words: [2]I am the Lord your God, who brought you out of the land of Egypt, out of the house of slavery; [3]you shall have no other gods before me.
>
> [4]You shall not make for yourself an idol. . . .
>
> [12]Honor your father and your mother. . . .
>
> [13]You shall not murder.
>
> [14]You shall not commit adultery.
>
> [15]You shall not steal. . . . (Exodus 20:1–15)

In the Biblical passage, "You shall not steal" (verse 15) is based on the same principle of the sanctity of other people's property on which the injunction in the Qur'ānic passage about orphans' property (verse 34) is based. The injunction about giving full measure in the Qur'ānic passage (verse 35) is also akin to the same principle since to give short measure is to steal.

Leviticus 19, too, is relevant:

> [1]The Lord spoke to Moses, saying:
>
> [2]Speak to all the congregations of the people of Israel and say to them: You shall be holy, for I the Lord your God am holy. [3]You shall each revere your mother and father . . . I am the Lord your God. [4]Do not turn to idols or make cast images for yourselves: I am the Lord your God. . . .
>
> [9]When you reap the harvest of your land, you shall not reap to the very edges of your field, or gather the gleanings of your harvest. [10]You shall not strip your vineyards bare, or gather the fallen grapes of your vineyards; you shall leave them for the poor and the alien: I am the Lord your God.
>
> [11]You shall not steal; you shall not deal falsely. . . .

> [13]You shall not defraud your neighbor; you shall not steal; and you shall not keep for yourself the wages of a laborer until morning. . . .
>
> [35]You shall not cheat in measuring length, weight, or quantity. [36]You shall have honest balances, honest weights. . . . [37]You shall keep all my statues and all my ordinances, and observe them: I am the Lord.

The Qur'ānic passage begins and ends with a statement of monotheism, and the same is the case with this chapter of Leviticus, although the phrase "I am the Lord" also occurs several times in this chapter.

26 God Makes Moses a Prophet

20 Ṭā-Hā 9–36

[9]And has the story of Moses reached you? [10]When he saw a fire, and said to his family, "Stay here awhile. I have glimpsed a fire; perhaps, I will bring you a firebrand, or will find guidance at the fire."

[11]When he reached it, it was proclaimed: "O Moses, [12]I am your Lord; so, take off your shoes—you are in the holy valley, Ṭuwā. [13]And I have elected you; so, listen carefully to what is being revealed. [14]I, indeed, am God. There is no deity but I, so worship Me, and establish the prayer to remember Me. [15]The Hour is going to come—I will just about keep it hidden, so that every being is recompensed for the effort it puts forth. [16]So, let not those who do not believe in it and follow their caprice keep you from it, lest you perish. [17]And what is that in your hand, Moses?"

[18]He said, "It is my staff; I lean on it and beat down with it leaves upon my sheep, and I have other uses for it, too."

[19]He said, "Put it down, Moses."

[20]So, he put it down, and there it was—a serpent running about!

[21]He said, "Seize it, and do not be afraid. [22]We will restore it to its original state. And draw your hand in to your side, and it will come out white, without any illness, being another sign!—[23]that We may show you of Our great signs. [24]Go to Pharaoh; he has rebelled."

[25]He said, "My Lord, open up my breast for me, [26]and make my task easy for me, [27]and untie the knot in my tongue, [28]that they may understand me. [29]And appoint, for me, an aid, from among my family—[30]Aaron, my brother; [31]back me up with him, [32]and make him a partner in my task, [33]that we may glorify You a great deal [34]and remember You a great deal. [35]You have been watching over us."

[36]He said, "You are granted your petition, O Moses!"

Sūrah 20 is Makkan.

I. Introduction

In this passage, Moses is vested with prophecy and charged with preaching to Pharaoh. According to the Qurʾān, Moses, who had grown up as a member of Pharaoh's household, accidentally killed a Copt and, afraid of being wrongly accused of willful murder, fled Egypt, ending up in Midian (Qurʾānic Madyan). In Midian, Moses met the prophet Shuʿayb, served him for many years, and married one of his daughters. The incident narrated in the passage takes place when Moses, accompanied by his family, is returning from Midian. As the family passes through a wilderness in Sinai, Moses spots a fire in the distance.

II. Commentary

Verse 9: "And has the story of Moses reached you?" This question, addressed to Muḥammad, is a question only in form and does not require an answer. It is asked only to alert Muḥammad that the story of Moses, which is about to be narrated, carries instructive lessons for him.

As a rule, the Qurʾānic stories of earlier prophets have a bearing on Muḥammad's prophetic career. By telling Muḥammad that those prophets, too, faced difficulties in carrying out their mission, that their nations' response to them was similar to the response of Muḥammad's nation to him, and that, like those prophets, Muḥammad, too, will be vindicated by God in the end, the stories guide, instruct, and console Muḥammad. The question—"And has the story of Moses reached you?"—is, thus, prefatory to providing direction, encouragement, and solace to Muḥammad at a certain juncture in his struggle against his Makkan opponents.

Verse 10: On spotting a fire in the distance—it is a cold night, and Moses and his family appear to be lost—Moses asks his family to stop and wait for him so that he may go up to the fire and either bring back from it a firebrand to keep his family warm or, with help obtained from someone who might be present at the fire, find a way out of the wilderness. The verse depicts a scene that would be familiar to people in nomadic lands. In early Arabia, for example, some people, wishing to help stray travelers to find their way through the desert, lit a fire at a place visible from a distance, and, at times, had food ready for the weary and hungry travelers.

"I have glimpsed a fire." The base form of the Arabic verb used in the text, *ānastu*, literally means "to sense *or* discern [the presence of something]." The implication is that Moses glimpsed a flash of fire that others, probably, did not see at that particular moment. Even Moses, it seems, saw the fire only for a moment or so. That would explain the use of the word "perhaps" in Moses' "perhaps, I will bring you a firebrand, or will find guidance at the fire."

Verses 11–16: Upon reaching the fire, Moses hears a loud voice addressing him. The speaker is God Himself, who instructs Moses to take off his shoes because he is treading the holy ground of the Ṭuwā valley. The Ṭuwā valley became holy on account of its association with God, and Moses is required to show respect for the place by taking off his shoes as he walks in it. Incidentally, Muslims are required to show the same respect on entering a mosque.

God informs Moses that He has "elected" him (verse 13)—that is, chosen him to be a prophet—and that he should pay close attention to what God is about to reveal to him. The Divine monologue continues in the next three verses, 14–16, in which Moses is enjoined, first, to serve God alone; second, to establish the formal prayer in order to remember God always; and, third, to ensure that those who do not believe in the Last Hour—whose occurrence is certain but whose timing is known only to God—do not succeed in keeping him from establishing the prayer. In verse 16—"So, let not those who do not believe in it and follow their caprice keep you from it"—the first "it" stands for the "Last Hour," the second, for "prayer." The verse implies that disbelief in the afterlife or pursuit of wayward desires is likely to lead to dereliction of the obligation to establish the prayer. "Lest you perish" reinforces the idea that disregard of the injunction just given will lead a person irretrievably away from the right path.

This part of the passage underscores the importance of the prayer: the first commandment received by every prophet after the commandment to serve God alone was that of establishing the prayer.

The words "so that every being is recompensed for the effort it puts forth" (verse 15) state the rationale of the afterlife: in the present life, one cannot receive complete recompense for one's actions; as such, an afterlife is needed in which such recompense could be made.

Verses 17–18: These verses introduce a lighter moment in the encounter between God and Moses. They make a serious point, however. Until now, only God has spoken: God's commanding voice has not allowed Moses to speak. With these verses begins a dialogue between God and Moses. God asks Moses affectionately what he is holding in his hand (literally, "right hand," but the Arabic word *yamīn* often has the simple generic meaning of "hand"). By asking the question, God does not mean to elicit information from Moses, but only to have Moses confirm that he is, indeed, holding a staff in his hand, a staff that will, to Moses' astonishment, soon turn into a serpent. Moses, both surprised and delighted at the honor of being God's dialogue partner, is not content to provide a brief, to-the-point answer but dwells at some length on the subject of his beloved staff; an all-purpose "and I have other uses for it, too" betrays Moses' barely concealed wish to continue the dialogue if God were to exhibit any interest in doing so. An amusing situation is created by Moses' failure to appreciate a discrepancy between the profoundly significant nature of the question asked by God and the rather literal interpretation placed on it by Moses. The significance of the question, of course, is that God is about to demonstrate to Moses that his ordinary staff will serve as a miracle-performing instrument, one that will aid him in performing his role as a prophet. In his response, Moses comes across as a simple shepherd who has no inkling that he is about to be made a prophet.

Verses 19–23: Moses is given two miracles by God. First, he is asked to put down his staff on the ground, and, when he does so, the staff becomes a serpent. Moses is terrified, as verse 21 suggests (and Q 27:10 and 28:31 confirm). God tells Moses to seize the serpent without being afraid, for it will become a staff again as soon as Moses takes hold of it. The second miracle is that Moses' hand, when drawn in by him toward his side, will become shiny bright, but not on account of any illness.

In "that We may show you of Our great signs" (verse 23), the preposition "of" suggests that the demonstration seen by Moses is only a preview, and that the staff and the shiny white hand will generate other great miracles as well.

Verse 24: Moses is instructed to "Go to Pharaoh," for "he has rebelled." No details of Pharaoh's rebellion against God are provided, but, according to other Qur'ānic verses (for example, Q 2:49; 28:38; 43:54), Pharaoh's rebellion consisted of his claim to deity, his tyrannical rule over his subjects, and his oppression of the Israelites. Since Moses, who has grown up in Pharaoh's household, is well aware of Pharaoh's rebellion, the brief reference made in the verse to Pharaoh's conduct suffices.

Verses 25–35: Acutely conscious of the difficult nature of his assignment, Moses makes a fourfold prayer to God:

First, he prays for internal resolve; the request to God to "open up my breast" (verse 25) means: Give me singleness of purpose and remove any hesitation on my part about my ability or willingness to take on this exceedingly difficult task.

Second, he prays that external circumstances be made favorable for him (verse 26): "and make my task easy for me."

Third, he prays for the gift of eloquence. In the context of an age in which the power of oratory was crucial to the success of a mission like Moses', the prayer "untie the knot in my tongue, that they may understand me" (verses 27–28) means: Give me an eloquent tongue so that I can make my message clear to my audience beyond the shadow of a doubt. The words "untie the knot in my tongue" do not necessarily mean that Moses had a speech impediment.

Fourth, he prays for a lieutenant—he proposes the name of his brother, Aaron—who could help him in discharging the duties associated with prophecy so that he and his lieutenant may glorify God and remember Him (verses 29–34)—that is, may carry out the assigned mission. "And make him a partner in my task" is a prayer that God may make Aaron, too, a prophet so that Aaron may share prophetic responsibilities with Moses.

Moses caps off his prayer by referring to God's blessings upon him and his brother in the past—"You have been watching over us" (verse 35). The reference is, in fact, an appeal to God for help, the verse meaning: You have watched over us in the past, and we request you to watch over us in the future as well.

Verse 36: As soon as Moses finishes his prayer, God tells him that his prayer is granted. The swiftness with which Moses' prayer is granted suggests that Moses will succeed in his mission.

III. Issues

1. Prophecy as a Gift. That Moses becomes frightened on seeing the staff turn into a serpent has, from a theological standpoint, twofold significance. First, it underscores Moses' humanity: fear is a natural human feeling, and, like all other human beings, Moses was subject to it. From this, the Qur'ān draws the further conclusion that a prophet—Moses, Jesus, Muḥammad, or any other prophet—even though he receives revelation from God and is close to God—remains a human being, does not come to partake of divinity, and must not be raised to the status of deity. Second, Moses' fright also constitutes a certain proof of the authenticity of his prophecy. Prophecy is a gift, not an acquisition: it is something that God may decide to bestow on one and is not something that one can acquire through effort and planning. Moses had not, in the least, expected or hoped to be vested with prophecy. Had he entertained a desire to become a prophet, he would have regarded the staff turning into a serpent as a materialization of his wish or ambition and would have been thrilled instead of being fear-stricken.

2. Prophet and Politician. Moses' prayer for an associate in carrying out his prophetic mission (verses 29–32) points up, within the context of the Qur'ān, a major difference between a divinely-appointed prophet and a worldly politician. The latter, offered a leadership position, would hardly want to share the laurels with anyone else. The former, on the other hand, would be overwhelmed by the sense of duty when charged with the mission of inviting people to submit to God. A politician—the Qur'ān presents Pharaoh as one—would like to set himself up as an all-powerful ruler and, if the opportunity presents itself, would not hesitate to claim to be a real or virtual deity. A prophet, on the other hand, would always take pains to emphasize his humanity and direct his followers to give homage not to his own person but to God, who alone, in the prophet's eyes, deserves to have the allegiance of all humankind.

IV. Literary Notes

1. The use of the word "guidance" (Arabic: *hudā*) in verse 10 has ironic significance. Moses, lost in the wilderness, uses the word in the simple sense of "guidance through the wilderness." What he gets is much more than that—guidance in the form of prophecy.

2. On being appointed a prophet, Moses wishes to have someone who would assist him in carrying out his prophetic assignment. He has his brother, Aaron, in mind, but the language he uses in his prayer for an aid (in verses 29–30) suggests that he is hesitant to mention him, as if he were afraid of being accused of promoting a member of his own family, so he puts off mentioning his name until the very end. As a

result, Moses' prayer for an aid comes to have the quality of a statement whose full meaning unfolds only gradually. Moses begins by making a request for an aid in the most general terms ("And appoint, for me, an aid"). Next, he requests that the aid be a member of his family ("from among my family"). Moving further, he identifies the aid by name ("Aaron"). Finally, he specifies that, by "Aaron," he means his brother and not a namesake in the family. Reading the two verses haltingly, pausing for a moment at each of the points marked by dashes in the following will give some idea of Moses' hesitation in making the request for an aid: "And appoint, for me, an aid—from among my family—Aaron—my brother."

V. A Comparison with the Bible

In the Qur'ān, the story of Moses is told in greater detail than that of any other prophet. The Biblical canvas is, of course, even larger. Limiting ourselves to the Qur'ānic passage under study, we will make a few remarks comparing the Biblical and Qur'ānic accounts. The Bible and the Qur'ān agree on some counts but differ on others.

In the Biblical story as in the Qur'ānic, Moses sees a fire. But, in the Qur'ān, Moses sees—or rather, glimpses—a fire as he is traveling with his family through the wilderness on a cold evening and is unsure of the direction in which he is moving, whereas, in the Bible, Moses, leading his father-in-law's flock "beyond the wilderness," comes to "Horeb, the mountain of God," where "the angel of the Lord appeared to him in a flame of fire out of a bush; he looked, and the bush was blazing, yet it was not consumed" (Exodus 3:1–2). In the Bible, too, Moses is asked—this time, he is being addressed by God rather than by the angel of the Lord—to take off his shoes: "Remove the sandals from your feet, for the place on which your are standing is holy ground" (Exodus 3:5). In the Qur'ān, God says, first, "I am your Lord," and, then, "I, indeed, am God. There is no deity but I." The Biblical statement is essentially similar: "I am the God of your father, the God of Abraham, the God of Isaac, and the God of Jacob" (Exodus 3:6). The Biblical account does not, however, mention the commandment about establishing the prayer and does not introduce the subject of the Last Hour.

In the Bible, as in the Qur'ān, God asks Moses what he is holding in his hand, and Moses replies, "A staff" (Exodus 4:1–2), although, in the Qur'ān, Moses offers some detail of the uses of the staff (Q 20:18). But the Biblical context of the exchange between God and Moses is different from the Qur'ānic. In the Qur'ān, the exchange occurs soon after Moses has been instructed to establish the prayer and is told about the certainty of the coming of the Last Hour. In the Bible, on the other hand, it occurs after Moses, having been asked to convey to Pharaoh God's command to let the Israelites depart from Egypt, expresses his doubt that Pharaoh will listen to him (Exodus 4:1–2) and is given the miracle in order to reassure him. Thus, whereas, in the Qur'ān, Moses is serenely unaware of the significance of God's question, the Biblical account strongly suggests, first, that the miracle of the staff has a bearing on Pharaoh's expected denial of Moses, and, second, that Moses himself is aware of the meaning of the miracle he is about to receive. In other words, the Qur'ānic account gives rise to an amusing moment because of a gap between the objective situation and Moses' perception of it, whereas the Biblical account is marked by a high degree of seriousness. The actual Biblical account of the staff turning into a snake is, however, quite similar to the Qur'ānic account:

> [3]And he [the Lord] said, "Throw it on the ground." So he [Moses] threw the staff on the ground, and it became a snake; and Moses drew back from it. [4]Then the Lord said to Moses, "Reach out your hand, and seize it by the tail"—so he reached out his hand and grasped it, and it became a staff in his hand—[5]so that they may believe that the Lord, the God of their ancestors, the God of Abraham, the God of Isaac, and the God of Jacob, has appeared to you. (Exodus 4:3–5)

In verse 22 of the Qur'ānic passage, God tells Moses to draw his hand in to his side, telling him that, when he brings it forth, "it will come out white, without any illness." In the Bible, God twice asks Moses to "put your hand inside your cloak"; the first time Moses takes it out, "his hand was leprous, as white as snow," but it is healed the second time he takes it out (Exodus 4:6–7). The Qur'ānic phrase "without any illness" seems to be an explicit reference to and a conscious departure from the Biblical "his hand was leprous, as white as snow."

Aaron's role in the Qur'ān is different from his role in the Bible. In the Qur'ān, as in the Bible (Exodus 4:10–16), Aaron serves as Moses' spokesman. In the Qur'ān, but not in the Bible, Aaron is a coprophet of Moses.

But, perhaps, the most fundamental difference between the Biblical and Qur'ānic accounts is that the former assumes a nationalistic context, whereas the latter assumes a more general context of struggle between right and wrong or between truth and falsehood. In the Bible, God intends to put an end to Israel's suffering under Pharaoh by sending Moses to Pharaoh with the command to let the Israelites depart from Egypt:

> [7]Then the Lord said, "I have observed the misery of my people who are in Egypt; I have heard their cry on account of their taskmasters. Indeed, I know their suffering, [8]and I have come to deliver them from the Egyptians. . . . So come, I will send you to Pharaoh to bring my people, the Israelites, out of Egypt. (Exodus 3:7–10)

The Qur'ānic passage under discussion does not mention Moses' demand that Pharaoh allow the Israelites to depart from Egypt. Elsewhere, the Qur'ān does speak of that demand (for example, 7:105; 20:47; and 26:17). But, in the Qur'ān, the demand represents a secondary mission or, rather, a fallback position of Moses, and the making of that demand by Moses is contingent on the outcome of his effort to fulfill his primary mission—namely, that of persuading Pharaoh and his chiefs to submit to God and accept Him as Lord (for example, 79:17–19). In other words, had Moses succeeded in converting Pharaoh and the notables of Egyptian society to the right belief, there would have been no need for Moses to demand that Pharaoh allow the Israelites to leave Egypt.

27 War in Self-Defense

22 Pilgrimage 38–41

[38]God will, indeed, defend those who believe; indeed, God does not love any inveterate betrayer of trusts, confirmed ingrate. [39]Permission is given to those against whom war is being waged, for they have been wronged; and God is fully capable of coming to their aid—[40]those who have been expelled from their homes without any justification, except that they say, "Our Lord is God!" And were it not for God's repulsing of some people by means of others, monasteries, churches, synagogues, and mosques, in which God's name is remembered a great deal, would have been demolished. And God will most definitely help those who help Him—indeed, God is Powerful, Mighty!—[41]those who, if We give them a position of power in the land, will establish the prayer and give *zakāh*, and enjoin good and forbid evil. And with God rests the final outcome of matters.

Sūrah 22 is Makkan.

I. Introduction

Sūrah 22, from which this passage is taken, is generally considered Madīnan, but it is unmistakably Makkan—if Late Makkan (see General Introduction, III.3). The four verses that make up this particular passage, though, are Madīnan since the permission given in them to fight in self-defense could not have been given in Makkan circumstances. The inclusion of a Madīnan passage in an otherwise Makkan sūrah does not, however, make the whole sūrah Madīnan; it only signifies that the principle underlying the inclusion of verses in a sūrah was thematic relevance, and that thematic identity or similarity could cause some Makkan sūrahs to be, if relevant, included in a Madīnan sūrah and vice versa. The passage immediately preceding this one in the sūrah consists of verses 25–37, and its very first verse refers to the efforts of the Quraysh, the rulers of Makkah, to keep the Muslims, who were still in Makkah, from performing the pilgrimage rites at the Kaʿbah; the rest of that passage talks about Abraham, the builder of the Kaʿbah, and the rituals associated with the pilgrimage. After their emigration to Madīnah, the Muslims wished to affirm and establish a close link with the Kaʿbah. The Quraysh, on the other hand, were determined to use any means to prevent that from happening. Since Arab consensus prohibited fighting during the pilgrimage or in the vicinity of the Kaʿbah, the Muslims wondered how they might respond to an aggressive action by the Quraysh to stop Muslims from performing the pilgrimage. This question, which the Muslims mulled over after their arrival in Madīnah, is addressed in the passage under discussion. As can be seen, the subject matter of this—Madīnan—passage dovetails with that of the preceding—Makkan—passage, and that explains why these Madīnan verses were placed in sūrah 22 alongside thematically congruent Makkan verses.

II. Commentary

Verse 38: Before the Muslims are actually permitted—in the next verse—to fight in self-defense, this verse promises them victory. "God will, indeed, defend those who believe"—that is, God has a stake in the fight between the believers and the disbelievers and will ensure victory to those who truly believe in Him. The implication is that the Quraysh, the opponents of the Muslims, are not true believers. This verse calls the Quraysh breakers of trusts and ungrateful people, for they owed their prestige, affluence, and power in Arabia to their custodianship of the Kaʿbah, which was built and dedicated to monotheistic worship by Abraham but which had been turned into a den of polytheism by the Quraysh. The Quraysh's verbal acknowledgment of Abraham as their great ancestor but their practical violation of everything that Abraham held sacred is termed in the verse a betrayal of a trust and ingratitude on their part.

Verse 39: This verse permits Muslims to take up arms against aggression. Two reasons are given to justify this permission: (1) The Muslims are the object of aggression—the mere fact of aggression against them justifying armed counteraction by them. (2) The Muslims have been wronged, that is, they have been expelled from their homes in Makkah (see verse 40, below).

The fact that the permission to fight back was given only in Madīnah, where the Muslims had organized themselves into a body politic, and not in Makkah, where no organized Muslim state existed, implies that only a properly constituted state can call for armed action against aggression.

"And God is fully capable of coming to their aid" is both a promise and a threat. It is a promise to the believers: God will aid them; and it is a threat to their opponents: God will defeat them.

Verse 40: The wrong committed against the Muslims (verse 38) is now explained: The Muslims were, without any justification, forced to leave their homes in Makkah by the Quraysh, to whom the Muslims' declaration—"Our Lord is God!"—was a great offense.

On the face of it, the declaration of "Our Lord is God!" sounds innocent enough, and one wonders why the Quraysh should have found it so offensive. In the context of the struggle between the Quraysh and the Muslims, however, it represented the main point at issue between the two parties. Both parties understood very well the fateful implications of that declaration. Above all, the declaration posed a challenge to the religious, political, and economic establishment that the Quraysh presided over, and the Quraysh could not afford to ignore the challenge.

The stated purpose of God's repulsion of one nation by means of another—namely, protection of the places of worship of Christians (churches and monasteries), Jews (synagogues), and Muslims (mosques)—signifies that, had God not sanctioned the taking up of arms against oppression, the aggressors would have torn down the places of worship of various religions—places where God is worshipped and remembered a great deal. In other words, piety and fighting are not mutually exclusive: taking up arms for a noble cause does not contravene piety.

The verse's reference not only to mosques, but also to synagogues, churches, and monasteries as places "in which God's name is remembered a great deal" indicates a recognition, on the Qur'ān's part, of the special status of the Jewish and Christian places of worship. This recognition is in keeping with the fact that Islam accords Jews and Christians the special status of the "People of the Book."

The statement "And God will most definitely help those who help Him" reinforces the promise of victory made earlier in the passage (verse 38). It also implies that, to serve in the way of God—for example, by protecting sanctuaries where God is worshipped and remembered—is actually to help God, and that those who help God can rest assured that He will help them in return.

Verse 41: The words "if We give them a position of power" are a foretelling or a promise: the people in question—the Muslims in this particular case—are going to be put in a position of power by God. That these people "will establish the prayer and give *zakāh*, and enjoin good and forbid evil" is not only a statement of what they will do on coming to power, but also an admonition to them to remember the real purpose of possessing power—namely, establishment of a society whose hallmark is piety, reflected, on the one hand, in submission to God (prayer) and, on the other hand, in a socioeconomic system based on the principle of ensuring the well-being of the poor and the disadvantaged (*zakāh*). Such a society will "enjoin good and forbid evil" in the sense that it will promote all forms of good at all levels and will endeavor to root out evil, endeavoring to bring an ethical society into existence.

"And with God rests the final outcome of matters"—that is, how things eventually turn out in this world and the next will be determined by certain laws bearing on the relationship between human actions and their consequences, laws that have been laid down by God. The proper course of action for human beings, therefore, is to submit to God, carry out His commandments, and ask Him for help and success.

III. Religion and War

Verse 40 provides a moral sanction for fighting and war. Fighting and war may, at times, become necessary to guarantee the security of places of worship—in more general terms, to guarantee the practice of religion in a state of peace and freedom. Since the verse speaks of non-Islamic as well as of Islamic places of worship, it would seem to follow that an Islamic state is obligated to prevent—and, if necessary, to use force to prevent—any damage to, among other things, all places of worship, whether Muslim or non-Muslim, under its jurisdiction.

The verse's reference to Jewish and Christian places of worship suggests that the permission to fight with a view to protecting places of worship is not being given for the first time; that such permission must have been given to earlier religious communities as well since protection of houses of worship has always been important, in Islam and before Islam; and that the Qur'ānic permission to fight to protect such sanctuaries is, therefore, only the latest instantiation of a universally and permanently valid rule.

IV. Literary Notes

1. Verse 38 contains one instance of prolepsis, or foretelling, and one of litotes, or understatement. The promise of victory, given before any fighting has taken place, is proleptic. The words "God does not love" in the statement "God does not love any inveterate betrayer of trusts, confirmed ingrate" are an understatement, for they mean that God hates such people and will deal sternly with them.

2. The two clauses that make up verse 38 each have an omission suggested by the other sentence. The meaning in full may be stated as follows (the italicized portions represent the omissions):

> *God loves those who believe, for they fulfill trusts and show gratitude.*
> *Therefore,* God will, indeed, defend those who believe.
> Indeed, God does not love any inveterate betrayer of trusts, confirmed ingrate, *for such people do not believe.*
> *Therefore, God will withdraw His support from such people.*

Once noted, the omissions add a certain nuance to the statements made in the verse: It is not enough to claim that one believes; one must give proof of the genuineness of one's belief by fulfilling trusts and showing gratitude. It is only such believers whom God will aid. Conversely, one who betrays trusts and shows ingratitude cannot be a true believer. God does not like such people and will not come to their aid.

3. In permitting war for self-defense, verse 39 uses the passive voice—"Permission is given." Furthermore, we are not told, in this verse or in the rest of the passage, who gave the permission or what is being permitted. Keeping in mind the context of the passage—namely, that fighting during the pilgrimage or near the Kaʿbah was considered condemnable by all Arabs (see section I, above)—will help us to see the significance both of the use of the passive voice and of the aforementioned lack of specification about who is permitting what. One can gather from the context that the permission being given is that of fighting—of fighting back, to be precise—but the Qur'ān, it seems, is reluctant to use explicitly the word "fighting," the omission of the word indicating a certain hesitation to get involved, even at a verbal level, with the idea of fighting. Likewise, it is not difficult to infer that God is giving the permission to fight, but, again, the verse's omission to refer explicitly to God as the one giving the permission is a subtle way of saying that God does not wish to be associated with the granting of the permission. The use of the passive voice in the verse heightens yet further the mood of reluctance in giving the permission to fight. The net effect of the construction "Permission is given" (the Arabic, incidentally, employs a single word, a verb, *udhina*) and of the absence of specification about the giver of the permission and the content of the permission is to suggest that war has been imposed on Muslims, who are now left with no choice but to fight back.

4. In verse 40, the words "Powerful" and "Mighty" appear to be synonyms, but they are not: The Arabic word for "Powerful," *qawī*, denotes the *presence* of power, whereas the Arabic word for "Mighty," *ʿazīz*, denotes the *absence* of weakness. The two words, thus, complement each other in thought.

5. The sequence in which the places of worship are mentioned in verse 40—monasteries, churches, synagogues, and mosques—may be significant. The first two are Christian places of worship, the third, Jewish, and the fourth, Muslim. A strictly historical sequence would have been as follows: synagogues, churches, monasteries, and mosques. In this sequence, however, monasteries would have been, so to speak, the odd institution out since the ordinary or regular places of worship in the three religions are synagogues, churches, and mosques. The Qur'ān here seems to be interested in grouping synagogues, churches, and mosques together in view of their equal status as places of worship and, consequently, in keeping any other institution—monasteries, in the present case—from breaking the integrity of that group. But the Qur'ān seems to be equally interested in maintaining the integrity of each religion's places of worship and, therefore, in listing each religion's places of worship as a solid bloc, which means that monasteries are to be paired off with churches. Since Islam is, chronologically, the last of the three religions in question, mosques are appropriately mentioned last. As such, the only possible sequence of the four places of worship is the one found in the verse, with monasteries leading off the series.

28 God Is the Light of the Heavens and the Earth

24 Light 35

God is the light of the heavens and the earth! His light, in terms of a parable, is like a niche in which there is a lamp; the lamp is in a glass; the glass is, as it were, a brilliant star; it is kindled from a blessed olive tree that is neither of the eastern nor of the western side—its oil would all but light up, even if no fire touched it. Light upon light! God guides to His light whomever He wishes. And God cites parables for people. And God has knowledge of all things.

Sūrah 24 is Madīnan.

I. Introduction

This is the celebrated Light Verse of the Qur'ān. It relates a parable. The basic meaning of the parable is that God, being the light of the heavens and the earth, is the source of all knowledge and goodness: those who believe in Him and follow His commandments walk in the full light of Divine guidance and will reach their destination—that is, will attain success in this world and salvation in the next. By implication, those who disbelieve in Him and reject His guidance are hopelessly surrounded by darkness and will fail to attain success and salvation. This implication is brought out explicitly only a few verses later in the sūrah, in verses 39–40, in which the disbelievers' deeds are compared to a "mirage" (verse 39) and to "deep darkness" (verse 40), indicating that the larger passage, starting with verse 35 and ending with verse 40, is meant to contrast the situations and destinies of the believers and the disbelievers.

II. Commentary

After making what may be called a thesis statement—"God is the light of the heavens and the earth"—the verse cites a parable about the Divine light. It compares the Divine light to a lamp that sits in a niche. The niche, being a recess at a certain height in the wall, diffuses the light of the lamp widely. The lamp is enclosed in a glass case, which, besides helping to spread the light, makes the light steady, focused, and bright. The glass, moreover, looks like a brilliant star, which means that it allows the light to shine through bright and clear. The oil of the lamp comes from a "blessed"—that is, fruitful—tree that is "neither of the eastern nor of the western side," and the oil would catch fire, it seems, even if no fire were to touch it. To the Arabs, the best trees in a garden were those that stood in the middle of a garden and, unlike the trees on the periphery—on the eastern or western sides, for example—got neither too much nor too little sunshine and were protected against floods, thus getting just the right amounts of sun and rain. Such trees were prized for the high quality of their yield. Coming as it does from a similarly situated tree, the oil of the lamp in question will, it appears, start burning even if it makes no contact with fire. The cumulative effect of all these elements of the parable is to enhance, to an exceedingly high degree, the light given off by the lamp. The verse itself sums up the scenario best: "Light upon light!"

This parable, as the last part of the verse indicates, is about guidance: "God guides to His light whomever He wishes." The verse opens with the statement "God is the light of the heavens and the earth" and closes with the statement, "God has knowledge of all things." The key word "light" in the first statement and the key word "knowledge" in the second, seen in relation to each other, yield the essential meaning of the parable: God is the source of all knowledge, and it is knowledge drawn from this fount that lights up the heavens and the earth, dispelling the darkness of ignorance and doubt. Conversely, without God, the world does not make sense and remains a dark enigma.

The statement, made toward the end of the verse, that "God guides to His light whomever He wishes" does not mean that God arbitrarily chooses people to whom He will grant His light, but only that God's will is not subject to any outside constraints, though He may, of His free will, impose certain constraints on Himself. In Qur'ānic theology, the Divine attributes do not exist in isolation from one another but are integrally related to one another. Accordingly, God's will bears a close relationship to God's knowledge. In fact, the concluding part of this verse—"And God has knowledge of all things"—clearly signifies that God's will is informed by His knowledge, and also that God, since He has complete knowledge of the earthly careers of all human beings, will, on Judgment Day, give all human beings their deserved recompense.

In interpreting a parable, it is not necessary to establish a one-to-one correspondence between the elements that are compared with each other; the crucial thing is the total effect created by the elements of the parable taken together. Thus, in the parable, it is possible, and certainly tempting, to interpret the niche as representing a certain object or idea, the lamp as representing another object or idea, and so on, but the main point of the parable—underscored cumulatively by all the elements of the parable—is that God is the true source of enlightenment about existence and about such major issues and questions of life as the origin and destiny of the human race, right and wrong conduct, and freedom and determinism. God is the master reference point that human beings must use in their attempt to understand themselves, the society of which they are members, the nature that surrounds them, and the universe they exist in.

III. Literary Notes

This verse, in which a series of phrases—starting with "God is the light of the heavens and the earth!" and ending with "Light upon light!"—is arranged in ascending order of force, is a good example of the figure of speech called climax. After a crescendo is reached, there begins, with "God guides to His light whomever He wishes," what may be called a dénouement, releasing the tension generated by the earlier accumulation of detail. By the time it ends, the verse regains the calm tone that marks its beginning. The verse may be called a vignette in that it presents a fairly complete description of a scene.

29 Qualities of the Servants of God

25 Criterion 63–76

63 And the servants of the Compassionate One are those who walk on the
ground modestly, and, when thoughtless people try to engage them in discussion,
they say, "Peace!"
64 And those who spend the night before their Lord in prostration and standing.
65 And those who say, "Our Lord, avert from us the punishment of hell."
Indeed, its punishment is a permanent liability. 66 What a bad dwelling and a bad
lodging it is, indeed!
67 And those who, when they spend, are neither extravagant nor stingy, but stay
in the middle.
68 And those who do not call upon another deity along with God, and do not
kill a being that God has declared inviolate—except with just cause—and do not
engage in illicit sex. And he who does that will face the consequences of sin; 69 the
punishment will be multiplied for him on the Day of Resurrection, and he will
remain in it forever, humiliated. 70 But those who repent, believe, and perform good
deeds, they are the ones whose bad deeds God will convert into good deeds; and
God is Very Forgiving, Very Merciful. 71 And he who repents and does good deeds
will be making his return to God.
72 And those who do not witness falsity, and, when they pass by frivolity, pass
with dignity.
73 And those who, when they are reminded by means of the verses of their
Lord, do not drop down upon them deaf and blind.
74 And those who say, "Our Lord, give us, in our spouses and children, coolness
of eyes, and make us leaders of the pious."
75 These are the ones who will be recompensed with lofts on account of their
steadfastness, and they will be accosted in them with salutations and "Peace!"
76 They will remain in them forever. What fine dwellings and lodgings!

Sūrah 25 is Makkan.

I. Introduction

This passage, which occurs at the end of sūrah 25, describes the ideal character of the believers. While it can be read and understood as an independent piece, implicitly present in its background, for purposes of contrast, is the character of the rich and arrogant rulers of Makkah of Muḥammad's period—the Quraysh. Accordingly, the traits enumerated as meritorious in this passage are to be taken as wanting in the Quraysh. Verse 77, the last verse of sūrah 25, has not been included in this passage since it is a comment on the entire sūrah and, as such, can be said to be separate from this passage.

II. Commentary

Verse 63: The reference to God as "the Compassionate One" in this verse becomes significant when read in light of one of the verses preceding this passage—verse 60, in which the idolaters of Makkah disdainfully speak of "the Compassionate One" (one of God's names—*Raḥmān* in Arabic): "When it is said to them, 'Fall prostrate before the Compassionate One,' they say, 'And what is "the Compassionate One?" Shall we prostrate ourselves before what you command us to?'" Alluding to this background, verse 63 now says that, on the one hand, there are those who do not wish to hear the name "the Compassionate One" spoken, and, on the other hand, there are those who, as the true servants of the Compassionate One, have such and such fine qualities.

The servants of God "walk on the ground modestly"—that is, they walk in a gentle and dignified manner rather than arrogantly or bumptiously—their modest gait reflecting their inner humility. And when ignorant and rude people try to argue with them, the servants of God say goodbye and move away. The Arabic word here translated as "Peace!" is *salām*, which is used in the language both as a greeting one offers on meeting someone and, in some situations, as a polite farewell one bids to someone whom one wishes to avoid. It has the latter sense in the verse. The verse means, then, that the servants of God, when foolish people try to wrangle with them, wash their hands of them by politely saying goodbye to them. In brief, their humility is evidenced both by the way they carry themselves and by their reluctance to boost their ego by trying to defeat in argument a thoughtless and ill-bred adversary.

Verses 64–65: If verse 63 describes the public aspect of the conduct of God's servants during the day, then verse 64 talks about their conduct in the privacy of their homes at night: the servants of God spend their nights worshipping God in prostration and standing—that is, in prayer. The reference here is to the optional late-night prayer, the implication being that, if these people show such earnestness in performing optional prayers in the small hours, then it is easy to imagine the degree of earnestness with which they must perform the obligatory prayers and carry out the other duties imposed by the religion.

The constant supplication of these people is that God may save them from the punishment of hell (verse 65). In other words, far from being proud of the good deeds they may have done and being cocksure that those deeds will earn them a ticket to paradise, they are acutely conscious of their lapses and are afraid that they will be punished for them in the next life. The last part of verse 65, which says that the punishment of hell is a "permanent liability," is causally connected to the preceding part of the verse: If the servants of God stay up at night to offer prayers, then it is because they realize that the punishment of hell is something that will stick on to one and never leave one, and that only in this world—through good actions, prayer, and God's help—can one endeavor to avert that punishment.

Verse 66: This Divine comment confirms the view that the servants of God have of the punishment of hell and approves of their attempt to avert that punishment: hell, indeed, is a very bad place to end up in. The words "dwelling" (*mustaqarr*) and "lodging" (*muqām*), when used together, come to have different shades of meaning: a "dwelling" becomes a permanent abode, whereas a "lodging" becomes a temporary staying place. The verse means that hell is a place where one cannot live even for a short while, not to speak of taking up permanent residence in it.

Verse 67: The servants of God, when it is a matter of satisfying their legitimate needs, neither squander money nor keep their purses shut. Instead, they walk the path of moderation, recognizing fully that, besides meeting their own needs, they must share their wealth with the less fortunate members of society.

Verses 68–69: The people in question worship God alone; they do not kill—for they believe in the sanctity of human life; and they refrain from engaging in illicit sex (verse 68), that is, in any sexual activity outside marriage. The exception drawn to killing—"except with just cause"—does not mean that, if just cause exists, then they take the law into their own hands and avenge themselves. Since "just cause" (*ḥaqq*) is defined by the law, enforcement of the law becomes the responsibility of the relevant agencies or institutions of the state.

"And he who does that" (verse 68) means: he who commits any of the three forbidden acts—namely, worshipping anyone other than God, taking a human life, and engaging in illicit sex. Punishment for these acts will not only be multiplied—the Arabic word used in the original text can mean "doubled" or "more than doubled"—but will also be accompanied by humiliation (verse 69).

Verses 70–71: Only those people who resolve to change the course of their life by repenting of their sins, reposing belief, and performing good deeds will be spared the above-mentioned punishment. God, since He is forgiving, will forgive such people. Since He is also very merciful, God will show His mercy by converting those people's bad deeds into good ones.

"And he who repents and does good deeds will be making his return to God" (verse 71) means that, although the grave nature of the above-mentioned sins (verse 68) may make some of the guilty persons doubtful about the possibility of forgiveness for those sins, such people should remember that, in repenting of those sins, they are returning to a most forgiving God. A further connotation is that such a "return" to God—in the afterlife—will be an honorable return: one who makes such a return will be received, honored, and rewarded by God Himself, so one can imagine the kind of reception, the degree of honor, and the amount of reward one will get. Finally, the verse implies that a person who repents and performs good acts need have no fears or concerns about finding an environment that will facilitate his change of conduct: he should be comforted by the thought that, since he is returning to God, God will make it easy for him to find and adjust to a new, favorable environment.

Verse 72: That the servants of God "do not witness falsity" means that they do not like to be present at any place where a falsehood is being spoken or a wrong act is being committed. And if they must pass by something that constitutes a frivolity, they do not stop and become part of it, but rather, pass on without compromising their dignity. The Arabic word here translated as "frivolity" is *laghw*, which literally means "nonsense." Otherwise a rather innocuous word, *laghw*, in this context, comes to have a meaning of certain gravity—it means "sinful act" (see III.4, below).

The Arabic verbal phrase here understood as meaning "to witness falsity" primarily means "to be present at a place where a sinful act is being committed." The phrase, however, can also be interpreted to mean "to bear false witness." The translation given in the passage under discussion attempts to combine the two meanings.

Verse 73: God's servants, if they happen to make a mistake and are made conscious of it by means of Qur'ānic verses, are quick to accept their mistake and show regret. They are not like those who would become defensive and start attacking or scoffing at the Qur'ānic verses, as if, being deaf or blind, they could not hear or see the truth. The real stress in the verse falls on the implied opposite of the behavior here depicted, the verse saying: When they are reminded by means of Qur'ānic verses, the servants of God, far from dropping down on them like deaf and blind people, eagerly listen to those verses, for they can clearly see and recognize the truths contained in them.

Verse 74: The servants of God are concerned not only about their own welfare and salvation, but also about the welfare and salvation of the other members of their families, and so they pray that God may keep the latter on the right path and make their conduct pleasing. The Arabic idiomatic expression here translated as "coolness of eyes" means "delight," "joy," or "happiness," for, in the hot environment of Arabia, cold was associated with comfort, and heat, with discomfort. But the use of the idiom, with its aforesaid meanings, in this verse also has a special historical significance. Muḥammad's prophecy caused a division in families, with some members in the families converting to Islam while others continuing to adhere to the idolatrous religion of their ancestors.

Since belief or disbelief in Muḥammad had important consequences—nothing short of one's salvation was at stake—those who had embraced Islam were deeply concerned about the fate of those members of their families who were still outside the fold of Islam. The prayer that God may give them, in their spouses and children, "coolness of eyes" reflects both the deep concern and the profound wish of the converts—namely, the concern that those members of their families who had not yet converted would meet a terrible fate, and the wish that such members of their families would, like them, see the light and join them in the new faith, thus completing the joy and happiness of those who had already adopted Islam.

The prayer "make us leaders of the pious" is made by the servants of God in their capacity as heads of their households and represents a wish to have a household whose members would cultivate piety. The prayer is not political in intent or character.

Verses 75–76: It is people possessing the traits listed in the foregoing verses who will be housed with honor in the afterlife—"lofts" signifies upper levels of paradise (verse 75). The phrase "on account of their steadfastness" (verse 75) is significant. It implies that the above-mentioned traits are a permanent part of the character of those people, who persevere in the path of righteousness regardless of any difficulties they may face in doing so. Such people will be accosted in their dwellings with salutations and with greetings of peace. Notably, the verse mentions the "steadfastness" of the people in question but does not state in what way they show their steadfastness. The omission, in fact, widens the scope of the steadfast action: the servants of God give proof of the constancy of their obedience to God by carrying out His commandments, by shunning vices, and by resolutely facing any hardships they may have to undergo in the course of serving God.

"What fine dwellings and lodgings!" (verse 76) is in contrast to verse 66, in which hell is described as "a bad dwelling and a bad lodging." It means: The lofts of paradise are fine places even as temporary lodgings; how much better they would be as permanent abodes!

III. Literary Notes

1. In the translation offered of this passage, the phrase "And the servants of the Compassionate One" in the opening verse is taken as the subject, with the rest of the verse taken as the predicate. In verses 64, 65, 67, 68, 72, 73, and 74, likewise, the phrase starting with "And those who" is, in each case, interpreted as a predicate of the aforementioned subject, the several predicates, all joined by conjunction, making up one long predicate. In other words, verses 63–74 are to be read as: "And the servants of the Compassionate One [*subject*] are those who . . . and those who . . . and those who . . . [*predicate*]." It is, however, also possible to take the entire set of the first twelve verses (63–74) as one long subject. In this case, each instance of "And those who" will serve as a relative clause qualifying "And the servants of the Compassionate

One," with the predicate now beginning with verse 75, "These are the ones who will be recompensed. . . ." On the latter interpretation of the structure of the passage, the incremental enlargement of the subject through verses 63–74 will, on account of the long delay in the supplying of the predicate, generate heightened suspense that will find a powerful release in verse 75.

2. The repetition of "And those who" at the beginning of a number of verses in the passage furnishes an example of anaphora.

3. The Arabic word *salām* ("Peace!") is used in the passage in two senses. In verse 63, it means "goodbye!"—meaning that the speaker is disinclined to talk and wishes to avoid the person being addressed with the word. In verse 75, it is used as an expression of welcome.

4. It was noted above that the Arabic word used for "frivolity" in verse 72 is *laghw*, which ordinarily means "nonsense" but has the meaning of "sinful act" in the verse. This is an example of how, in the Qur'ān, context imparts to a word a meaning quite different from its dictionary meaning. The use of *laghw* in the verse is reflective not so much of the objective meaning of the word as it is of the state of mind of the servants of God, who are being talked about. To these people, a sinful act is something they wish to avoid completely, for they view such an act as a senseless or pointless thing that does not concern them at all.

5. The passage makes a subtle contrast between the "high" and the "low." At the beginning, the servants of God are said to walk on the ground *modestly* or *humbly* (verse 63); at the end, their reward is said to be *lofts* in paradise (verse 75). In other words, their *self-abasement* in worldly life earns the servants of God the reward of *exaltation* in the afterlife.

30 Luqmān's Advice to His Son

31 Luqmān 12–19

[12]We gave Luqmān wisdom: "Be grateful to God!" And he who shows
gratitude does so to his own good. But he who disbelieves, God is Self-Sufficient,
Worthy of Thankful Praise.

[13]And when Luqmān said to his son—he was giving him advice—"My son, do
not set up copartners with God; indeed, the setting up of copartners is a very great
wrong."

[14]And We advised man concerning his parents—his mother carried him in her
womb, suffering one debility after another, his weaning taking two years: "Be
grateful to Me and to your parents; the return is to Me.

[15]"But if they should put pressure on you to set up, as My copartners, what you
have no knowledge of, do not listen to them. Keep company with them in a kindly
way in worldly life, though, and follow the path of those who turn to Me. Then you
will come back to Me, and I will apprise you of what you did.

[16]"O my son, if it be of the weight of a mustard seed—be it in a rock, in the
heavens, or in the earth—God will bring it forth; God is Subtle, Aware. [17]O my
son, establish the prayer, enjoin good and forbid evil, and be steadfast in the face of
what befalls you: this, indeed, is one of the acts of resolution. [18]And do not be wry-
faced with people, and do not walk on the ground with a swagger; God does not
like any vain, conceited person. [19]And be modest of gait, and keep your voice low;
indeed, the most disgusting voice is that of a donkey."

Sūrah 31 is Makkan.

I. Introduction

Luqmān was a wise patriarch of ancient Yemen, in southern Arabia. This passage cites the advice that Luqmān gave his son, presumably when, nearing death, Luqmān wished to transfer the mantle of leadership to him. The Qur'ān's purpose in quoting the advice is to show that the wise men of Arabia taught the same essential message that Muḥammad was teaching. In other words, human reason leads one to the same broad and general truths to which Divine revelation leads. (As some Muslim theologians have argued, possession of reason by human beings, quite apart from the availability of revelation to them, is grounds for at least basic human accountability in the hereafter.) There is also the implication that the Makkans, who, like other Arabs, held Luqmān in high esteem, ought to remember what Luqmān stood for and propagated. In the larger Qur'ānic perspective, then, Arabia's wisdom tradition, represented by Luqmān, complements Arabia's revelatory tradition, represented by Abraham at an earlier period and by Muḥammad at a later time. There is one other important point to consider.

After Muḥammad had preached in Makkah for several years, his message began to attract the attention of people who were relatively free from the pull of the ancestral tradition of idol worship. Among such people were youths who were being pressured by their parents and the elders of Makkah to remain faithful to their ancestral religion. Understandably, not a few young people in the city were torn between accepting the message of Islam and remaining loyal to the idolatrous ways of their parents. In this passage, the Qur'ān exhorts such youths to rise above clannish loyalties and embrace the message of Islam, assuring them that, in doing so, they will be continuing the noble tradition of Luqmānian wisdom. At the same time, the Qur'ānic passage can be seen as warning the parents and the Makkan elders against using tactics to stop these youths from converting to Islam. The passage expresses surprise that the leaders of Makkah should show such diligence in persecuting their youths to force them to remain idolaters, whereas Luqmān, a well-wisher of his son, gave his son advice of a very different kind.

II. Commentary

Verse 12: God is the speaker in this verse. The opening statement, "We gave Luqmān wisdom," is immediately followed by "Be grateful to God!" implying, first, that the gist or sum and substance of all wisdom consists in offering gratitude to God, and, second, that Luqmān, indeed, was possessed of that wisdom.

"And he who shows gratitude does so to his own good." That is, by being grateful, one does not do any favor to God but does something that will benefit one's own self, especially in the hereafter.

"But he who disbelieves, God is Self-Sufficient, Worthy of Thankful Praise." The point made by the preceding phrase is here repeated, but in a negative way: If one does not do God any favor by believing in God, one does not take anything from Him by refusing to believe in Him. God is not dependent upon anyone for anything. Being self-sufficient, He deserves gratitude and praise irrespective of whether anyone believes in Him or whether anyone offers praise and gratitude to Him.

A phrase like "We gave Luqmān wisdom" in the Qur'ān might mean that a person was appointed a prophet by God. It, thus, raises the possibility that Luqmān was a prophet. But Luqmān, probably, was not a prophet. Arabian tradition also regards him as a wise man rather than as a prophet. That the Qur'ān says that Luqmān received the gift of wisdom from God does suggest, however, that Luqmān's wisdom was of a superior quality, and that Luqmān, though not a prophet, spoke and acted within the larger prophetic tradition of Arabia.

Similarly, while the sentence "Be grateful to God!" is in the form of a commandment given by God to Luqmān, it is not necessary to assume that God actually spoke to Luqmān, instructing him to be grateful. It is more probable that, having been blessed with wisdom by God, Luqmān realized that gratitude to God is the beginning and end of wisdom. Since this insight was the fruit of the wisdom he had received from God, it is here presented as if it had been taught by God to Luqmān direct.

Verse 13: Having introduced Luqmān as a wise man, the Qur'ān now quotes the advice that he gave his son, obviously implying that the advice is wisdom-filled and has perennial relevance. The very first piece of advice is "do not set up copartners with God." There is a connection between the imperative to show gratitude to God and the imperative to shun idolatry: the proper way to show gratitude to God is by avoiding setting up copartners with God.

The parenthetical phrase, "he was giving him advice," suggests that Luqmān spoke to his son on a special occasion, most probably when he was on his deathbed and wished to appoint his son as his successor. The Arabic word used in the text to denote the giving of advice (*ya'iẓu*) suggests, on the one hand, the content of the advice—it was an admonition, a warning—and, on the other hand, the manner of giving the advice—Luqmān spoke in an affectionate manner. In other words, the most important counsel that caring and loving parents can give their children is that of declaring the oneness of God and shunning the setting up of copartners with Him. In view of the importance of the advice, one can assume that Luqmān must have given the same advice to his son on many previous occasions as well, and that, on his deathbed, he reemphasized it since it represents what the Qur'ān calls the essence of all wisdom.

Verses 14–15: In the Qur'ān, the theme of monotheism is often paired with that of filial obligation—for example, in 17:23 (see chapter 25, "Commandments," section II, verse 23).

According to verse 14, the period of suckling lasts for two years. On the basis of this statement, Islamic law regards two years as the upper limit of the period of suckling.

The concluding part of verse 14 mentions God and parents as the joint object of the same verb—"Be grateful to Me and to your parents"—elevating the status of parents. The admonition, "the return is to Me," coming as it does on the heels of the commandment to honor God and parents, implies that, upon their return to God on Judgment Day, people will be held accountable not only for their belief about God, but also about their conduct toward their parents.

Verse 14 enjoins showing gratitude to one's parents. Verse 15 adds the rider that one must not succumb to any pressure put on one by one's parents to set up copartners with God. The obligation to obey God takes precedence over the obligation to obey the parents. One must honor and serve one's nonbelieving parents and treat them with kindness, discharging one's responsibilities toward them in worldly matters, even praying that they may be guided to the right path, but in matters of belief and worship, one must follow in the footsteps of those who have made submission to God. Addressing parents as well as their offspring, the concluding part of verse 15 says that, on the Last Day, God will judge and evaluate the conduct of all people—including all parents and all descendants: "Then you will come back to Me, and I will apprise you of what you did."

The injunction that one must refuse obedience to one's parents if they ask one to set up copartners with God is derived from a rule succinctly stated in a *ḥadīth*: "No obedience is due to a created being in defiance of the Creator."

"What you have no knowledge of" means "that for which you are not presented with any proof," and hence "for which no proof exists."

Verse 16: After forbidding his son to set up copartners with God—and, thus, underscoring the importance of monotheism, the most fundamental of all truths (verse 13)—Luqmān now speaks of the hereafter, another fundamental truth: omniscient and omnipotent, God will bring forth every single act performed by every single human being—even if that action is of the weight of a mustard seed, which is hidden in a rock or anywhere else in the heavens and the earth—and will recompense that act. In the translation of the verse, the pronoun "it" in "if it be of the weight of a mustard seed" refers to an act, good or bad, performed by a human being.

"God is Subtle, Aware" refers to the comprehensive range of Divine knowledge: God perceives both what is obvious and what is not, both what can be perceived by the senses and what cannot be so perceived, both what has been and what will be.

Verse 17: Verse 12 spoke of gratitude as the essence of the wisdom given to Luqmān. Turning now to the ways in which gratitude ought to be expressed or manifested in the believer's life, this verse presents Luqmān as enjoining his son to establish the prayer and—what will befit his successor and the new ruler—to command good and forbid evil. Luqmān warns his son that the carrying out of these responsibilities will require patience and steadfastness in the face of hardship and criticism by others, but that resolute action will help him discharge the responsibilities properly.

Verses 18–19: These verses, which continue the theme of verse 17, present no special difficulty. The advice given in them holds good for all people, though it has especial relevance for those who enjoy a position of authority in society, for they are, by virtue of their position, more liable to behave in a conceited way. The aim of the verses is not to make people adopt a show of humility—such that people should, for example, feign to walk gently and speak in low tones—but to cultivate true inner piety, which should then be manifested in gentle speech and in a humble gait.

In verse 18, the Arabic phrase that has been translated as "And do not be wry-faced with people" draws the picture of a camel whose neck has become crooked on account of a certain illness. It is to this animal that the verse likens the haughty individual who is contemptuous of ordinary people.

III. Literary Notes

1. We noted above that the Qur'ān often discusses the theme of filial obligation together with that of monotheism. An interesting thing happens in this passage, though: the doctrine of monotheism is stated by Luqmān (verse 13), but the subject of filial obligation is addressed by God Himself (verses 14–15). This change of speakers from verse 13 to verses 14–15 tells us something about Luqmān. Since he is counseling his own son, Luqmān, out of modesty and humility, omits to instruct his son to honor his parents since Luqmān himself would be the claimant and recipient of such honor. The omission is supplied by God Himself, and this explains the change of speakers. The joining of the Divine voice to Luqmān's is meant to honor Luqmān. From verse 16 onward, Luqmān again becomes the speaker, with verses 14–15, thus, constituting a kind of parenthetic addition but being integral to the theme of the passage.

2. Notably, while the opening and concluding parts of verse 14 refer to both parents, the middle part of the verse refers only to the mother. The omission to mention the father implies that, while one must discharge one's duty to both parents, one's mother is especially deserving of one's affection and kindness since it is she who, among other things, undergoes the pain of pregnancy. Since the speaker in verse 14 is God, one's greater obligation to one's mother would seem to carry Divine sanction behind it.

3. The strategic placement of "he was giving him advice" in verse 13 is notable. The phrase, a circumstantial clause in Arabic, is interposed between "And when Luqmān said to his son" and "My son, do not set up copartners with God." By temporarily stopping the flow of the main sentence, the clause focuses attention on the following prohibition against idolatry.

4. The tone of a statement often suggests the presence of a nuanced meaning. Verse 16 is a case in point. As noted above, the pronoun "it" in the initial part of the verse may refer to a good or a bad action (see II, verse 16). The tone of the statement, however, suggests that the primary reference is to a bad action. As a rule, human beings try to hide their bad actions. Luqmān is warning his son, telling him that every action, especially every bad action—even if it were of the weight of a mustard seed and were hidden from the eyes of people—will be brought forth and recompensed by God. The last part of the verse—"God is Subtle, Aware"—reinforces the same point.

31 Behavior Unbecoming of a Believer

49 Apartments 11–13

[11]O you who believe, one group of men should not make fun of another group of men; it is possible that they are better than them. And neither should women, of women; it is possible that they are better than them.

And do not make yourselves the objects of sarcasm.

And do not give one another insulting nicknames. How bad is the very name of wickedness after belief! And those who do not repent, they are the wrongdoers.

[12]O you who believe, avoid making too many conjectures; some conjectures, indeed, are a sin.

And do not pry.

And you should not backbite one another. Would any of you like to eat the flesh of his—dead—brother? You would detest it! And fear God; God is Most Forgiving, Very Merciful.

[13]O people, We have created you from one male and one female, and have made you into races and tribes that you may get to know one another. Indeed, the noblest of you in the sight of God is the one most pious of you. God is All-Knowing, Aware.

Sūrah 49 is Madīnan.

I. Introduction

In the last few years of Muḥammad's prophethood, with Islam established as the dominant power of Arabia, quick and frequent conversions to Islam started to take place. Many new converts had had few opportunities to receive adequate training in Islam and, consequently, their social conduct as Muslims left much to be desired. Sūrah 49 draws attention to some of the problems that arose in this connection. In the verses immediately preceding this passage in the sūrah, Muslims are urged to effect a reconciliation between Muslim groups if these should happen to fight with one another. Those verses conclude with the reminder, "The believers are but brothers to one another" (verse 10). This statement becomes the basis of an appeal, on the one hand, to the Muslim community to make peace between warring Muslim parties (verse 10) and, on the other, to the believers to mend certain types of unseemly behavior (verses 11–13).

II. Commentary

Verse 11: As in other cases, the invocation "O you who believe" enjoins the believers, especially the new converts, to fulfill their obligations as members of the Muslim community and to abide by the commandments that are about to be set forth.

This verse prohibits Muslims, men and women both, from ridiculing one another. It is possible, it says, that those who are being ridiculed are morally superior to those who ridicule them. The verse is not to be taken as proscribing good-natured fun; it only seeks to prohibit derisive talk and disdainful, haughty behavior.

Since Muslims are brothers to one another, one who heaps sarcasm on one's brother heaps sarcasm on oneself—hence the statement, "And do not make yourselves the objects of sarcasm." In other words, in diminishing others, one diminishes oneself.

Like the Arabic word of which it is a translation, "sarcasm" may be verbal, gestural, or both, and the Qur'ānic prohibition applies to both types.

After prohibiting sarcasm, which is an implicit way of showing contempt for others, the verse prohibits using abusive names for others, which is an explicit way of showing contempt. Using sarcastic remarks or gestures may give rise to suspicion and animosity, while calling others by insulting nicknames will openly fan the flames of hatred. Both are unacceptable to the Qur'ān.

"How bad is the very name of wickedness after belief!" means that, after becoming a believer, one should not only shun wicked acts, but also drive the very thought of wickedness out of one's mind. One should detest "the very name"—that is, the very word or the very idea—of wickedness. Belief and wickedness are, thus, mutually exclusive. If, however, through human weakness, one commits an act that is contrary to the dictates of the religion, then one should make repentance. God will look kindly upon those who repent. It is only those who refuse to repent who will be called wrongdoers and meted out the punishment due to them.

Verse 12: It does not behoove the believers to prejudge other believers. As an operating assumption and in the absence of any evidence to the contrary, Muslims should think well of one another. Indulging in baseless speculation about other people's motives, attitudes, and actions frequently leads one to harbor ill will toward others, and, sometimes, to act toward them in an unreasonable, even hostile, way.

"And do not pry" means, in a general way: Do not be overly inquisitive. But the Arabic text often has connotations of mischief and malice, and, in the present context, therefore, it has a more specific meaning as well: Do not try to ferret out the weaknesses, faults, or vices of people with a view to embarrassing those people or putting them to shame.

In the next part of the verse, the backbiter is likened to one who eats the flesh of his own brother. The analogy has to be understood in the Arabian cultural and literary context. To the Arabs, a backbiter was like a predator. Spotting carrion, a predator comes up to it and, feeling secure against retaliation by the dead animal, starts nibbling at its flesh. That is exactly how the backbiter was pictured as doing: Since the object of his attack was not there to rebut him, the backbiter, with the psychology of a predator, thought of his victim as a dead animal whose flesh he could devour with shameless impunity. The idiomatic expression "to eat somebody's flesh," thus, came to mean in Arabic "to backbite somebody." (On the use of the word "brother" in the idiom, as used in verse 12, see section IV.2, below.)

The concluding part of the verse calls upon the believers to fear God and refrain from committing the acts proscribed in this verse and the preceding one. As at the end of verse 11, so at the end of verse 12, the believers are reminded that they must live up to the standard that is being set for them, and that, should they fall short of that standard in practice, they must turn in repentance to the Forgiving, Merciful God.

Verse 13: The vices that verses 11–12 asked the believers to shun originate in certain perceptions that people sometimes form of themselves and of others. Those perceptions are now addressed in this verse.

According to the Qur᾽ān, all human beings are descended from the same pair of ancestors (see chapter 14, "One God, One Humanity"). As such, all human beings are essentially equal and none has the right to assert superiority over any other. As for groupings like family and tribe, they are approved by God because they are practical, manageable social units that make it easy for people to establish their identities and deal with one another in harmonious ways: they are meant to create bonds and relationships, not hostile groups or antagonistic units—and certainly not to give the members of some families, tribes, or nations the right to claim racial or some other kind of superiority over other families, tribes, or nations. While the above-mentioned social units serve an important purpose, their importance is, essentially, functional; they must not be allowed to obscure the fact that, in the sight of God, the only criterion of nobility is piety rather than racial stock, economic affluence, or social status, and that, in the hereafter, only the criterion of piety will be used by God to judge human beings. And God, who knows the inmost secrets of the human heart, is fully aware of the quality of an individual's piety and will give due recompense to every individual.

III. Two Types of Vices

Verses 11–12 list six vices, which can be divided into two types: those committed in public and those committed in relative secrecy. Verse 11 lists the first type: derision, sarcastic behavior, and use of insulting nicknames; verse 12 lists the other type: speculating about other people's actions and motives, prying, and backbiting. By covering both types of vices, the Qur'ān is saying that both the public and the private life of a Muslim should be above reproach.

IV. Literary Notes

1. In verse 11, the prohibition against ridiculing others is laid down twice, once with reference to men and once with reference to women. The repetition indicates that members of both sexes are equally liable to fall prey to the bad habit and must, therefore, make an effort to avoid indulging in it. Also, from the relative brevity of the repeated prohibition ("And neither should women, of women"), it appears that, according to the Qur'ān, the vice of ridiculing one another is found mainly among men.

2. The Arabic idiom "to eat someone's flesh," meaning "to backbite someone," was discussed in reference to verse 12. While the idiom was familiar to the Arabs of Qur'ānic times, the Qur'ān gives it a typical Islamic slant by adding the word "brother" to it, implying that, while the act of eating somebody's flesh is bad enough, the act of eating the flesh of one's brother is heinous beyond measure—"You would detest it!" as verse 12 puts it. Since the word "brother" in the reworked idiom means "brother in faith," the idiom comes to have religious and ethical connotations. To eat the flesh of one's brother is, therefore, grossly to violate the bonds of brotherhood that hold a Muslim society together. Thus, the strategic use of a single word—"brother"—transforms an ordinary Arabic literary expression into a characteristically Islamic literary expression.

3. The invocation "O you who believe," first used in verse 11 of the passage and repeated in verse 12, changes to "O people" in verse 13. The reason is that, in verse 13, the statement following the invocation—namely, "We have created you from one male and one female"—is true of all members of the human race, the pronoun "you" in the statement referring to humankind in general rather than to Muslims specifically, as was the case in verses 11 and 12.

4. The appeal to faith as the basis of conduct serves to knit the passage together. As already noted (see section I, above), the verse immediately preceding this passage declares all Muslims to be brothers, and, from that declaration, the verses of this passage derive implications for Muslim social conduct.

32 Relations with Non-Muslims

60 Women Tested 8–9

[8]God does not forbid you to act charitably toward and deal justly by those who have not fought against you in the matter of religion and have not expelled you from your homes; indeed, God loves those who are just in their dealings. [9]He only forbids you to take as friends those who have fought against you in the matter of religion and have expelled you from your homes and have aided in your expulsion. And those who take them as friends, they are the wrongdoers.

Sūrah 60 is Madīnan.

I. Introduction

By emigrating from Makkah to Madīnah in 622, Muḥammad and his followers made a complete break with the city of Makkah and its idolatrous residents. But some of the emigrant Muslims still maintained secret contacts with the idolatrous members of their families in Makkah. The opening verse of sūrah 60 prohibits such Muslims against taking as friends those Makkans who had shown hostility toward Islam and Muslims. This passage now further clarifies the matter by saying that the ban against befriending the idolaters of Makkah applies only to those Makkans who took up arms against the Muslims and threw Muslims out of their homes when the latter were in Makkah, and that it does not apply to those Makkans who were not guilty of any such act.

II. Commentary

Verse 8: "God does not forbid you to act charitably toward and deal justly by . . . " means, in effect: God commands you to act charitably and deal justly by . . . . The particular phrasing used in the verse is meant to preempt the thought—not uncommon among the Arabs of pre-Islamic times—that a tribe, while at war with another tribe, did not have to discriminate between legitimate and non-legitimate targets in the enemy tribe. In prosecuting a war, a tribe felt unconstrained by any considerations of charity, virtually acting as if it had been "forbidden" to deal justly by the enemy. It is this mindset that is being criticized in this verse, which says that, in contradistinction to the above-stated Arabian tribal approach to warfare, God does not forbid the believers to act in a just and charitable manner toward the enemy. The principle of justice, the verse is saying, has to be upheld under all circumstances: Muslims may *not* inflict any harm on those who have inflicted no harm on them.

This verse has a historical context—it makes reference to the non-Muslims of Makkah. But the principle stated in the verse is not restricted, in its application, to the Arabian situation of Muḥammad's time, but has general validity, forming as it does a part of the Islamic doctrine of war and peace.

The two injunctions, "to act charitably toward [non-Muslims]" and "deal justly by [non-Muslims]," refer, respectively, to the ethical and to the legal aspects of the normative Muslim treatment of non-Muslims. The injunction about charitableness means that those non-Muslims who have caused no harm to Muslims must be treated by Muslims with kindness. The injunction about just treatment means, in a general way, that Muslims' dealings with non-Muslims must be based on the principle of justice. More specifically, it means that non-Muslims must be treated by Muslims in accordance with the law (the law making no distinction between a believer or a disbeliever) or in accordance with the terms of a pact if a pact governing the relationship between Muslims and non-Muslims exists.

Verse 9: "Those who have fought against you in the matter of religion" means: those who have fought against you because your religious belief happens to differ from theirs. Befriending those who have been hostile to Muslims means befriending such people with a view to making a personal gain at the expense of the larger interest of the Muslim community. To take such hostile people as friends is to commit a wrong, and, in the hereafter, God will take such wrongdoers to task.

33 The Hypocrites

63 Hypocrites 1–4

[1]When the hypocrites come to you, they say, "We bear witness that you, indeed, are the Messenger of God." And God knows that you, indeed, are His Messenger; and God bears witness that the hypocrites, indeed, are liars. [2]They have taken their oaths to serve as a shield, and so have kept off from the path of God. How bad, indeed, is what they have been doing! [3]This is because they believed and then disbelieved, so their hearts were sealed, so they lack understanding. [4]And when you look at them, you admire their bodies. And should they speak, you would listen to their speech. As if they were propped-up blocks of wood! Every shout, they think, is upon them! They are the enemy, so be on your guard against them. May God strike them! How they are straying off!

Sūrah 63 is Madīnan.

I. Introduction

In Madīnah, the Muslims had to contend with, besides other religious groups, a group of opponents whom the Qurʾān calls "hypocrites." These people had embraced Islam not out of conviction, but out of a desire to protect their political and economic interests, reference to which is made in two verses (7–8) immediately following this passage in the sūrah. Like the other opponents of Islam, the hypocrites fell into more than one category. Those discussed in this passage had, as the verses indicate, gone far afield in their hypocrisy.

II. Commentary

Verses 1–2: An expression like "We bear witness that . . ." signifies an oath. Since their actions belie their words, giving rise to questions about their intentions, and since they have a guilty conscience, which makes them doubt their own credibility, the hypocrites, on coming into Muḥammad's presence, seek to assure him of the genuineness of their faith by swearing oaths.

The hypocrites' statement—"We bear witness that you, indeed, are the Messenger of God"—is technically correct, but, since they do not mean it, they give themselves the lie and are, therefore, speaking a falsehood. "And God knows that you, indeed, are His Messenger" means that the hypocrites, who swear by God to convince Muḥammad that they believe in him as God's messenger, forget that they cannot deceive God, that God, who raised Muḥammad as a prophet, does know that he is a messenger of God. They do not need to establish the already well-established, objective truth of Muḥammad's prophethood; they need to realize, though, that, by taking a hypocritical stance on the matter, they are perjuring themselves. Their intention in professing Islam is to protect themselves and their interests against what they fear is the rising power of a religion for which they have no love lost but which they are unable to defeat or stem. Using their oaths as a defense against possible criticism of their duplicity, they have, after taking a few tentative and halfhearted steps toward Islam, stopped in their tracks. They think that they will succeed in pulling the wool over the Muslims' eyes, but, in fact, they are playing a dangerous double game and will, one day, face the consequences of their actions.

Verse 3: This verse explains why the hypocrites are acting the way they are: They disbelieved after reposing belief, thus making light of the guidance God had given them. Since they chose to reject the guidance that had come to them from God, they no longer deserved to receive Divine guidance. In this way, they incurred God's punishment: God sealed their hearts, rendering them incapable of distinguishing between truth and falsehood and, consequently, of understanding and accepting the truth and taking the right path.

Verse 4: The duplicitous character of the hypocrites is symbolized, as it were, in the disparity between the bright veneer of their personalities and their dark souls. Their affluence is reflected in their well-fed and well-groomed bodies, but the hearts inside those bodies are dead. They are glib talkers and can convince a Muslim audience of their sincere commitment to Islam, but their words lack substance. In brief, they are comparable to nice-looking but lifeless blocks of wood that have been propped up against a wall, creating the false impression that they are alive.

"Every shout, they think, is upon them!" That is, whenever a sign of danger appears, they fear for their safety. They would like you to believe that they are willing to sacrifice their all in the cause of Islam, but that is empty talk; in reality, they are great cowards.

Because of their machinations and seditious plans, the hypocrites are the real enemy of Islam, and, therefore, Muslims need to be on their guard against them. "How they are straying off!" can be interpreted both as a cause and as an effect of a chain of events. It is a cause in that the hypocrites' decision to depart—or stray off—from the right path has shaped their typical personality; it is an effect in that their attitude and behavior have caused them to depart—or stray off—from the right path, such that there is little hope of their getting back to that path.

The idiomatic "May God strike them!" (literally, "May God fight them!") is a curse.

III. Literary Notes

Verse 4 is one of the most compactly drawn portraits in the Qur'ān of the hypocrites of Madīnah. More suggestive than graphic in respect of the details it provides, the verse appeals to the reader's or listener's imagination to draw both the outward appearance and the inner state of mind of the hypocrites. The verse is made up of eight short, crisp sentences:

(1) And when you look at them, you admire their bodies.
(2) And should they speak, you would listen to their speech.
(3) As if they were propped-up blocks of wood!
(4) Every shout, they think, is upon them!
(5) They are the enemy,
(6) So be on your guard against them.
(7) May God strike them!
(8) How they are straying off!

The first two sentences describe the outward aspect of the hypocrites' personalities: Their well-nourished bodies give them a striking physical appearance, and their eloquence charms the audience. The third sentence deflates their pomposity: they are bodies without souls and images without substance. The next two sentences depict the inward aspect of the hypocrites' personalities: Contrary to the impression they would like to give, they are cowards at heart; far from offering any sacrifices in the cause of Islam, they are afraid that any impending danger will claim them as its first casualty. They would like to be taken as the supporters and well-wishers of Islam and Muslims, but they are deeply hostile to Islam and Muslims. In the sixth sentence, therefore, Muslims are commanded to be on their guard against the hypocrites. The seventh sentence puts a curse on the hypocrites for their treacherous conduct. The concluding sentence traces that conduct to a perversion of reason on the part of the hypocrites, the tone of the sentence indicating both surprise and regret at their state.

34 An Argument for the Afterlife

78 News 1–17

1What are they querying one another about?
2About the Momentous News!—
3Concerning which they are in disagreement.
4Certainly not! They will soon find out.
5Again, certainly not! They will soon find out.
6Have We not made the earth a cradle,
7And the mountains stakes?
8And We created you in pairs;
9And We made your sleep a comfort;
10And We made the night a garment;
11And We made the day a time for earning a livelihood;
12And We built, above you, seven Firm Ones;
13And We installed a blazing lamp;
14And We sent down, from the wringing-wet ones, streaming water,
15That We may grow, by means of it, grains and vegetables,
16And dense gardens.
17Indeed, the Day of Decision is an appointed time.

Sūrah 78 is Makkan.

I. Introduction

Addressing the idolaters of Makkah, this sūrah presents one of the several types of Qur'ānic arguments to establish the truth of the afterlife. The argument is based on the principle that privilege entails accountability: the fact that human beings are the recipients of many blessings of God strongly suggests that they will, one day, be held accountable for the attitude they adopt toward those blessings (see chapter 1, "The Essence of the Qur'ān," sections IV.3 and V.4). After introducing the subject of the afterlife in an indirect but dramatic way, the sūrah cites a series of familiar existential phenomena as evidence of the various ways in which God has blessed human beings, with the final verse deducing the conclusion that the Day of Judgment must come to pass.

II. Commentary

Verses 1–3: Verse 1 asks a question, verse 2 supplies the answer, and verse 3 makes a comment.

Verse 1, actually, is a question about a question. A group of people are referred to as asking one another questions about a certain matter, which is not stated in explicit terms but which, one soon finds out, has to do with the possibility of the afterlife. The wording and tone of the verse suggest that the querying about the afterlife is derisive and dismissive in character. Accordingly, the question asked in the verse about the querying is itself somewhat satirical.

Verse 2 identifies the question under discussion with some specificity: It is the Momentous News. Again, though, a precise identification is not made.

Verse 3 remarks that the query makers, who are scoffing at the Momentous News, are themselves in disagreement over it—that is, over the question of the afterlife: the suggestion made is that some of them are skeptical of the occurrence of an afterlife, others have a vague belief in it, and still others, while believing that an afterlife will occur, are confident that intercession by someone close to God will save them any punishment due to them for their actions in worldly life. These different attitudes of the idolaters toward the afterlife are attested in the Qur'ān.

Verses 4–5: The two occurrences of "Certainly not," once in each verse, mean that the reality about the hereafter is not what the query makers—the Qur'ān would probably call them querymongers—have made it out to be. The hereafter will occur, and it will occur to fulfill certain purposes in accordance with the will and wisdom of God. The query makers are told, in a threatening tone, "They will soon find out." It is not stated what they will find out, but the reference, obviously, is to the dire consequences they will face for rejecting and making fun of the Momentous News—the afterlife.

The repetition, in verse 5, of the threat made in verse 4, "Certainly not! They will soon find out," is not for emphasis only. The punishment with which the Qur'ān threatens nations is of two types: punishment in this life and punishment in the afterlife. Verse 4 refers to the first type; verse 5, to the second.

Verses 6–17: These verses argue that the existential scheme of the universe contains ample and striking evidence to support the idea of an afterlife. The evidence of the many blessings bestowed by God upon human beings (verses 6–16) points to the conclusion (verse 17)—namely, that God will bring about a time when He will call human beings to account for all those blessings. To explain these verses briefly:

- God has created the earth to be a cradle-like place of comfort and held the earth in place by means of huge pins called mountains, so that the earth might serve as a stable base of operations, as it were, for human beings (verses 6–7).
- He has provided for the continuation of the human race by creating the two complementary genders of male and female, such complementarity, since it is a

feature of all existence, implying that the next world is a necessary complement to this world (verse 8).

- He has made sleep a remover of fatigue that refreshes and reinvigorates one—fatigue and freshness complementing each other in the sense that each gives rise to the other: freshness, through activity, turns into fatigue, which, when disspelled, produces freshness (verse 9).
- He has made the night a dress that enwraps human beings, holding them and giving them comfort, and He has made the day a time for economic activity—the day and the night, thus, representing another set of complements (verses 10–11).
- He has built, above the earth, seven heavens, which, being "Firm Ones," give the assurance that they will not collapse, and which, like a roof, complement the floor called the earth, mentioned in verse 6, above (verse 12).
- He has installed in the sky a blazing lamp, the sun, whose heat and light have a direct impact on the continuation and prosperity of life on the earth below (verse 13).
- From the skies, again, God sends down streaming rain, by means of which He causes to grow, on earth, not only grains and vegetables for human beings, but also fodder for animals, which, too, serve human beings (verses 14–16).
- Reflection on this vast and complex providential arrangement, built on the principles of interconnection and complementarity, leads one to conclude that life in this world would not make much sense if taken in isolation from its complement, the afterlife, for the Day of Judgment, or Decision, alone will give meaning and substance to the relationship between privilege and accountability (verse 17).

III. Literary Notes

This passage illustrates one of the special ways in which economy of expression is achieved in the Qurʾān. Verses 6–7 are interrogative in form: "Have We not made the earth a cradle, and the mountains stakes?" The next nine verses, starting with "And We created you in pairs" (verse 8) and ending with "And We sent down . . . dense gardens" (verses 14–16), are declarative in form, but, conceptually, they, too, are interrogative. They are presented in declarative form for the following reason: The question asked in verses 6–7 requires an affirmative answer, which is assumed to have been given in the form of a declaration: "Of course, We have made the earth a cradle, and the mountains stakes." It is to this unstated affirmative assertion that verses 8–16 are joined by conjunction. Thus, verses 6–17, together with explanatory material (in italics), will read as follows:

6Have We not made the earth a cradle,

7And the mountains stakes?

Of course, We have made the earth a cradle,

And the mountains stakes.

[8]And We created you in pairs;

[9]And We made your sleep a comfort;

[10]And We made the night a garment; . . .

[17]Indeed, the Day of Decision is an appointed time.

Alternatively, we can assume that, in the original text, the statements made in verses 8–16 are, in each case, responses to questions that are present in thought but have been omitted in the interest of brevity:

[6]Have We not made the earth a cradle,

[7]And the mountains stakes?

[8]And *did We not create you in pairs?*

Of course, We created you in pairs;

[9]And *did We not make your sleep a comfort?*

Of course, We made your sleep a comfort;

[10]And *did We not make the night a garment?*

Of course, We made the night a garment; . . .

[17]Indeed, the Day of Decision is an appointed time.

35 Muḥammad Consoled

93 Bright Morning

In the name of God, the Most Compassionate, the Very Merciful.

1 By the bright morning,
2 And by the night, when it becomes tranquil,
3 Your Lord has neither forsaken you nor hates you.
4 And the end is going to be better for you than the beginning.
5 And He will soon award you, and you will be gratified.
6 Did He not find you an orphan and give you refuge?
7 And He found you lost and guided you.
8 And He found you in want and enriched you.
9 So, as for the orphan, do not oppress him;
10 And as for the supplicant, do not rebuke him;
11 And as for the blessing of your Lord, tell of it.

Sūrah 93 is Makkan.

I. Introduction

This sūrah seeks to assure Muḥammad that the difficulties he is facing in presenting his message in Makkah will soon come to an end. It informs him that God will help him in the future just as He has helped him in the past. Thus, the purpose of the sūrah is to comfort Muḥammad and keep his spirits up in his confrontation with his Makkan opponents, whose conduct is critiqued in the sūrah.

II. Commentary

Verses 1–3: The Qur'ānic oaths provide supporting evidence for Qur'ānic theses. The bright, sunny morning (verse 1) and the dark, still night (verse 2) are opposites in respect of their time frames, their properties, and their overall character, but, in the larger scheme of existence, both the light and heat of the day and the darkness and stillness of the night are equally needed, the day and the night thus becoming complementary to each other. In the same way, both ease and hardship, activity and repose, and scarcity of means and abundance of resources are necessary for the spiritual and ethical training of human beings. If, therefore, in presenting his message, Muḥammad is facing difficulties—whether caused by a lack of support or resources or by enemy hostility—then those difficulties do not signify that he has lost favor with God, for he has done nothing to deserve God's wrath or indifference. Hardships are a part of the program of training and discipline that God wants him to go through, so that he may develop the ability to carry out his mission effectively.

Verses 4–5: These verses promise success in the near future. "The end is going to be better for you than the beginning" (literally, "The last is better for you than the first") (verse 4) means that the difficulties besetting Muḥammad at present will eventually come to an end, his prophetic ministry meeting with much greater success in the concluding phase than it has in the initial phase. Verse 5 ("And He will soon award you, and you will be gratified") promises that the change in Muḥammad's situation—which will occur as a blessing from God that will gratify Muḥammad—will happen sooner rather than later.

Verses 6–8: To reinforce the above-stated promise of success (verses 4–5), these verses cite God's support of Muḥammad in the past. The verses refer to three crucial periods in Muḥammad's past life:

(1) Muḥammad became an orphan at an early age: his father died before he was born, and his mother died when he was quite young. Verse 6 says that God gave refuge to the orphan Muḥammad when he needed such refuge the most.

(2) Like a number of other thinking individuals of Arabia, Muḥammad, in his preprophetic life, was in search of answers to the larger questions of life. Verse 7 refers to this search: "And He found you lost and guided you." The word "lost" (Arabic: *ḍāll*) in this case is best interpreted as "searching for the way," for one who is lost is, by implication, in search of the way. The two meanings of "being lost" and "searching for the way," thus, imply each other. Examples of such a relationship between the seemingly different meanings of a word are found in many languages. For example, the English verb "to miss" means both "to be lacking" and "to desire what is lacking." The same is the case with the French verb *manquer*. It, too, means "to be lacking," but, again, that which is lacking is also missed—in the sense of being desired and sought after—hence a usage like *Vous me manquez*, "I miss you."

(3) Whereas verse 7 refers to the initial change, in Muḥammad's case, from the state of being lost to the state of being guided, verse 8 refers to the abundance of revelatory guidance and wisdom that Muḥammad received from God after he was made a prophet. In "And He found you in want and enriched you," the primary meanings of the words "want" and "enriched" are, respectively, "want of Divine guidance" and "enriched by means of Divine guidance."

Verses 9–11: Verses 9–10 are, apparently, addressed to Muḥammad, who is being told not to oppress orphans and not to rebuke those who petition him for something. They do not imply, however, that Muḥammad used to commit either of the two acts. The verses exemplify a characteristic feature of Qurʾānic style—namely, that of indirect reference: the rich, powerful, and arrogant Quraysh are the ones who are being criticized here (as they are elsewhere in the Qurʾān—for example, 51:19; 70:25; 107:2). The indirect reference here shows disregard for the real addressees—the Quraysh—who are presented as being unworthy of being addressed direct. Thus, verse 9 commands the Quraysh to desist from their practice of oppressing orphans. At the same time, it tells Muḥammad to adopt toward orphans an attitude that is the exact opposite of the Quraysh's attitude. Muḥammad must remember that he himself was an orphan, and he must, therefore, treat orphans kindly. Likewise, verse 10 instructs Muḥammad to treat with kindness those who come to him for help in any matter—financial, intellectual, or religious. The actual criticism, again, is directed at the Quraysh.

The word "blessing" in verse 11 ("And as for the blessing of your Lord, tell of it") refers to the guidance and wisdom given to Muḥammad, who is instructed to proclaim this blessing—that is, by propagating the truth and wisdom it represents.

III. Literary Notes

1. It was noted above that the bright morning of verse 1 and the tranquil night of verse 2 are, both from a literary and from a conceptual standpoint, complementary opposites.

2. In verse 5—"And He will soon award you, and you will be gratified," we are not told what will be awarded to Muḥammad by God, this lack of specification indicating the great magnitude of the promised award. The extraordinary nature of the award is further emphasized by the phrase "and you will be gratified."

3. This passage illustrates one of the ways in which the Qurʾān employs the principle of verbal economy. Verse 6 is a question: "Did He not find you an orphan and give you refuge?" Conceptually, verses 7–8, too, are interrogative but have been put in the declarative. As in the case of Q 78:1–17 (see chapter 34, "An Argument for the Afterlife," section III), so in the present case, there are two explanations. First, potentially present in the text is the response to the question in verse 6: "Of course, He found you an orphan and gave you refuge." To this unstated response, which is in the form of a declarative sentence, the next two verses (7–8), declarative in form, are conjoined by conjunction, thus (the italicized portions are supplied):

> 6Did He not find you an orphan and give you refuge?
> *Of course, He found you an orphan and gave you refuge.*
>
> 7And He found you lost and guided you.
>
> 8And He found you in want and enriched you.

Alternatively, a question like the one that makes up verse 6 can be taken as implied before each of the two questions in verses 7–8, thus:

> 6Did He not find you an orphan and give you refuge?
> *Of course, He found you an orphan and gave you refuge.*
>
> 7And *did He not find you lost and guide you?*
> *Of course,* He found you lost and guided you.
>
> 8And *did He not find you in want and enrich you?*
> *Of course,* He found you in want and enriched you.

In either case, the verses would achieve economy of expression.

4. The last six verses of the passage have the following parallel structure: ABCA′B′C′. Each of the three reminders in verses 6–8—namely, that God found Muḥammad an orphan and gave him refuge (verse 6), found Muḥammad lost and guided him (verse 7), and found him in want and enriched him (verse 8)—is paired off with a prescription in verses 9–11—namely, that the orphan must not be oppressed (verse 9), the supplicant must not be rebuked (verse 10), and God's blessing must be proclaimed (verse 11).

36 Judgment Day

101 Striker

In the name of God, the Most Compassionate, the Very Merciful.

1 The Striker!
2 What is the Striker?
3 And how would you know what the Striker is!
4 The day on which people will be like scattered moths,
5 And the mountains will be like carded wool.
6 So, as for those whose scales are heavy,
7 They shall live a pleasant life.
8 But, as for those whose scales are light,
9 Their abode shall be Hāwiyah!
10 And how would you know what Hāwiyah is!
11 A raging fire!

Sūrah 101 is Makkan.

I. Introduction

Sūrah 101 depicts the cataclysmic events that will take place on the Day of Judgment. At the start of the day, a general panic will prevail, with resurrected human beings scattered all over and the physical world going through a massive upheaval. The day will conclude with the passing of Divine judgment: one whose life has been predominantly good will be sent to live a blissful life in paradise, whereas one who has lived a predominantly evil life will end up in hell, which is a raging fire. The sūrah's name hints at the moral of the sūrah: Judgment Day will arrive all of a sudden, so one must not allow oneself to be caught unawares; rather, one must always be prepared for the day.

II. Commentary

Verses 1–3: The sūrah's name refers to the Last Hour. It is a translation of *al-Qāriʿah*, which, since it comes from a root that means "to knock" or "to hit," ordinarily carried the meaning of "calamity." The Arabic word signifies that the Last Hour, which will usher in the Day of Judgment, will strike all of a sudden—like a stranger who arrives in the middle of the night and knocks on the door, causing worry and consternation—and that the best attitude for one, therefore, is to be prepared for it.

As just noted, the word *al-Qāriʿah*, in the sense of "calamity," was familiar to the Arabs (Q 13:31 uses it in this sense). The Qurʾānic use of the word for the Last Hour, though, was something of a novelty, and, reflecting the Qurʾānic audience's implied demand for a precise meaning of *al-Qāriʿah* in this sūrah's context, the Qurʾān says, "What is the Striker?" Anticipating that the audience, no matter how hard it tried, would fail to comprehend the magnitude of the *al-Qāriʿah*-related events, the Qurʾān presses ahead with the remark—the tone is exclamatory now—"And how would you know what the Striker is!" (literally, "And what will inform you what the Striker is?")

Verses 4–5: After the first three verses, there is an omission that a little reflection will supply: The Striker is the Day of Judgment. With verse 4 begins the description of some of the happenings of that day. Two images depict the dreadful confusion of the Day of Judgment: (1) Human beings, having been resurrected, will come out of their graves and run about in a state of anarchy, like moths scattered all around in the rainy season. The point of the image is that, on Judgment Day, all individuals will be fending for themselves, and no one will be in a position to help anyone else. (2) The mountains will float about in the air as if they were combed wool—the fibers of the combed wool being exceedingly fine. The point of this image is that, on Judgment Day, even seemingly enduring phenomena like mountains will lack all substance. Taken together, the two images depict a scene of total panic and disarray.

The Qurʾānic statement that, on the Last Day, mountains will float in the air like wool fibers was meant to address a certain issue. Elsewhere in the Qurʾān, we are told that, when the Qurʾān said that the Last Day would disrupt the structure of the world, the opponents of the Qurʾān sarcastically asked whether such a dislocation would affect the immovable mountains as well, and the Qurʾān responded that, on that day, the mountains would be pulverized (Q 20:105).

Verses 6–7: These verses introduce an element of order in the chaos of the Day of Judgment—though this order is ominous in its own way. On that day, the deeds of every individual will be weighed—in the Divine Court, it is implied. Only those people whose good deeds will tip the balance in their favor will enjoy a life of peace and happiness. The point of these verses—as also of verses 8–9 (below)—is that, on the Day of Judgment, one's final destination will be determined by the acts that one has performed in this world.

Verses 8–11: Those who have performed few good deeds will find that their evil acts have tipped the balance against them. The destination of such people will be Hāwiyah. The question, in verse 10—"And how would you know what Hāwiyah is!"—is similar to the question asked about "the Striker" at the beginning of the sūrah, and the last verse provides the answer: Hāwiyah is the fiercely and violently burning fire of hell.

III. The Scales

The Qur'ān uses the concept of the balance to express its view of justice in the next world. Both good and bad deeds will be weighed in a balance, good deeds being placed in one scale and bad deeds, in the other. What kind of balance and scales will be used to weigh deeds the Qur'ān does not say. The essential point is that, on Judgment Day, God will deal with people in accordance with the principle of justice, the balance and scales symbolizing that principle.

The statement in the sūrah about Divine judgment (verses 6–9) only lays down the principle of judgment. There is plenty of evidence in the Qur'ān to support the view that Divine judgment will be heavily tempered by Divine mercy.

IV. Literary Notes

1. This sūrah is a good example of the little-noticed feature of suspense in Qur'ānic narrative. The sūrah opens with the words "The Striker," a translation of the Arabic word *al-Qāri'ah*. We are a little puzzled at a sūrah starting on a seemingly enigmatic note. With its ordinary meaning of "calamity" in mind, one suspects that something ominous is meant, but no precise definition of the word is given. Nor can we determine whether *al-Qāri'ah* is (1) the subject of an omitted predicate: "*Al-Qāri'ah* [is such and such]," (2) the predicate of an omitted subject: ["Such and such a thing is] *al-Qāri'ah*"; or (3) the object of an omitted verb: ["Remember *or* Think of] *al-Qāri'ah*." Before we can form an opinion, the next verse, by asking a question—"What is *al-Qāri'ah*?"—confirms our suspicion that the word has, indeed, been used in a special, but until now unexplained, sense. As we search for an explanation, verse 3 takes away all hope of finding one: "And how would you know what *al-Qāri'ah* is!" Interrogative in form but exclamatory in spirit, the verse, by virtue of its construction, deepens the mystery about *al-Qāri'ah* and, by virtue of its import, suggests that a precise understanding of *al-Qāri'ah* is hard to come by.

Tantalized, we look to the Qur'ān itself for an explanation of *al-Qāri'ah*. Verse 4 appears to supply an explanation, but the explanation offered is circuitous—and also partial: "The day on which people will be like scattered moths." From this, we do gather that *al-Qāri'ah* is some kind of an event that will take place on a certain day, but the construction of the verse is such that our attention is immediately deflected from the word "day" and is focused on the graphic simile, which, we feel, has diverted us from our quest for an explanation of *al-Qāri'ah*. The structurally similar verse 5, which, by piling another simile on top of that in verse 4, further confirms our impression that only a roundabout and partial explanation of *al-Qāri'ah* has been offered so far.

At this point, the sūrah's mood undergoes a radical change. Up to this point, the sūrah has been marked by commotion and intensity. Starting with verse 6, a calm seems to prevail in the sūrah. Verses 6–9 lay down, in a firm, matter-of-fact manner, the principle of recompense in accordance with which, on Judgment Day, human beings will be evaluated by God. Verses 8–9 are parallel in structure to verses 6–7. But verse 9, by saying that Hāwiyah shall be the abode of those whose scales turn out to be light, makes one wonder about the exact meaning of "Hāwiyah," with verse 11 eventually providing the answer.

On reviewing the sūrah's contents, we may now ask, "Did the sūrah ever define *al-Qāri'ah*?" The answer is both no and yes—in that order. No, because a dictionary definition is not supplied. Yes, because the description and information provided in verses 4–11 leave no doubt in one's mind that *al-Qāri'ah* stands for the calamity that ushers in the Day of Judgment.

2. "Hāwiyah," in verse 9, is one of the Qur'ānic names for hell. The root of the Arabic word for "Hāwiyah" denotes "fall." Hāwiyah, thus, represents the embodiment, in the afterlife, of the "fall" in this world: those who fail to perform good deeds in this world and, as a consequence, fall from the position they could have kept had they performed good deeds will receive the punishment of being thrown into Hāwiyah. The Arabic word also connotes that Hāwiyah is an abyss.

3. The word "abode" in verse 9 is a translation of *umm* (literally, "mother"), which has been used in an ironic sense. A panicked, terrified child runs into its mother's arms for refuge and consolation. On the Day of Judgment, those whose scales have few good deeds in them will find no refuge anywhere against God's punishment; they will be "lovingly" embraced by Hāwiyah, their "mother" and their "refuge"!

37 Serving Only God

112 Sincerity

In the name of God, the Most Compassionate, the Very Merciful.

1 Say: He—God—is Unique.
2 God is the Sheet Anchor.
3 He did not beget and is not begotten.
4 And He has no peers.

Sūrah 112 is Madīnan.

I. Introduction

Some consider this a Makkan sūrah, but its contents include not only a critique of the idolatry of the Makkans, but also a critique of the People of the Book's view—more specifically, the Christians' view—of monotheism; it was in Madīnah that the Muslims had a serious theological confrontation with the People of the Book.

This sūrah's Arabic name is *Ikhlāṣ*, which, though not derived from the sūrah itself, accurately sums up the sūrah's contents. The essential meaning of the word is "purity" and "exclusivity"; the word is used to denote, for example, one's exclusive love for someone or one's pure and unmixed devotion to someone. As the sūrah's name, *Ikhlāṣ* means "to give one's allegiance only to God, to obey God to the exclusion of any other being or power, to worship God single-mindedly." Monotheism, the central doctrine of Islam, became and remained the most celebrated issue in Arabia after Muḥammad's announcement of his prophecy. Toward the end of Muḥammad's ministry, a need was felt to offer a succinct and definitive statement of that doctrine, and this sūrah supplies that need.

This is one of the most frequently recited sūrahs of the Qur'ān.

II. Commentary

Verse 1: The imperative "Say" has the sense of "proclaim." That is: declare openly and definitively so that everyone comes to know the truth in clear, unmistakable terms. The imperative also signifies that the proclamation to be made by the Prophet originates with God and is being made by the Prophet only on behalf of God.

The pronoun "He," referring to God, is anticipatory. Its use in the verse indicates that the subject to be discussed is so familiar to the audience that reference to it by means of a pronoun would suffice to direct attention to it. The use of the noun "God"—*Allāh* in Arabic—immediately after the pronoun confirms that the referent of "He" is, indeed, God. Used together in this way, the pronoun and the noun represent a unity of the signifier and the signified.

God is "Unique" both in the sense that He is One and in the sense that there is none like Him. "There is nothing like Him," as Q 42:11 says.

Verse 2: "Sheet Anchor" is a translation of the Arabic *Ṣamad*, used in the verse as a name of God. Literally, a huge rock that serves as a refuge for a people under attack, the word *ṣamad* came to mean a leader who serves as people's recourse at a time of need and without whose advice and guidance no important decision is made. As a name of God, *Ṣamad* means that God provides the best protection against all danger, is the refuge of those in crisis, and is the one to whom all petitions must be directed and all matters referred. "Sheet Anchor," with its meaning of "someone or something that can be depended on in a time of difficulty," is an English expression very close in meaning and spirit to the Arabic *Ṣamad*; another possible English translation would be "Mainstay."

This verse complements verse 1 by guarding against a possible misinterpretation of that verse. Verse 1 may be understood by some to mean that God is so unique, so different, so far removed from human beings as to be completely unapproachable. In other words, taken by itself, verse 1 may be understood to signify the absolute transcendence of God. Verse 2 corrects such a misunderstanding by stating that God, though transcendent, is not unconcerned or unconnected with the world or with the affairs of human beings: if, on the one hand, God is Unique, then, on the other hand, He is the Sheet Anchor as well. In a word, God is both transcendent and immanent.

Verse 3: God has no offspring and no ancestors. This verse rejects all kinds and shades of idolatry or polytheism—or all types of "association" (the literal meaning of the Arabic *shirk*, the Islamic term for idolatry or polytheism) of any being or object with God. The verse would apply, most directly and unambiguously, to the *shirk* that was committed by the people of Arabia at Muḥammad's time. The Qur'ān, while it does not call Jews and Christians idolaters, rejects the Christian interpretation of monotheism and criticizes the Israelites, on the one hand, for having worshipped the golden calf (for example, Q 2:51; 4:153) and, on the other, for having raised Ezra to the level of deity (Q 9:30) on account, probably, of such signal contributions of his as recovery of the Lost Torah. (The Qur'ānic reference to Ezra's deification may mean that only some Israelites were involved in the deification, just as, according to the Qur'ān itself, only one segment of the Israelite population was involved in calf-worship.) In brief, verse 3 would cover all those cases in which monotheism is, in any shape or form, compromised. Needless to say, the verse would equally apply to all historical instances of the violation of the monotheistic principle, committed under one guise or another, by Muslims themselves.

Verse 4: Not only does God have no family tree, He has no peers and no equals. In other words, He alone is Eternal, and He is Unique in respect of each one of His many attributes.

III. God as Necessary Existence and as the Author of Creation

This sūrah is, probably, the pithiest definition of Islamic monotheism in the Qur'ān. Since God is Unique, has no parent and no offspring, and is unlike any creature, it follows that He exists in His own right—or that, in philosophical language, His existence is necessary. Since no time can be posited at which He did not or will not exist, it follows that He has always existed and will always exist, that only His existence is absolute or underived, the existence of everything else being contingent or derived. Thus, the universe depends for its existence on God, the creator or maker of the universe who is also *Ṣamad*—that is, the recourse, refuge, and support of all.

Concluding Remarks

I have presented and tried to explain what I believe are some of the significant passages in the Islamic Scripture. My concern throughout this book has been to make the subject comprehensible to a general audience—an audience that is seriously interested in learning about one of the most important religious texts but has no special training to deal with that text. How far I have succeeded in the task is for the readers to judge.

The passages discussed in this work deal with a variety of themes, but it will appear from those passages that the Qur'ān's prime concern is with the moral life. The ethical focus of the Qur'ān is in evidence in the description of the building of the Ka'bah by Abraham and his son Ishmael (chapter 3) and in the narration of the battle between the Israelites and the Philistines (chapter 5); in the statement of the principle of lack of coercion in the matter of religion (chapter 7) and in the instructions about documenting a loan (chapter 9); in the recounting of the events of Jesus' life (chapter 12) and in the affirmation of the oneness of God and oneness of humanity (chapter 14); in the comments on previous prophetic dispensations (chapter 19) and in the reference to nature as a repository of signs (chapter 20); in the relation of a significant incident in the life of the prophet Joseph (chapter 23) and in the laying down of a series of commandments (chapter 25); in the summing up of the qualities of those devoted to God (chapter 29) and in the criticism of the so-called hypocrites (chapter 33); and in the presentation of an argument for the hereafter (chapter 34) and in the portrayal of scenes of the Last Day (chapter 36). It is well to remember that the Qur'ānic ethical focus is itself the product of a conception of a faith whose cornerstone is recognition, with understanding, of God as the central reality of all existence and whose principal requirement of its adherents is submission to that God in all spheres of human life. But the Qur'ān's concern with the reality of God should not obscure from view the Qur'ān's concern with another reality—that of the human being. In a certain sense, in fact, the Qur'ānic concern with the human reality takes precedence over its concern with any other reality, for the Qur'ān says everything that it says—including what it says about God—with the express purpose of guiding human thinking and effort in specific ways.

I hope I have been able to show that the Qur'ān is not just a bland theological book. The present book does not purport to parse and analyze Qur'ānic Arabic in much detail. Still, the brief discussions offered of the literary aspect of the Qur'ān have, perhaps, suggested that the Qurʾānic word choice, verbal economy, repetition, shifts of person and number, idioms, images, figures of speech, and narrative devices require careful attention and are fruitful subjects of study. I have tried to indicate that the literary aspect of the Qurʾān bears an intimate relationship to the Qurʾānic ideation, that the Qurʾānic literary and stylistic devices often acquire interpretive significance in that they help to bring out or highlight certain meanings or shades of meanings that make for a richer understanding of the Qurʾān.

Taken together, the passages included in this volume form a small part of the Qurʾānic text. It need hardly be said that they are not meant to serve as a substitute for the full text of the Qurʾān. It is my hope, though, that a study of this book will give the readers some idea of the character and range of the Qurʾān and will also initiate them, if to a very limited extent, into some of the ways of studying and reflecting on the Islamic Scripture. I also hope that this book will prompt some of the readers to undertake an in-depth study of the Qurʾān by acquiring the linguistic and other skills necessary to the task.

Notes

1 The Essence of the Qur'ān

1 Opening

I. *Al-Fātiḥah as the very first revelation:* See Rāzī, 1:177; Bayhaqī, *Dalā'il an-Nubuwwah*, quoted in Ibn Kathīr, 1:19. *Manār*, on the strength of a report by ʿAlī, calls *Al-Fātiḥah* the first sūrah to have been revealed (1:66).

Basmalah *as a self-standing verse of the Qur'ān:* Iṣlāḥī, 1:49. In one case, the *basmalah* occurs inside a sūrah (27:30) and is, therefore, counted as a regular Qur'ānic verse.

II. ***Verse 1:*** *Primary meaning of* ḥamd*: Lisān*, s.v. *ḥ-m-d*. Ṭabarī defines *ḥamd* as *shukr* (1:46; also Ibn Kathīr, 1:41–42). Qurṭubī cites Qur'ānic usage to argue that *shukr* is the predominant part of the meaning of *ḥamd* (1:134; also Iṣlāḥī, 1:55–56).

Meaning of "the Lord of the worlds": Cf. Ibn Kathīr, 1:43–44; Qurṭubī, 1:138–139.

Verse 3: *Why the "Day of Recompense" is singled out:* Ibn Kathīr, 45–46; Qurṭubī, 1:143.

III. *Al-Fātiḥah encapsulates the main themes of the Qur'ān:* Cf. Rāzī, 1:173–175. Since *Al-Fātiḥah* succinctly summarizes the contents of the Qur'ān, some *aḥādīth* refer to the sūrah as *Umm al-Qur'ān* ("Mother *or* Essence of the Qur'ān"; in one *ḥadīth*, it is called "the greatest sūrah in the Qur'ān" (*aʿẓamu s-suwari fī l-Qur'āni*). Qurṭubī, 1:108, 112.

To the petition made in Al-Fātiḥah, *the rest of the Qur'ān is a response:* Mawdūdī, 1:42.

IV. This is based on Iṣlāḥī's commentary, 1:61–66.

VI. 2. *Omission of the preposition* ilā *creates emphasis:* Iṣlāḥī, 1:59 (cf. Ibn Kathīr, 1:49, 51).

2 The Story of Adam

2 Cow 30–39

II. The interpretation presented here of verses 30–33 is borrowed from Iṣlāḥī (1:160–161). Ṭabarī, commenting on "if you are right" (verse 31), cites but disagrees with the interpretation that the phrase means: If you are right in thinking that the human race will include only mischief-makers (1:161–162). Iṣlāḥī's exegesis, taken in its details, yields a more coherent explanation of the several issues of language and thought raised by verses 30–33.

Verse 30: *Basis of the angels' apprehension on hearing the appointment of a caliph:* Qurṭubī, 1:274; *Manār*, 1:255, 281.

Verse 32: *Generic use of the word "caliph": Manār:* "Evidently—and God knows best—by *khalīfah* is meant Adam and all of his progeny" (1:258). A number of Qur'ānic verses call particular nations or individuals *khalā'if al-arḍ*, "caliphs of the earth," or *khalā'if fī l-arḍ*, "caliphs on the earth" (6:165; 7:69, 74; 10:14, 73; 27:62; 35:39; 38:26).

Verse 34: *Iblīs:* This is the personal name of Satan. The name comes from a root (*b-l-s*) that means "to despair"; Iblīs is so called because, after his fateful refusal to obey God's command to bow before Adam, he despaired of ever receiving God's mercy (*Lisān*, s.v. *b-l-s*; also Ṭabarī, 1:180).

Iblīs as a jinnī*:* In light of this explanation, the exceptive particle *illā* in verse 34 is disjunctive (*munqaṭi'*), signifying that what is excepted (Iblīs) is not a member of the class (angels) to which the exception is drawn.

According to a ḥadīth, *the angels are made of light:* Rāzī, 2:214.

Verse 36: *Satan as the cause of Adam and Eve's expulsion:* Ṭabarī, 1:186.

Human beings and satanic beings as natural enemies of each other: Manār: "For the enmity is between man and Satan, not between the members of man's progeny" (1:278). Also Iṣlāḥī, 1:167.

"On earth, you shall have a dwelling place and a provision for a certain time": See Iṣlāḥī, 1:169, and Abū Ḥayyān, 271.

Verse 38: *The command "Descend" does not signify punishment for Adam and Eve and their progeny:* Qurṭubī, 1:221.

Emphatic verb in verse 38: Daryābādī, 18, n. 142; Iṣlāḥī, 1:170.

Possession of reason as grounds for basic accountability: Zamakhsharī, 1:64; Abū Ḥayyān, 1:272.

III. 1. *Human beings' mandate as caliphs: Manār*, 1:258–260. Qurṭubī: "He [Adam] was the caliph of God in respect of implementing his commands and injunctions" (1:263).

Human caliphate is essentially moral in character: Nevertheless, this verse has been used to justify the political institution of caliphate in Islam. Qurṭubī discusses the matter at great length (1:264–274); for a compact statement, see Ibn Kathīr, 1:125–126.

2. *Human beings are attracted to the forbidden:* Abū Ḥayyān, quoting Qushayrī, 1:257; Iṣlāḥī, 1:267.

IV. 4. *Use, for God, of the first person plural pronoun to signify Divine majesty:* Abū Ḥayyān, 1:245–246, 272; Qurṭubī, 1:291.

Use, for God, of the first person singular pronoun to signify Divine affection: Daryābādī, 18.

Use, for God, of the first person singular pronoun to suggest God as the only source of guidance: Abū Ḥayyān, 1:272.

V. *God's plan to send Adam and Eve to earth preceded Adam and Eve's temptation by Satan:* Mawdūdī, 68–69, n. 53 (*ad* Q 2:38); also Rāzī, 3:26, explaining the imperative *ihbiṭū*, "Descend," in Q 2:38. Abū Ḥayyān observes that, if the Garden of Eden had been meant to be a permanent dwelling place for Adam and Eve, then (1) Iblīs would not have been allowed to enter it and tempt them (1:254), and (2) Adam and Eve would not have been placed under the prohibition of eating the fruit of a certain tree (1:256). Qurṭubī reaches the same conclusion—namely, that Adam and Eve's stay in the Garden of Eden was, from the very beginning, meant to be temporary—from the imperative "reside" (*uskun*) in verse 35 (1:299).

Qur'ān does not identify the forbidden tree: After listing the names of trees that Muslim scholars have suggested for the tree, Abū Ḥayyān remarks: "It is a tree about whose type God has not informed us, and this is the most obvious thing, for the purpose is only to inform us that commission of a forbidden act will entail punishment" (1:256); also Ṭabarī, 1:183–185, and Ibn Kathīr, 1:138.

Dominant perspectives on the story of Adam in the Bible and the Qur'ān: *Manār*, 1:279–280.

3 Abraham Builds the Kaʿbah and Prays for a Prophet

2 Cow 124–129

II. ***Verse 124:*** *Kalimah in the sense of "command":* Qurṭubī, 2:97; Abū Ḥayyān, 1:601; *Manār*, 1:453. See also Iṣlāḥī, 1:325.

Abraham as a "leader of humankind": Abū Ḥayyān, 1:601. The word "leader" (*imām*) in this verse has also been interpreted in a political sense, with several injunctions derived from its use in that sense. See Zamakhsharī, 1:92; Abū Ḥayyān, 1:605–607.

Verse 125: *"Abraham's staying place":* *Manār*, 1:461–462; Iṣlāḥī, 1:329–330.

Abraham and Ishmael are instructed to purify the Kaʿbah: Abū Ḥayyān, 1:601; *Manār*, 1:462.

Prayer is the main form of worship to be performed in the Kaʿbah: Iṣlāḥī, 1:331.

Bowing and prostration formed elements of the Abrahamic prayer: Manār, 1:463.

Verse 126: *Historical fulfillment of Abraham's twofold prayer:* Abū Ḥayyān, 1:608–609; Iṣlāḥī, 1:333–335.

Prayer for "produce of various kinds" is a prayer for the change of the nomadic lifestyle to a settled lifestyle: Iṣlāḥī, 1:335–337.

Issue of leadership of humankind is distinct from the issue of providing sustenance: Zamakhsharī, 1:93; Rāzī, 4:61; Qurṭubī, 2:119–120.

IV. 1. *The demonstrative "this" in verse 126:* Elsewhere in the Qur'ān, in referring to Makkah, Abraham does use the expression "this land" (14:35; 90:1), but that does not invalidate the point made here. Cf. Rāzī (4:61) and Abū Ḥayyān (1:612), who bring up the matter indirectly while discussing the issue of definiteness and indefiniteness of the relevant words in Q 2:126 and other Qur'ānic verses.

2. *Bifurcated subject: Manār*, 1:469.

4 True Piety

2 Cow 177

I. *Piety and* pietās*:* See section II, below, *note on "piety as dutifulness."*

II. *Generic use of the singular "Book":* Zamakhsharī, 1:109; *Manār*, 2:115.

Piety as dutifulness: For the essential meaning of "piety," which is here offered as the translation of the Arabic *birr*, see *Lisān*, s.v. *b-r-r*, and Farāhī, *Mufradāt* (Sarā'e Mīr, A'zam Garh, India: Ad-Dā'irah al-Hamīdiyyah, 1358/1939), 264–267. Cf. the definition of *pietās*: "dutiful conduct towards (and from) gods, country, parents, brothers and sisters, etc." *(Chambers Murray Latin-English Dictionary*, s.v. *pietās*).

"In spite of their love of it": The Arabic, *'alā ḥubbihī*, may also mean "on account of their love of Him [God]." The translation "in spite of their love of it [wealth]," however, is inclusive of the first meaning—for, one who spends wealth in spite of one's love of it does so on account of one's love of God. Iṣlāḥī, 1:425–426.

"The needy": *Manār*, 1:368 (*ad* Q 2:83). The Arabic word, *masākīn*, literally means "those whom poverty and need have humbled or brought low." See Ṭabarī, 1:309.

"In the cause of slaves": The meaning, of course, is "in the cause of setting slaves free," but the preposition *fī* in the original (*fī r-riqāb*—literally, "in the necks [of slaves]") opens up the possibility of spending one's wealth in a number of ways, direct and indirect, to achieve the desired goal of setting slaves free and of abolishing slavery.

The exhortation to spend money, besides the mandatory zakāh, *on social causes:* The commentators cite a *ḥadīth* in this connection: *Inna fī l-māli la-ḥaqqan siwā z-zakāti*, "Inherent in one's wealth, indeed, is an obligation besides *zakāh*." Ṭabarī, 1:56–58; Qurṭubī, 2:242. Rāzī, 5:44–45, offers a fairly detailed discussion.

"Always": This is an attempt to translate the emphasis arising out of the use of the nominal rather than of the verbal form—of *al-mūfūna bi-'ahdihim* rather than of *awfā bi-'ahdihī*, which, had it been used, would have been analogous in construction to the preceding *wa-aqāma ṣ-ṣalāta wa-ātā z-zakāta*. On the Qur'ān's omission to use a verbal form, see Abū Ḥayyān, 2:140.

'Ahd *is general in import:* Rāzī, 5:48.

The pious keep their commitments at all costs: Iṣlāḥī, 1:429. Proper intonation of the particle *idhā*, "when," will bring out the full force of the phrase *wa l-mūfūna bi-'ahdihim idhā 'āhadū*.

"In particular": This phrase is meant to indicate the meaning of the accusative of praise (*naṣb 'alā l-madḥ*) of *aṣ-ṣābirīn*.

Meaning of "These are the ones who have proven truthful": Abū Ḥayyān, 2:141–142. *Manār*, 2:122.

"And these are the godfearing": The Arabic, *wa-ulā'ika humu l-muttaqūn*, may also be translated—taking *an-nār*, "the fire," as the omitted object of *al-muttaqūn*—"And these are the ones who will avoid *or* be saved from the fire." Ṭabarī, 1:60; Abū Ḥayyān, 2:142.

IV. *The various parties to which the admonitory statement about facing the east or the west in prayer may be addressed:* Ṭabarī, 2:56; Rāzī, 5:38, 40.

5 A Battle Between the Israelites and the Philistines

2 Cow 246–251

I. *Reason for the Israelites' demand for a king:* Rāzī, 6:182. Ibn Kathīr offers a brief account, representative of Muslim exegesis, of the oppression of the Israelites by their enemies and of the rise of the prophet Samuel (1:533–534).

II. ***Verse 246:*** *Meaning of "Did you not see?" (a-lam tara):* Iṣlāḥī, 1:563; *Manār*, 2:456–457 (*ad* Q 2:243).

Samuel's question expresses certain reservations: Zamakhsharī, 1:148; Rāzī, 6:183.

Samuel's understanding of the Israelites' weakness: Iṣlāḥī, 1:569.

Omission between "when, already, we have been expelled from amidst our homes and our children" and "But when fighting was prescribed for them": Ṭabarī, 2:377.

Verse 247: *Ṭālūt's humble background:* Ṭabarī, 2:378, 379–380.

"And he has not been given an abundance of wealth either" means that Ṭālūt is poor: Rāzī, 6:185. The construction and tone of the sentence in the original text imply: And he is, *moreover*, poor (see Ibn Kathīr, 1:534), hence the translation, "And he has not been given an abundance of wealth *either*."

Ṭālūt's qualifications as king: Zamakhsharī, 1:148–149; Qurṭubī, 3:246; Ibn Kathīr, 1:534. *Manār*, commenting on the Qur'ānic reference to Ṭālūt's physical and intellectual traits, remarks that Ṭālūt possessed *al-ʿaql as-salīm fī l-jism as-salīm* (2:477), this Arabic phrase being a literal translation of *mens sana in corpore sano*.

Meaning of "And God is Wide-Ranging, All-Knowing": Iṣlāḥī, 1:571.

Intonation of "God, indeed, has chosen him over you": Ibn Kathīr, 1:534.

Rulership is not by heredity: Ṭabarī, 2:381; *Manār*, 2:477.

Verse 248: *Israelites were not fully convinced by the evidence presented by Samuel in support of Ṭālūt's kingship:* Ṭabarī, 2:381; *Manār*, 2:482.

Contents of the Ark: Ṭabarī, 2:387–388; Ibn Kathīr, 1:535–536; *Manār*, 2:484 (quoting Deuteronomy 31:24–30).

Meaning of "[A]ngels will be carrying it": *Manār*, 2:485 (the second of the two interpretations); Iṣlāḥī, 1:572–573.

Verses 249–250: *Omission between these verses and verse 248:* Ṭabarī, 2:390; Abū Ḥayyān, 2:585.

Identification of those who crossed the river along with Ṭālūt: Ṭabarī, 2:394–395.

Why Ṭālūt tests his troops: Rāzī, 6:192, 195; Iṣlāḥī, 1:577; *Manār*, 2:486–487.

The test was commissioned by God: Iṣlāḥī, 1:577.

Only the true believers crossed the river: Rāzī, 6:195–196; Iṣlāḥī, 1:577–578.

Belief in God and the afterlife as a source of strength: Iṣlāḥī, 1:578.

"And God is with the steadfast" as a Divine comment: Rāzī, 6:198.

Verse 251: *Omission between this verse and verse 250:* Ṭabarī, 2:396.

Divine law of removing oppressor nations by means of other nations: Iṣlāḥī, 1:581–582.

Divine law concerning the removal of evil: Rāzī, 6:204–205; Qurṭubī, 3:259–261.

David integrates, in his person, the functions of king and prophet: Ibn Kathīr, 1:538; Qurṭubī, 3:257; Abū Ḥayyān, 2:593.

III. 1. *The Muslims' fight for their* qiblah, *the Kaʿbah, is comparable to the Israelites' fight for their* qiblah, *the Ark of the Covenant:* Iṣlāḥī, 1:557.

IV. 5. *Reason for the use of the present tense rather than the past:* Iṣlāḥī, 1:581.

V. 2. *Saul as proper name and Ṭālūt as nickname:* Iṣlāḥī, 1:570.

3. *Importance of the Ark of the Covenant for the Israelites*: Ṭabarī, 2:374; Mawdūdī, 1:189–190, n. 270; Iṣlāḥī, 1:571–572.
5. *"And [God] taught him [David] of what He wishes" refers to David's expertise in certain arts and crafts:* Ṭabarī, 2:403.

6 The Throne Verse

2 Cow 255

I. *Incompatibility between monotheism and intercession:* Iṣlāḥī, 1:584, 586, 589–590.

Throne Verse as the greatest verse of the Qur'ān: Qurṭubī, 3:268, 271, 278; Zamakhsharī, 1:154, especially the Prophet's statement: "The greatest discourse [*sayyid al-kalām*] is the Qur'ān, the greatest part of the Qur'ān is *Sūrat al-Baqarah* [sūrah 2], and the greatest part of *Sūrat al-Baqarah* is the Throne Verse"; also Abū Ḥayyān, 2:607. According to some scholars, the Throne Verse is the greatest verse because it refers to God, by name or by pronoun, no fewer than eighteen times (Qurṭubī, 3:271).

II. *God alone deserves to be worshipped:* Ṭabarī, 3:4; *Manār*, 3:23, quoting and supporting *Jalālayn*. Rāzī advances an argument from linguistic usage to establish that, as deity (*ilāh*), God alone is to be worshipped (*ma'būd*) (4:196, *ad* Q 2:163).

God is eternally living: Ṭabarī, 3:4.

God does not suffer death: Daryābādī, 106, n. 979.

Attribute of Qayyūm *negates deification of any being other than God:* Iṣlāḥī, 1:588.

God's existence is absolute, with all else possessing contingent existence: Rāzī, 7:4, 5.

Being subject to sleep or drowsiness would diminish Divine life and Divine sustainership: Iṣlāḥī, 1:588; Zamakhsharī, 1:153.

God is never unmindful of His creation: Rāzī, 7:6.

God is the creator and master of all things: Rāzī, 7:9.

Exception made for intercession negates the possibility of intercession: Manār, 3:31.

Intercession will not be allowed because the intercessor does not add to God's knowledge: Manār, 3:31; Iṣlāḥī, 2:589.

Permission to intercede represents an honor conferred on the intercessor: Iṣlāḥī, 1:590.

God does not need help in watching over the universe: Iṣlāḥī, 2:590.

God possesses perfection and is above imperfection, "Exalted" and "Great," thus, being complementary: Daryābādī, 107, n. 988.

God is too "Exalted" and too "Great" to depend on anyone else: Rāzī, 7:6.

God's greatness must not to be measured by ordinary yardsticks: Iṣlāḥī, 1:590.

III. *Division of the verse into components:* See Zamakhsharī, 1:154, for a fivefold division of the verse and for a comment on the feature of asyndeton in the verse.

Throne Verse equals one-third of the Qur'ān: Qurṭubī, 3:270.

Throne Verse is comparable to sūrah 112: Zamakhsharī, 1:152.

7 No Compulsion in the Matter of Religion

2 Cow 256

I. *"Guidance has become distinct from misguidance" as rationale for "There is no compulsion in the matter of religion":* Abū Ḥayyān, 7:616.

II. *Meaning of "There is no compulsion in the matter of religion":* Zamakhsharī, 1:155; Rāzī, 7:15; Abū Ḥayyān, 2:616.

Abundant proofs have distinguished truth from falsehood: Rāzī, 7:16.

"There is no compulsion in the matter of religion" enunciates the principle that force may not be used to compel anyone to accept Islam: Manār, 3:36–37.

Ṭāghūt *is any being, power, or entity that bids defiance to God:* Ṭabarī, 3:13; *Manār,* 3:37.

The form of the word Ṭāghūt *denotes intensity* (mubālaghah*): Manār,* 3:35.

"There is no compulsion in the matter of religion" does not refer to the use of force in implementing Islamic law: Qurṭubī, 3:279; Iṣlāḥī, 1:592–593.

Ad-dīn *means "Islam":* Grammatically, the definite article of the Arabic word denotes *ʿahd* or *iḍāfah*. Rāzī, 7:616; Abū Ḥayyān, 2:616.

"The Firmest Tie" refers to the means of securing salvation in the afterlife or to faith or Islam: Ṭabarī, 3:13; see also Abū Ḥayyān, 7:617.

"The Firmest Tie" will not crack—not to speak of breaking: Qurṭubī, 3:282; also Rāzī, 7:17; Abū Ḥayyān, 2:617.

"The Firmest Tie" belongs to a strong rope: Zamakhsharī, 1:155; see also *Manār,* 3:35, 37–38.

Those who take hold of the "Firmest Tie" will not stray from the right path: Manār, 3:37.

Meaning of "And God is All-Hearing, All-Knowing": Iṣlāḥī, 1:594.

8 Spending in the Way of God

2 Cow 261–269

I. *Meaning of "to spend in the way of God":* Rāzī, 7:47; *Manār,* 3:60; Iṣlāḥī, 1:613.

Relationship of the passage to Q 2:245: Ṭabarī, 3:41; Rāzī, 7:47.

II. ***Verse 261:*** *Meaning of "for whomever He wishes":* Iṣlāḥī, 1:613; also Zamakhsharī, 1:159–160.

Meaning of "And God is Wide-Ranging, All-Knowing": Iṣlāḥī, 1:613; Ṭabarī, 3:42.

Verse 262: *Favor-reminding and infliction of hurt as major sins:* Rāzī, 7:51.

Verse 263: *Bothersome attitude of some petitioners:* Zamakhsharī, 1:160; Rāzī, 7:52; Iṣlāḥī, 1:614.

Meaning of "And God is Opulent, Forbearing": Rāzī, 7:53; *Manār,* 3:64.

Implicit threat in the word "Forbearing": Rāzī, 7:53; *Manār,* 3:64.

Verse 264: *"God will not guide the ungrateful people" means that God will keep them from entering heaven:* Iṣlāḥī, 1:616–617.

Verse 265: *Spending in the way of God as a means of self-fortification:* Zamakhsharī, 1:16; Rāzī, 7:60; Abū Ḥayyān, 2:667; *Manār*, 3:67; Iṣlāḥī, 1:617.

The kind of spending that fortifies one's self: Iṣlāḥī, 1:616.

Meaning of "a garden on an elevation": Ṭabarī, 3:48; Zamakhsharī, 1:161; Abū Ḥayyān, 2:667–668; *Manār*, 3:68; Iṣlāḥī, 1:618. The Arabic word used in the original text for "elevation" is *rabwah*, which, following Qurṭubī (3:315), I have interpreted as a slightly raised piece of land rather than one that rises sharply above the surrounding land.

Meaning of "And God observes what you do": Iṣlāḥī, 1:618. See also Rāzī, 7:62.

Verse 266: *Elements of the analogy:* See Ṭabarī, 3:50–52; Zamakhsharī, 1:161; Ibn Kathīr, 1:567.

Misfortune of loss of good actions befalling one in the hereafter when one needs good actions the most: Ṭabarī, 3:50–52; Rāzī, 7:62, 63, 64.

"A whirlwind, with fire in it" means a hot wind or sandstorm: Ṭabarī, 3:53; Abū Ḥayyān, 2:674.

Verse 267: *"Choice possessions" and "what lacks worth":* In the translation of this verse of the Qur'ānic passage, "choice parts" and "what is of poor quality" are renderings, respectively, of *ṭayyib* interpreted as *jayyid* and of *khabīth* interpreted as *radī'*: See Ṭabarī, 3:55; also Qurṭubī, 3:321; Ibn Kathīr, 1:568.

One would accept a worthless offering only grudgingly: Ṭabarī, 3:56–57.

Meaning of "And know that God is Opulent, Worthy of Thankful Praise": Ṭabarī, 3:58–59; Qurṭubī, 3:328; Iṣlāḥī, 1:620.

Verse 268: *Satan's strategy to keep one from spending in the way of God:* Qurṭubī, 3:328; Iṣlāḥī, 1:620–621.

Meaning of "from Him" after "forgiveness": Rāzī, 7:70.

Verse 269: Iṣlāḥī, 1:621.

III. 2. *Generic use of* alladhī *in verse 264:* Zamakhsharī, 1:161.

3. *Mention of two types of fruits followed by a mention of many types of fruits (verse 266):* Zamakhsharī, 1:163.

4. *Juxtaposition of "tree" with "fruit" (verse 266):* Abū Ḥayyān, 2:672; *Manār*, 3:69.

5. *Reverse parallelism (verse 268):* The chiasmus is hinted at in Ṭabarī (3:59) and in Iṣlāḥī (1:620).

9 Making a Loan Transaction

2 Cow 282–283

II. 1. *Taking witnesses over spot trading:* Zamakhsharī, 1:169; Abū Ḥayyān, 2:740; Thānawī, 1:171, 172; Iṣlāḥī, 1:641.

Loan transactions made between relatives and friends: Mawdūdī, 1:219.

"For a stated term" does not mean that some loans are not for specified periods of time: Abū Ḥayyān, 2:723.

Implications of the phrase "between you": Qurṭubī, 3:383–384; Abū Ḥayyān, 2:723–724.

2. *Why the debtor is asked to dictate:* Zamakhsharī, 1:168; Rāzī, 7:120; Thānawī, 1:169.
3. *Not everyone is fit to serve as a witness:* Rāzī, 7:122; Abū Ḥayyān, 3:730.

Examples of situations in which the debtor is unable to dictate: Rāzī, 7:120; Abū Ḥayyān, 2:726.

Scribe should benefit society with the expertise with which God has endowed him: Zamakhsharī, 1:167; Rāzī, 1:119; Abū Ḥayyān, 2:724; Iṣlāḥī, 1:640.

Obligation of witnesses to bear true and complete witness: Thānawī, 1:172.

In certain cases, the testimony of a single female is decisive: Qurṭubī, 3:391; Abū Ḥayyān, 2:729.

Neither scribe nor witness should be reluctant to perform his obligation: Rāzī, 7:123.

Scribes and witnesses must not be harmed: Thānawī, 1:171.

The best witness according to Muḥammad: Rāzī, 1:131; Ibn Kathīr, 1:596.

III. *Detail and repetition in Q 2:282:* Rāzī, 7:115.

10 Creed and Commitment

2 Cow 285–286

II. ***Verse 285:*** *Purpose of reporting that Muḥammad and the believers believe:* Iṣlāḥī, 1:648.

The Prophet also is subject to Divine commandments: Iṣlāḥī, 1:648.

"We do not discriminate between any of His messengers": This is a critique of the People of the Book—of Jews, who believe in Moses but not in Jesus, and of Christians, who believe in Moses and Jesus but not in Muḥammad. Ṭabarī, 3:101; Rāzī, 7:143.

"We hear, and we obey" signifies that belief must be followed by action: Manār, 3:144–145.

Omission of "We seek" before "Your forgiveness, our Lord!" Rāzī, 7:147–148.

Verse 286: *"Our Lord, do not hold us accountable if we should forget or make a mistake" as an indication of modesty:* Iṣlāḥī, 1:651.

Difference between "Do not lay on us a burden the way you laid it on those before us" and "do not burden us with what we lack the ability to bear": Iṣlāḥī, 1:652; see also Ṭabarī, 3:104–105.

Difference between "overlook our failings" and "forgive us": Following Ṭabarī, 3:105. For a somewhat different interpretation of these two phrases and also of the third phrase, "have mercy on us," see Rāzī, 7:160–161; Abū Ḥayyān, 2:766–767.

"And have mercy on us": Ṭabarī, 3:105–106.

III. 2. *Shift from the third person to the first:* Iṣlāḥī, 1:649.

3. *Difference between* kasabat *and* iktasabat: Two other interpretations of the difference may be mentioned. Zamakhsharī and Ibn ʿAṭiyyah both proceed from the premise underlying the

explanation given here—namely, that, compared with *kasabat*, *iktasabat* connotes effortfulness. According to Zamakhsharī, *iktasabat* is used in the verse in connection with bad deeds since human beings, drawn by the seductive charm of evil, make a greater effort to pursue evil (1:172). According to Ibn ʿAṭiyyah, the verb *kasabat* is used in connection with good actions since it denotes that one who obeys God is able to perform good actions effortlessly, whereas *iktasabat* is used in connection with bad actions since it denotes that one who performs bad deeds does so effortfully, trying to force his way through the barrier of prohibitions erected by the religion (quoted in Qurṭubī, 3:431, and Abū Ḥayyān, 2:762).

Iktasabat *signifies one's doing of something for one's own sake:* Rāzī, 7:152.

11 Love of Desirable Things

3 Family of ʿImrān 14–17

I. *Context of the passage:* Ṭabarī, 3:133.

Verse 14: *Both God and Satan may be taken as the one who has made "the love of desirable things" glamorous to people:* Abū Ḥayyān, 3:50 (basic statement of the issue); Rāzī, 7:207–208 (theological discussion of the issue).

Meaning of "glamorization": Iṣlāḥī, 2:40.

"Branded horses": Ṭabarī, 3:135–136; Iṣlāḥī, 2:41.

Importance of cattle in the bedouin economy: Iṣlāḥī, 2:41.

"Tilled land": Iṣlāḥī, 2:41.

"The good return" means "heaven": Ṭabarī, 3:137.

The worldly provision is transient, whereas the blessings of the hereafter are enduring: Abū Ḥayyān, 3:53.

The order in which the "desirable things" are listed: Abū Ḥayyān, 3:50 ff. See also *Manār*, 2:239–245.

Referent of "people": Iṣlāḥī, 2:41.

III. 1. *Difference between normal love and excessive love of worldly things:* Iṣlāḥī, 2:40.

One should make use of the worldly provision with a view to earning a good reward in the hereafter: Rāzī, 7:212.

God makes the love of worldly things glamorous in order to put human beings to the test: Zamakhsharī, 1:178 (Zamakhsharī cites Q 18:7 as supporting evidence). Another sense in which God may be understood as having invested worldly things with glamor can be stated as follows: According to the Qurʾān, those people who persist in evil and do not mend their ways despite reminders and warnings are, as punishment, confirmed in evil by God—some Qurʾānic verses (for example, 2:7; 4:155; 16:108; 40:35) speak of this punishment in terms of God's "sealing" of the hearts and senses of those. In line with this argument, one might say that those who fall for this world and are utterly heedless of the afterlife are confirmed by God in their love for this world—such love assuming glamor in their eyes.

2. *Verse 16 does not mean that faith alone suffices for salvation:* Rāzī, 7:215; Abū Ḥayyān, 3:56.

IV. 1. *Shift of person from verse 14 to verse 15 implies conferral of honor or prestige:* Abū Ḥayyān, 3:55.
2. *Shift of number in verse 14 implies disdain for worldly things:* Abū Ḥayyān, 3:53.

12 Jesus: Birth, Miracles, and Mission

3 Family of ʿImrān 45–51

II. ***Verses 45–46:*** *Jesus as* kalimah: Rāzī, 8:50; Iṣlāḥī, 2:39.

Jesus as Messiah: Abū Ḥayyān, 3:152; Ibn Kathīr, 2:39; Iṣlāḥī, 2:91–92.

The name "Jesus son of Mary" makes it clear that Jesus was born of one parent only: Rāzī, 8:53; *Manār*, 3:306.

The name "Jesus son of Mary" signifies that Jesus was neither the son of God nor had a human father but was a human being born of a female human being: Ṭabarī, 3:186; Daryābādī, 133, n. 117.

(2)(c) *That Jesus is known as the son of Mary is Mary's distinction as well:* Zamakhsharī, 1:190.

(3) *Use of the word* wajīh *for Jesus:* Iṣlāḥī, 2:92.

(4) *Jesus' speech during his infancy served to vindicate his mother:* Rāzī, 8:55–56 (Rāzī also discusses the Christians' denial of Jesus' talk in infancy); Iṣlāḥī, 2:93.

That Jesus will speak to people at an advanced age implies that he will have a relatively long life: Abū Ḥayyān, 3:156.

Even during his infancy, Jesus' speech will be marked by maturity and wisdom: Zamakhsharī, 1:190; Iṣlāḥī, 2:94.

(5) *That Jesus is "one of the intimates" of God and "one of the virtuous" means that he is not a deity:* Daryābādī, 134, nn. 117 and 118; Iṣlāḥī, 2:94.

Verse 47: *"Thus does God create what He wishes" indicates that Jesus is a created being:* Abū Ḥayyān, 3:158; Ibn Kathīr, 2:40; *Manār*, 3:307.

Several systems of causation may possibly exist: Cf. *Manār*, 3:308.

Verses 48–50: *In the phrase "the Book and wisdom, and the Torah and the Evangel" (verse 48), the second conjunction "and"* (Arabic: *wāw) is explicatory or exegetical:* Iṣlāḥī, 2:94.

The singular "sign" (verse 49) has been used generically: Rāzī, 8:58; see also Iṣlāḥī, 2:96.

Those suffering from leprosy and congenital blindness (verse 49) were considered incurable: Ṭabarī, 3:192.

Jesus was sent specifically to Israel (verse 49): Iṣlāḥī, 2:94, 95.

Two meanings of muṣaddiq *(verse 50):* Iṣlāḥī, 2:96–97.

Jesus' making lawful of what had been made unlawful for the Israelites refers to the severities arising from subjective interpretations of the Law (verse 50): Iṣlāḥī, 2:97.

Jesus' mission was to restore the spirit of the Torah (verse 50): Iṣlāḥī, 2:94.

III. 4. *Indefiniteness of "a Word" (verse 45):* Iṣlāḥī, 2:80 (*ad* Q 3:39).

Indefiniteness of "a Straight Path" (verse 51): Iṣlāḥī, 2:98.

IV. 1. *Generic use of the plural* malāʾikah: Rāzī, 8:36 (*ad* Q 3:39), 50; Abū Ḥayyān, 3:128 (*ad* Q 3:39), 152.

2. *Jesus' advent was awaited by Israel:* Iṣlāḥī, 2:96–97 (including the citation of Luke 7:18–19).

5. *Resonance between Q 3:51 and John 20:17:* Iṣlāḥī, 97–98.

13 God's Blessing upon the Arabs

3 Family of ʿImrān 102–105

I. *Nature and context of God's blessing upon the Arabs:* Ṭabarī, 4:22–23, 24–25; Iṣlāḥī, 2:154.

II. ***Verse 102:*** *Meaning of "Fear God as He ought to be feared":* Iṣlāḥī, 2:152.

"And you must not die except that you be in submission" means that one must constantly be mindful of one's conduct: Abū Ḥayyān, 3:285–286; Ibn Kathīr, 2:83; *Manār*, 4:19; Iṣlāḥī, 2:152–153.

Verse 103: *Interpretations of the "Rope of God" and the* ḥadīth *comparing the Qurʾān to the "Rope of God":* Ṭabarī, 4:21; Zamakhsharī, 1:206; Rāzī, 8:173; Abū Ḥayyān, 3:286; Iṣlāḥī, 2:153.

Need for Muslims collectively to seize the "Rope of God": Iṣlāḥī, 2:152.

General and specific referents of God's blessings upon the Arabs: Ṭabarī, 4:22–23; Rāzī, 8:174; Abū Ḥayyān, 3:286–287, 289; Ibn Kathīr, 2:85; *Manār*, 4:21–22. See also I, above.

Verse 104: *Need for a political setup to accomplish the goal of enjoining good and forbidding evil and the establishment of the caliphate in Islamic history:* Iṣlāḥī, 2:155.

Referent of "It is they who are the successful ones": Iṣlāḥī, 2:155.

14 One God, One Humanity

4 Women 1

II. *The "single being" is Adam, and his "mate" is Eve:* Ṭabarī, 4:150; Ibn Kathīr, 2:196.

In "and [He] created, from it, its mate," the preposition "from" signifies genus: Iṣlāḥī, 245–246.

Elevation of the status of the "ties of kinship": Zamakhsharī, 1:241; Iṣlāḥī, 2:246.

Two possible meanings of "fear . . . the ties of kinship": Ṭabarī, 4:151–152.

III. 1. *Significance of the reference to* taqwā *at the beginning of sūrah 4:* Rāzī, 9:157.

2. *Women are men's equals in dignity and are not inferior to men:* Iṣlāḥī, 2:247.

4. *Ethical and legal dimensions of the statement that all human beings are descendants of Adam and Eve:* Ṭabarī, 4:149–150; Abū Ḥayyān, 3:492–493; Iṣlāḥī, 2:246, 247.

15 Orphans, Justice, and Polygamy

4 Women 2–4

II. ***Verse 2:*** *Those addressed by the verse:* Ṭabarī, 4:153; Iṣlāḥī, 2:251.

Prohibition of ways of embezzling orphans' property: Iṣlāḥī, 2:251.

Meaning of "And do not exchange the unwholesome for the wholesome": Qurṭubī, 5:9; *Manār*, 4:343.

Verse 3: In interpreting the word *nisāʾ* in this verse and in the next as "[the] mothers [of orphans]," I follow Iṣlāḥī, 2:251–254.

"What you possess in your hands": It is not necessary to translate the Arabic word *aymān* (sing. *yamīn*) in the original as "right hands," for, unless a contrast with *shimāl* ("left hand") is intended, *yamīn* may be taken simply to mean "hand."

Verse 4: *The verse strongly urges the giving of the dower:* Ṭabarī, 4:161; Iṣlāḥī, 2:254.

The last part of the verse forbids coercing the woman to forgo or return the dower in whole or in part: Zamakhsharī, 1:246; Rāzī, 9:182.

The phrase "with pleasure and relish" signifies lawfulness and absence of accountability: Zamakhsharī, 1:246; Rāzī, 9:182; Qurṭubī, 5:17.

III. 1. *In the passage, the discussion of polygamy is ancillary to the theme of the protection of orphans' rights: Manār*, 4:347.

Verse 3 attaches great importance to equal treatment of wives: Manār, 4:345.

The overall thrust of verse 3 is to discourage, even prohibit, polygamy: Manār, 4:350.

IV. *Significance of the conjunction "and" at the start of verse 2:* Iṣlāḥī, 2:251.

16 Structure of Authority in Islam

4 Women 59

I. *The verse as the most compact statement of authority in Islam:* Observing that this verse "contains most of the science of jurisprudence" (*mushtamilatun ʿalā akthari ʿilmi uṣūli l-fiqhi*), Rāzī discusses in detail the legal authority of the Qurʾān, Sunnah, *ijmāʿ* (consensus), and *qiyās* (analogy), the four fundamentals—or "roots," as they are called—of Islamic jurisprudence (10:143–148).

II. *Obedience to the Messenger is commanded by God, and to obey the Messenger is to obey God:* Ṭabarī, 5:93; Rāzī, 10:143.

The ulū l-amr *can be denied obedience if their command is at variance with the Divine or the Prophetic command:* Ṭabarī, 5:95; Ibn Kathīr, 2:324–325.

To obey God is to abide by the Qurʾānic commands and prohibitions, and to obey the Messenger is to follow Muḥammad and his Sunnah: Ṭabarī, 5:93, 95; Zamakhsharī, 1:275; Abū Ḥayyān, 3:687; Ibn Kathīr, 2:326.

The term ulū l-amr *applies primarily to those in positions of religious and political leadership:* Ṭabarī, 5:93–95; Abū Ḥayyān, 3:686; Ibn Kathīr, 326; *Manār*, 5:181, 187 (where the group of *ulū l-amr* is presented as including influential people from several spheres of society).

The ulū l-amr, *primarily, are those with the ability to discern the truth of a matter:* Ṭabarī, 5:95, 96.

"If you believe in God and the Last Day" contains an implicit threat: Rāzī, 10:149, 152; Abū Ḥayyān, 3:688. According to Ṭabarī (5:95), the phrase means that observance of the prescription will be rewarded and violation of the prescription punished in the afterlife.

The meaning of "This is better, and more excellent in respect of outcome": Ṭabarī, 5:96; *Manār*, 5:193; Iṣlāḥī, 2:324–325.

17 Matrimony: Some Issues

4 Women 127–130

I. *This passage addresses issues arising out of and pertaining to the sūrah's opening, namely, Q 4:2–4:* Qurṭubī, 5:402; also Rāzī, 11:62.

II. ***Verse 127:*** *The unspecified query about which the Prophet's ruling is being sought is elucidated by means of the answer given in the rest of the passage:* *Manār*, 5:443; Iṣlāḥī, 2:397.

The three issues raised and addressed in the verse: Iṣlāḥī, 2:397, 398.

"And that you should treat orphans justly" is joined by conjunction to an implied statement: Iṣlāḥī, 2:397–398.

Verse 128: *A woman may reach a compromise with her husband in the larger interest of safeguarding the marriage and avoiding a divorce:* Ṭabarī, 5:196; Zamakhsharī, 2:302; Qurṭubī, 5:406; Abū Ḥayyān, 4:86; Ibn Kathīr, 2:406, 409–410; *Manār*, 5:446; Iṣlāḥī, 2:399.

Meaning of "And souls are confronted with greed": Abū Ḥayyān, 4:87–88; also Zamakhsharī, 1:302.

Reason why "And if you do good . . . what you do" mentions only the possibility of doing good: Abū Ḥayyān, 4:85.

"And if you do good . . . what you do" is addressed to men: Qurṭubī, 5:407.

Verse 129: *Meaning of "And you will never be able . . . like one dangling":* Ṭabarī, 5:201, 203; Zamakhsharī, 2:302; Rāzī, 11:68; Qurṭubī, 5:407; Ibn Kathīr, 2:410.

Meaning of "And if you rectify things and cultivate piety": Rāzī, 11:68; Ibn Kathīr, 2:410–411; Iṣlāḥī, 2:399.

Verse 130: Ṭabarī, 5:204; Rāzī, 11:68; Abū Ḥayyān, 4:89; Ibn Kathīr, 2:411; Iṣlāḥī, 2:399–400.

Apparently addressed to both marriage partners, the verse primarily seeks to encourage and reassure the wife: Iṣlāḥī, 2:400.

IV. 2. Meaning of *istaftā* (base form of *yastaftūnaka*): Rāzī, 11:62; Abū Ḥayyān, 4:81; *Manār*, 5:443, 444.

5. See Rāzī, 11:67.

18 Prophets and Revelation

4 Women 163–165

I. *This passage responds to the People of the Book's demand made in Q 4:153:* Ṭabarī, 6:20; Zamakhsharī, 1:313.

The prophets whose stories have not been told in the Qur'ān far outnumber those whose stories have been told in it: Rāzī, 11:109.

II. *There is nothing extraordinary about the way God is sending revelation to Muḥammad:* See Rāzī, 11:108, 109, 110.

Relationship between the attributes of Divine power and Divine wisdom: Iṣlāḥī, 2:432.

IV. *Chronological and qualificative orders of naming the prophets:* Iṣlāḥī, 2:431; also Abū Ḥayyān, 4:137 (Jesus, Job, and Jonah).

19 Torah, Evangel, and Qur'ān

5 Feast 44–48

II. ***Verse 44:*** *Torah as "guidance and light":* Iṣlāḥī, 2:527.

Significance of rendering judgment in light of the Torah: Iṣlāḥī, 2:527–528.

Meaning of "who had submitted": Iṣlāḥī, 2:528.

Meaning of "on account of the fact that they had been given custody of the Book": Iṣlāḥī, 2:527.

Timing of the commandment "So, do not fear people, but fear Me, and do not take a small price for My verses": Iṣlāḥī, 2:528.

All worldly gains made through misinterpretation of Divine scripture are paltry in comparison with the reward of guidance in the hereafter: Manār, 6:399.

Verse 45: *The pronoun "him" in "it shall be an atonement for him" refers to the injured party:* Iṣlāḥī, 2:530.

Use of the word taṣaddaqa *is an exhortation to pardon the offender:* Zamakhsharī, 1:342.

Verse 46: *"Their" in "in their wake" refers to the above-mentioned prophets, making Jesus a prophet:* Abū Ḥayyān, 4:277.

Meaning of "in their wake": Iṣlāḥī, 2:531.

Meaning of muṣaddiq: Iṣlāḥī, 1:179 (*ad* Q 2:41).

Identity between prophet and scripture: Iṣlāḥī, 2:531.

Verse 47: *Timing of the commandment "And let the People of the Evangel judge in accordance with what God has revealed in it":* Abū Ḥayyān, 4:280; Iṣlāḥī, 2:532; also *Manār,* 6:402.

Verse 48: *Meaning of* muhaymin*:* Iṣlāḥī, 2:533; Abū Ḥayyān, 4:28; also *Manār*, 6:411–412.

Meaning of "a law and a path": Iṣlāḥī, 2:534–535.

Purpose of altering the outer form of religious truth is to test people: Zamakhsharī, 1:343; Iṣlāḥī, 2:534–536.

III. 1. *The statement that those who do not judge by revealed scripture are disbelievers, wrongdoers, and transgressors is general in its import:* Zamakhsharī, 1:341; Abū Ḥayyān, 4:269.

IV. 4. *Wordplay involving* hāda*:* Iṣlāḥī, 1:226–229 (*ad* Q 2:62), quoting Farāhī.

Contrast between "submitters" and "Jews": Abū Ḥayyān, 4:267.

V. *The principle of retribution cited from the Torah forms part of Islamic law:* Abū Ḥayyān, 4:273; Iṣlāḥī, 2:531.

Jesus' Sermon on the Mount in Matthew recommends forgiveness: *Manār*, 6:401.

20 Nature as a Repository of Signs

6 Cattle 95–99

II. ***Verse 95:*** *Criticism of those who set up other deities besides God:* Ṭabarī, 7:186; also Qurṭubī, 7:44.

Verse 96: *"One who rips out the morning!":* A word about the translation is in order. As noted in the commentary, the word *fāliq* occurs both in verse 95 and in verse 96. In verse 95, however, what is split open is the direct object of *fāliq*, namely, the grain and the fruit stone. In verse 96, however, it is not the direct object of *fāliq*—namely, the morning—that is split open, but the (implied) darkness of the night, with the morning wrenched out of it, so to speak. This understanding of verse 96 is close to the first of Zamakhsharī's two interpretations of the Qur'ānic phrase (*fāliq al-iṣbāḥ* = *fāliq ẓulmat al-iṣbāḥ*) (2:29; for more details, see Rāzī, 13:98).

Implication of "And He has made the night a source of rest": Iṣlāḥī, 3:119.

The sun and the moon follow designated courses: Ṭabarī, 7:188–189.

The sun and the moon are indicators of time: Zamakhsharī, 2:30; also Ṭabarī, 7:189.

Connection between the two meanings of the statement that God has made "the sun and the moon a reckoning": Ṭabarī, 7:189.

"This is the planning of the Almighty, the All-Knowing" contrasts God with the alleged deities: Ṭabarī, 7:189–190.

Heavenly bodies owe their existence to an outside power—to an Almighty and All-Knowing God: Rāzī, 13:100.

Being Almighty and All-Knowing, God harnesses the sun and the moon to certain ends: Zamakhsharī, 2:30.

God's power complements His knowledge: Iṣlāḥī, 3:120.

Possible referents of the demonstrative "this" in "This is the planning of the Almighty, the All-Knowing": Abū Ḥayyān, 4:595; also Iṣlāḥī, 3:119.

Verse 98: *Meaning of* mustaqarr *and* mustawdaʿ: Iṣlāḥī, 3:123.

Use of the word mustawdaʿ *suggests that those buried will be resurrected for judgment:* Qurṭubī, 7:47; Iṣlāḥī, 3:123.

It is pointless to put one's reliance on anyone other than God: Iṣlāḥī, 3:123.

Meaning of ansha'a*:* Iṣlāḥī, 3:122.

The human race has only one creator, God: Iṣlāḥī, 3:122.

Verse 99: *God provides human beings not only with basic foods, but also with fruits of various kinds:* Iṣlāḥī, 3:126.

Only a few of the fruits familiar to the Arabs are mentioned in the verse: Iṣlāḥī, 3:126.

Meaning of "alike and different," used of fruit trees: Ṭabarī, 7:195; Zamakhsharī, 2:31; Rāzī, 13:110; Iṣlāḥī, 3:126.

Trees and plants produced by rainwater provide food for human beings and fodder for animals: Ṭabarī, 7:194.

"Hanging low" means "within easy reach": Zamakhsharī, 2:31; Rāzī, 13:108.

Meaning of "Observe its fruit when it blossoms, and its ripening": Zamakhsharī, 2:31; Rāzī, 13:111; Iṣlāḥī, 3:127.

A single cause, water, produces effects of great variety: Ṭabarī, 7:197.

III. *Universal harmony as proof that there is only one God:* Iṣlāḥī, 3:117, 118, 119–121.

V. 3. *Omission in verse 99:* Iṣlāḥī, 3:127.

4. *Difference between "He brings forth . . ." and "He is going to bring forth . . .":* Iṣlāḥī, 3: 117–118.

6. *Shifts of person and number:* Iṣlāḥī, 3:124–125 (on verse 99).

21 The Primordial Covenant

7 Heights 172–173

II. *The singular may be interpreted to mean that many people are being addressed one by one:* Iṣlāḥī, 3:392.

"From out of their loins" signifies that all members of the human race are being referred to: Iṣlāḥī, 3:392.

III. 1. *The event described in the passage may be interpreted to mean that human beings have an intuitive understanding of God's oneness and providence:* Zamakhsharī supports this view, saying that the event narrated in the passage is allegorical (2:103). Abū Ḥayyān quotes Zamakhsharī approvingly (5:220–221). See also *Manār*, 9:386–387.

Prophetic message as a reminder: Iṣlāḥī, 3:395.

2. Iṣlāḥī, 3:393.

3. Iṣlāḥī, 3:392.

22 Charity Offerings

9 Repentance 60

I. Zamakhsharī, 2:159.

II. *It is assumed that a religiously or morally forbidden act is not the cause of the debt incurred:* Ṭabarī, 10:114.

Restricted and general meanings of "in the cause of God": See Rāzī, 16:113.

Meaning of "an obligation from God! And God is All-Knowing, All-Wise": Ṭabarī, 10:115; Rāzī, 16:115.

III. 1. *Like the administrators, "those whose hearts are to be won over" may be given a share of the charity offerings regardless of their financial status:* Ṭabarī, 10:112–113.

It is not necessary to divide the charity offerings equally among all the heads of expenditure or even to allocate some amount under each head: Ṭabarī, 10:112; Zamakhsharī, 2:158.

2. See Rāzī, 16:114.

23 Joseph Interprets the Dreams of His Prison-Mates

12 Joseph 36–42

II. ***Verse 36:*** *Meaning of "pressing wine":* Ṭabarī, 12:127; Rāzī, 18:134; Iṣlāḥī, 4:217.

Verses 37–40: *The fellow-prisoners' request for the interpretation of their dreams gives Joseph an opportunity to present his monotheistic faith to them:* Ibn Kathīr, 4:28.

Nature of God's bounty on people: Rāzī, 18:138.

Knowledge of the interpretation of dreams is definitively accurate only when it is based on revelation: Rāzī, 18:136, 137.

Joseph's reference to Abraham, Isaac, and Jacob (verse 38) implies that these personages were well-known in the region: Iṣlāḥī, 4:218–219.

"It does not behoove us to associate anything with God" (verse 38) means that there is no justification, rational or other, for setting up copartners to God: Iṣlāḥī, 4:219.

Verse 41: *Joseph avoids specifying which interpretation is meant for which prison-mate so as not to hurt the one who is destined to be crucified:* Ibn Kathīr, 4:28.

Verse 42: *The prisoner's heedlessness in mentioning Joseph to the king, since it is unvirtuous in character, is attributed to Satan:* Iṣlāḥī, 4:221.

III. 2. *Relationship between piety and the ability to interpret dreams:* See Rāzī, 18:135.

IV. 2. *Use of "over" rather than of "on" (verse 36):* See Mustansir Mir, "Irony in the Qurʾān: A Study of the Story of Joseph," Issa J. Boullata, ed., *Literary Structures of Religious Meaning in the Qurʾān* (Richmond, Surrey, United Kingdom: Curzon, 2000), 181 and n. 20.

3. *"I have abandoned the way of people who do not believe in God" (verse 37) does not necessarily mean that Joseph was previously a disbeliever in God:* Rāzī, 18:137.

   "I have abandoned the way of people who do not believe in God" (verse 37) implies that Joseph has made a conscious choice to adopt monotheism and reject polytheism: Iṣlāḥī, 4:218.

V. *Qur'ānic commentators' borrowing of information from Biblical or Jewish sources about the prisoners' identities:* Ṭabarī, 12:126–127; Rāzī, 18:133.

24 Inviting People to the Faith

16 Bee 125–128

I. Iṣlāḥī, 4:462.

II. ***Verse 125:*** *Meaning of "wisdom" and "good counsel":* Zamakhsharī, 2:349; Iṣlāḥī, 4:463, 464.

God knows who has strayed and who would accept guidance: Zamakhsharī, 2:349.

Verses 126–128: *Overretaliation is forbidden (verse 126):* Iṣlāḥī, 4:464.

Showing patience is better than exacting retribution (verse 126): Iṣlāḥī, 4:464.

Meaning of "God is with those who are godfearing and who perform good works" (verse 128): Ṭabarī, 14:134; Zamakhsharī, 2:349.

God will ensure the eventual success of those who are godfearing and do good works (verse 128): Iṣlāḥī, 4:465.

25 Commandments

17 Night Journey 22–39

I. *The passage consists of twenty-five commandments:* Rāzī, 20:213.

II. ***Verse 22:*** *The reduction to the state of "one censured, forsaken" will take place in the afterlife:* Iṣlāḥī, 4:495.

Meaning of "one censured, forsaken": Iṣlāḥī, 4:495.

The monotheist will earn praise and receive Divine support: Rāzī, 20:182.

The verse addresses Muḥammad, but only as a representative of the Muslim community: Iṣlāḥī, 4:495. To Ṭabarī, the verse addresses all those who are morally accountable (15:46). Rāzī, granting this latter interpretation, prefers to take "man" as the addressee (20:182). See also Ibn Kathīr, 4:297.

Verse 23: *It is to one's parents, after God, that one is most beholden:* Rāzī, 20:185.

Even parents—not to speak of others—may not be deified: Iṣlāḥī, 4:496.

The verse honors parents by placing the commandment about treating them well next to the commandment to serve only God: Zamakhsharī, 2:357.

The prohibition against saying Uff! *to one's parents in their old age underscores the need for one to be especially kind to them when they get old:* Iṣlāḥī, 4:496.

Meaning of Uff!*:* Zamakhsharī, 2:357; Iṣlāḥī, 4:496.

Meaning of "while they are with you": Zamakhsharī, 2:357.

Children should be patient with their old parents, just as the parents put up with their children when the latter were little: Ṭabarī, 15:47.

The prohibition against uttering Uff! *necessarily implies a prohibition against inflicting greater hurt on the parents:* Rāzī, 20:189.

Verse 24: *Meaning of the idiom "to lower the wing of humility for somebody":* Rāzī, 20:191; Iṣlāḥī, 4:496.

Need for the children to reverse roles by taking care of their old parents: Rāzī, 20:196; Iṣlāḥī, 4:496.

Significance of the phrase "out of mercy": Iṣlāḥī, 4:496–497.

Verse 25: Ṭabarī, 15:50; Rāzī, 20:192; Iṣlāḥī, 4:497.

Verses 26–28: *If one lacks the means to help needy people, one may promise to help them when one's circumstances improve (verse 28):* Ṭabarī, 15:54; Rāzī, 20:194.

Meaning of to "draw away" from people (verse 28): Rāzī, 20:194.

Verse 29: *Meaning of "to tie up one's hands to one's neck" and of "to spread out one's hands all the way":* Ṭabarī, 15:56; Rāzī, 20:195; Iṣlāḥī, 4:498.

Meaning of "lest you end up as one reproached, without resource": Iṣlāḥī, 4:498–499; also Ṭabarī, 15:56.

Verse 30: *The ultimate source of sustenance is God, who, in His wisdom, decides how much to give to whom:* Rāzī, 20:196; Ibn Kathīr, 4:304; Iṣlāḥī, 4:499.

Verse 31: Ṭabarī, 15:57; Rāzī, 20:196–197; Iṣlāḥī, 4:499.

Verse 33: *The verse orders a departure from the pre-Islamic practice of taking excessive revenge:* Ṭabarī, 15:59.

The survivor or heir of the person killed is the real plaintiff in a case of homicide: Iṣlāḥī, 4:501.

Verse 35: See Rāzī, 20:206–207; Iṣlāḥī, 4:502.

Verse 36: Iṣlāḥī, 4:502.

Verses 37–38: *That God dislikes the evil represented by the prohibited acts means that He dislikes those who perpetrate such acts:* Iṣlāḥī, 4:503.

One must be humble before God, who has limitless power: Iṣlāḥī, 4:502.

Verse 39: *The demonstrative "this" refers to all the commands and prohibitions stated in the preceding verses:* Rāzī, 20:213–214; Ibn Kathīr, 4:309; Iṣlāḥī, 4:503.

The verse addresses the Muslim community through the Prophet Muḥammad: Ibn Kathīr, 4:309.

III. 1. *That the passage begins and ends with a statement about monotheism implies that monotheism ought to frame all thought and action:* Rāzī, 20:214.

Monotheism is like a wall enclosing and guarding the teachings contained in the passage: Iṣlāḥī, 4:503.

26 God Makes Moses a Prophet

20 Ṭā-Hā 9–36

I. Ṭabarī, 16:107; Ibn Kathīr, 4:497–498; Iṣlāḥī, 5:30.

II. ***Verse 9:*** *"And has the story of Moses reached you?" is a question in form only and is meant to draw Muḥammad's attention to the story about to be related:* See Rāzī, 22:14–15.

The flash of fire glimpsed by Moses was probably not seen by his family: Iṣlāḥī, 5:30. Zamakhsharī (2:428)—and, following him, Rāzī (22:15)—interprets the relevant Arabic verb (*ānastu*) differently. Iṣlāḥī's interpretation seems to agree better with the Qur'ānic text.

Verses 11–16: *The Ṭuwā valley became sacred on account of its association with God (verse 12):* Iṣlāḥī, 5:31.

Taking off one's shoes is a mark of the respect one needs to show on entering a sacred place or a house of worship (verse 12): Iṣlāḥī, 5:31; also Zamakhsharī, 2:429.

That God has "elected" Moses means that He has chosen him to be a prophet (verse 13): Ṭabarī, 16:112; Zamakhsharī, 2:429; Rāzī, 22:16; Iṣlāḥī, 5:31.

The first commandment given to every prophet after the commandment to serve only God was that of establishing the prayer (verse 14): Iṣlāḥī, 5:32, 34.

Interpretation of the two occurrences of "it" in "So, let not those who do not believe in it and follow their caprice keep you from it" (verse 16): Iṣlāḥī, 5:33, citing Abū Muslim's opinion, for which, see Rāzī, 22:23.

Disbelief in the hereafter is likely to lead one to neglect the prayer (verse 16): Iṣlāḥī, 5:33.

Meaning of "lest you perish" (verse 16): Iṣlāḥī, 5:34.

Verses 17–18: Yamīn *often simply means "hand" (verse 17):* Iṣlāḥī, 5:34.

Purpose of asking the question, "And what is that in your hand, Moses?" (verse 17): Ṭabarī, 16:116. Zamakhsharī (2:430) and Rāzī (22:25) each cite an analogy from ordinary life to illustrate the nature of the question.

Verses 19–23: *The staff and the shiny white hand will generate other miracles also (verse 23):* Iṣlāḥī, 5:36.

Moses' fright as evidence of his prophecy (verse 21): Rāzī, 22:29 (quoting Abū l-Qāsim al-Anṣarī).

Verse 24: *A brief reference to Pharaoh's rebellion was sufficient:* Iṣlāḥī, 5:37.

Verses 25–35: *Meaning of Moses' prayer:* Iṣlāḥī, 5:38–42.

Moses' prayer, "untie the knot in my tongue," does not necessarily mean that he had a speech problem (verse 27): Iṣlāḥī, 5:39–40.

"And make him a partner in my task" is a prayer for Aaron's appointment as a coprophet with Moses (verse 32): Ṭabarī, 16:121; Qurṭubī, 11:194.

"You have been watching over us" (verse 35) is a request by Moses to God to bless him and his brother in the future as well: Qurṭubī, 11:194; Iṣlāḥī, 5:42.

III. 2. *Unlike a prophet, a politician craves leadership:* Iṣlāḥī, 5:37–38.

27 War in Self-Defense

22 Pilgrimage 38–41

I. *Sūrah 22 is unmistakably Madīnan:* Iṣlāḥī, 5:252.

II. ***Verse 40:*** *The Qur'ān recognizes the special status of the Jewish and Christian places of worship:* See Rāzī, 23:40.

III. *Fighting and war may be necessary to ensure the freedom of practice of religion:* Qurṭubī, 12:70; Abū Ḥayyān, 7:516.

IV. 4. ʿAzīz *literally means "one of unassailable strength."* An Arabic word very close to *ʿazīz* in meaning is *manīʿ*. See Ṭabarī, 17:126.

28 God Is the Light of the Heavens and the Earth

24 Light 35

I. Ṭabarī, 18:105; Iṣlāḥī, 5:409.

II. *The niche and the star-like glass help to diffuse the light of the lamp:* Iṣlāḥī, 5:410–411.

To the Arabs, the best trees in a garden were those situated in the middle of it: Iṣlāḥī, 5:410.

Meaning of "blessed," used of the olive tree: Iṣlāḥī, 5:410.

The elements of the parable combine to enhance the quality of the light: Zamakhsharī, 3:77.

God as the source of enlightenment about major issues of life: Iṣlāḥī, 5:409.

29 Qualities of the Servants of God

25 Criterion 63–76

I. *The meritorious character traits listed in the passage are lacking in the Makkan opponents of Muslims:* See Zamakhsharī, 3:104 (*ad* Q 25:68); Iṣlāḥī, 5:486.

II. ***Verse 63:*** *Makkan idolaters' disdain for the name "the Compassionate One":* Iṣlāḥī, 5:486.

Meaning of the word "modestly," used to describe the gait of the servants of God: Ṭabarī, 19:23; Zamakhsharī, 3:103; Rāzī, 24:107; Qurṭubī, 13:68–69; Abū Ḥayyān, 8:126; Iṣlāḥī, 5:486.

The humble gait of the servants of God is reflective of their inner humility: Iṣlāḥī, 5:486.

Meaning of salām *and the response of the servants of God to thoughtless people's attempt to debate with them:* Zamakhsharī, 3:103; Rāzī, 24:108; Qurṭubī, 13:69; Abū Ḥayyān, 8:126; Iṣlāḥī, 5:485, 486–487.

Verses 64–65: *Verse 64 describes the servants of God's conduct in private, just as verse 63 describes their conduct in public:* Rāzī, 24:108; Ibn Kathīr, 5:164; Iṣlāḥī, 5:487.

The reference in verse 64 is to the optional late-night prayer: Zamakhsharī, 3:103; Rāzī, 24:108; Iṣlāḥī, 5:487.

Even as they perform good deeds, the servants of God are afraid of punishment in the afterlife for their lapses (verse 65): Zamakhsharī, 3:104; Qurṭubī, 13:72; Abū Ḥayyān, 8:128.

Punishment of hell as a "permanent liability" (verse 65): Ṭabarī, 19:23; Qurṭubī, 13:72; Ibn Kathīr, 5:164.

Connection between the statement that hell is a "permanent liability" and the preceding part of verse 65: Iṣlāḥī, 5:487.

Verse 66: Iṣlāḥī, 5:487.

Verse 67: *The servants of God's moderation in spending:* Iṣlāḥī, 5:487–488.

Verses 68–69: *Punishment for committing any of the three forbidden acts:* Iṣlāḥī, 5:488.

Verses 70–71: *God forgives even grave sins (verse 71):* Ṭabarī, 19:26.

Those who repent of a sinful life should not worry about finding and adjusting to a new environment (verse 71): Iṣlāḥī, 5:489.

"And he who repents and does good deeds will make his return to God" (verse 71) means that such a person will be forgiven, and also handsomely rewarded, by God: Rāzī, 24:113; Abū Ḥayyān, 8:131–132; also Zamakhsharī, 3:105.

Verse 72: *Primary meaning of "to witness falsity":* Ibn Kathīr, 5:171.

"To witness falsity" may also mean "to bear false witness": Zamakhsharī, 3:105; Rāzī, 24:113; Ibn Kathīr, 5:171.

Demeanor of the servants of God on passing by a frivolity: Zamakhsharī, 3:105; Qurṭubī, 13:80–81.

Meaning of laghw: Qurṭubī, 13:81. Zamakhsharī (3:105) interprets the word to mean "anything that is fit to be nullified or discarded."

Verse 73: *The real stress of the verse falls on the implied opposite of the behavior here described:* Zamakhsharī, 3:105; Abū Ḥayyān, 8:132; Iṣlāḥī, 5:490.

Verse 74: *The servants of God's concern about the well-being of their families:* Iṣlāḥī, 5:490.

Explanation of the idiom "coolness of eyes": Qurṭubī, 13:82; Abū Ḥayyān, 8:133.

Historical significance of the use of the phrase "coolness of eyes": Ibn Kathīr, 5:173 (quoting Miqdād).

The prayer "make us leaders of the pious" is religious, not political, in character: Iṣlāḥī, 5:490–491; Qurṭubī, 13:83 (quoting Ibrāhīm an-Nakhaʿī and Makḥūl).

Verses 75–76: *Meaning of "on account of their steadfastness":* Iṣlāḥī, 5:491.

The omission to specify the areas in which the servants of God show their steadfastness broadens the scope of steadfast action: Zamakhsharī, 3:106; Rāzī, 24:116.

Fine dwellings and lodgings of paradise: Iṣlāḥī, 5:491.

III. 1. *Two possible interpretations of the structure of the passage:* Zamakhsharī, 3:103; Rāzī, 24:107. Zamakhsharī prefers the second interpretation, and Rāzī follows suit; Qurṭubī (13:82), too, seems to prefer this interpretation. Abū Ḥayyān (8:125–126) prefers the first interpretation.

5. *Contrast between self-abasement in this world and exaltation in the afterlife:* Iṣlāḥī, 5:491.

30 Luqmān's Advice to His Son

31 Luqmān 12–19

I. Iṣlāḥī, 6:124–125.

II. ***Verse 12:*** *Gratitude is the essence of all wisdom:* Iṣlāḥī, 6:127; also Ṭabarī, 21:44; Zamakhsharī, 3:211–212; Rāzī, 25:145.

Meaning of "And he who shows gratitude does so to his own good": Iṣlāḥī, 6:128.

Meaning of "But he who disbelieves, God is Self-Sufficient, Worthy of Thankful Praise": Zamakhsharī, 21:212; Rāzī, 25:145, 146; Iṣlāḥī, 6:128.

Luqmān was probably not a prophet: Iṣlāḥī, 6:125; see also Ṭabarī, 21:43; Qurṭubī, 14:59–60.

Verse 13: *Connection between verse 12's injunction to be grateful to God and verse 13's injunction to shun setting up copartners with God:* Iṣlāḥī, 6:128.

Significance of "he was giving him advice": Iṣlāḥī, 6:128, 133.

Verses 14–15: *The Qur'ān often discusses the themes of monotheism and filial obligation together:* Ibn Kathīr, 5:383; Iṣlāḥī, 6:129.

Implication of "the return is to Me" (verse 14): Ṭabarī, 21:45; Iṣlāḥī, 6:130.

Obedience to God takes precedence over obedience to parents (verse 15): Iṣlāḥī, 6:129.

One's obligations to one's parents (verse 15): Zamakhsharī, 21:212; Qurṭubī, 14:65; Iṣlāḥī, 6:129.

In matters of belief, one must follow those who have submitted to God (verse 15): Ṭabarī, 21:45; Iṣlāḥī, 6:130.

Meaning of "what you have no knowledge of" (verse 15): Zamakhsharī, 21:212; also Iṣlāḥī, 6:129.

The concluding part of verse 15 addresses parents as well as children: Iṣlāḥī, 6:130.

Verse 16: *This verse speaks of the hereafter:* Iṣlāḥī, 6:131.

Referent of "it" in "if it be of the weight of a mustard seed": Iṣlāḥī, 6:131.

Verse 17: *This verse talks of expressing gratitude to God through worshipful conduct and of the need to serve God steadfastly:* Iṣlāḥī, 6:131–132; also Rāzī, 25:148, 149; Qurṭubī, 14:68.

Verses 18–19: Iṣlāḥī, 6:132–133.

Image behind the phrase "And do not be wry-faced with people" (verse 18): Ṭabarī, 21:47; Qurṭubī, 14:69; Ibn Kathīr, 5:385.

III. 1. *Verses 14–15 as a kind of parenthetic addition*: The Arabic term for this kind of addition is *taḍmīn*, which may be translated as "implicative construction."

31 Behavior Unbecoming of a Believer

49 Apartments 11–13

I. Iṣlāḥī, 6:479.

II. ***Verse 11:*** *The invocation "O you who believe" exhorts Muslims to carry out the commandments about to be given:* Iṣlāḥī, 7:505.

Those ridiculed may be morally superior to those ridiculing them: Qurṭubī, 16:378; Iṣlāḥī, 6:506.

To heap sarcasm on a Muslim is to heap sarcasm on oneself: Ṭabarī, 26:83; Zamakhsharī, 4:13; Rāzī, 28:132; Qurṭubī, 16:327; Iṣlāḥī, 6:507.

Meaning of "How bad is the very name of wickedness after belief!": Iṣlāḥī, 6:508.

Verse 12: *As a matter of principle, Muslims should think well of one another:* Ṭabarī, 26:85; Iṣlāḥī, 6:509.

Speculation about other people's motives and actions may create in one ill will or hostility toward them: Rāzī, 28:134.

The Arabic for "And do not pry" has connotations of mischief and malice: Ibn Kathīr, 6:380.

"And do not pry" is a prohibition against finding other people's shortcomings and defects: Ṭabarī, 26:85; Zamakhsharī, 4:15; Rāzī, 28:134; Iṣlāḥī, 6:510.

Meaning of "to eat somebody's flesh": Iṣlāḥī, 6:510.

Verse 13: *The verse addresses perceptions that cause certain people to think of themselves as superior to others:* Iṣlāḥī, 6:506.

Purpose of the division of humankind into such groupings as races and tribes: Ṭabarī, 26:89; Iṣlāḥī, 6:512.

In the hereafter, God will judge human beings in accordance with the criterion of nobility only: Qurṭubī, 16:345–346.

III. Iṣlāḥī, 6:512.

IV. 1. *The vice of ridiculing one another appears to be more common among men:* Rāzī, 28:132; also Ibn Kathīr, 6:378.

2. *Use of the word "brother" in the idiom "to eat the flesh of one's brother" makes the act extremely heinous:* Zamakhsharī, 4:15; Rāzī, 28:134–135.

32 Relations with Non-Muslims

60 Women Tested 8–9

II. ***Verse 8:*** *The verse makes a principled statement about the conduct of Muslims toward all non-Muslims:* Ṭabarī, 28:43; also Iṣlāḥī, 8:332–333, 334.

Specific meaning of the injunction about treating non-Muslims justly: Iṣlāḥī, 8:335.

Verse 9: *To befriend those who are hostile to Islam and Muslims is to work against the interests of Islam and Muslims:* Iṣlāḥī, 8:334, 335.

33 The Hypocrites

63 Hypocrites 1–4

II. ***Verses 1–2:*** *"We bear witness that . . ." signifies an oath (verse 1):* Qurṭubī, 18:122; Iṣlāḥī, 8:398.

The hypocrites feel that they have to swear oaths to establish their credibility: Iṣlāḥī, 8:398.

What the hypocrites say is correct, yet they are lying: Ṭabarī, 28:69; Zamakhsharī, 4:100; Iṣlāḥī, 8:398.

Sense in which the hypocrites use their oaths as a shield: Ṭabarī, 28:69; Iṣlāḥī, 8:398–399.

Verse 3: Ṭabarī, 28:69; Iṣlāḥī, 8:399.

Verse 4: *The hypocrites' flashy personalities and dark souls symbolize their duplicity:* Iṣlāḥī, 8:400–401.

"Every shout, they think, is upon them": "Shout" is a translation of *ṣayḥah*, which, in some contexts, as here, means the shout raised at the approach of a danger and, therefore, comes to mean "danger." See Iṣlāḥī, 8:401.

"May God strike them!" is a curse: Zamakhsharī, 4:101.

34 An Argument for the Afterlife

78 News 1–17

II. ***Verses 1–3:*** *The querying about the hereafter is derisive and dismissive in character (verse 1):* Zamakhsharī, 4:176.

Nature of the idolaters' disagreement over the hereafter (verse 3): Iṣlāḥī, 9:157–158; Zamakhsharī, 4:176; also Rāzī, 31:2.

Verses 4–5: *It is the dire consequences of denying the hereafter that the sūrah's addressees will "find out" about:* Ṭabarī, 30:3; Zamakhsharī, 4:176.

Two types of punishment with which the Qur'ān threatens nations: Iṣlāḥī, 9:158.

Verses 6–17: Iṣlāḥī, 9:159–162.

35 Muḥammad Consoled

93 Bright Morning

I. Iṣlāḥī, 9:409.

II. ***Verses 1–3:*** Iṣlāḥī, 9:412–413.

Verses 4–5: Iṣlāḥī, 9:414–415; also Zamakhsharī, 4:219 (on verse 5).

Verses 6–8: *Meaning of "And He found you lost and guided you":* Iṣlāḥī, 9:415–417.

Verses 9–11: Iṣlāḥī, 9:418–419.

III. 3. *Potential presence of a declarative response in verse 6:* See Abū Ḥayyān, 1:242 (*ad* Q 2:33), where similar examples—Q 7:172, 18:26, and 94:1—are cited and briefly explained.

4. *Parallel structure of verses 6–11:* Iṣlāḥī, 9:418–419; see also Abū Ḥayyān, who allows another possibility as well—AA′BCC′B′—justifying the chiasmus BCC′B′ (10:498).

36 Judgment Day

101 Striker

II. ***Verses 1–3:*** Iṣlāḥī, 9:512–513.

Verses 4–5: Iṣlāḥī, 9:513–514.

Verses 6–7: *In the afterlife, one's acts will determine one's final destination:* Iṣlāḥī, 9:514.

IV. 2. *Hāwiyah is an abyss:* See Zamakhsharī, 4:230; Rāzī, 32:74.

3. *Ironic use of* umm *("mother"):* See Ṭabarī, 30:183; also Zamakhsharī, 4:230; Rāzī, 32:74.

37 Serving Only God

112 Sincerity

I. *Sūrah 112 is Madīnan:* Iṣlāḥī, 9:644.

Name Ikhlāṣ: Iṣlāḥī, 9:643.

II. ***Verse 1:*** *"Say" means "proclaim":* Iṣlāḥī, 9:648.

"Say" signifies that the proclamation is being made by the Prophet on behalf of God: Rāzī, 32:177–178.

Verse 2: *Meaning of* Ṣamad*:* Ṭabarī, 30:224; Zamakhsharī, 4:242; Rāzī, 32:181; Iṣlāḥī, 9:650.

Sense in which this verse complements verse 1: Iṣlāḥī, 9:650–651.

Verse 3: Iṣlāḥī, 9:651–652.

Verse 4: Zamakhsharī, 4:242; Rāzī, 32:185; Iṣlāḥī, 9:652.

Concluding Remarks

The Qur'ān's primary concern is the human being rather than God: See Fazlur Rahman, *Major Themes of the Qur'ān* (Chicago and Minneapolis: Bibliotheca Islamica, 1980), 1.

GLOSSARY

The chapter, or any other part of the book, in which a term appears is indicated at the end of a description.

Aḥādīth See **Ḥadīth.**

Anaphora Repetition of a word or phrase at the beginning of a series of statements. (Chapter 29)

Āyah (1) A "sign" of nature, that is, a natural phenomenon serving as a pointer to a higher reality, especially God. (chapter 20) (2) A "verse" of the Qur'ān. (chapter 20) Pl. *āyāt.*

Basmalah A shorthand reference to the invocatory formula *Bi smi llāhi r-Raḥmāni r-Raḥīm*, "In the name of God, the Most Compassionate, the Very Merciful." (Chapter 1).

Bifurcated Subject Division of a subject into two or more components, one or more of which are placed after the verb or the predicate. (Chapters 3, 10, 19)

Chiasmus See **Reverse Parallelism.**

Climax An arrangement of words or phrases in ascending order of force. (Chapter 28)

Dénouement The outcome of a complex series of events. (Chapters 2, 28)

Envelope Repetition, at the end, of a phrase that occurs at the beginning of a statement. (Chapters 20, 25)

Epic Simile A simile in which a comparison, once introduced, is developed at some length, the simile acquiring a kind of substantive presence of its own. (Chapter 8)

Evangel The scripture that, according to the Qur'ān, was revealed to Jesus (Arabic: *Injīl*). (General Introduction, Chapters 11, 12, 19)

Ḥadīth Literally, "report," *Ḥadīth* (with a capital *Ḥ*) is the transmitted record of the sayings, acts, and approvals of Muḥammad (Muḥammad's silence on witnessing one of his followers performing a certain act is construed as his approval); *ḥadīth* (with a small *ḥ*; pl. *aḥādīth*) is one such transmitted report. (General Introduction, chapters 2, 6, 13, 16, 18, 30)

Ḥajj Annual pilgrimage to the Kaʿbah in the city of Makkah in Arabia. According to ancient Arabian tradition, which was confirmed by Islam, the ḥajj was instituted by Abraham, who built the Kaʿbah. (Chapter 3)

Ḥuffāẓ Those who have memorized the Qur'ān (masc. sing. *ḥāfiẓ*; fem. sing. *ḥāfiẓah* [pl. *ḥāfiẓāt*]). (General Introduction)

Hysteron Proteron Transposition of two words, phrases, or statements—putting last that which comes first and putting first that which comes last. (Chapter 10)

Litotes Understatement. (Chapters 5, 17, 27)

Metonymy Substitution of a part for the whole or vice versa. (Chapter 4)

Parallelism Arrangement of several words and phrases in such a way that the first two or more words or phrases are paralleled by the next two or more words or phrases in the same order (for example, ABA′B′ or ABCA′B′C′). (Chapters 12, 35, 36)

Parataxis Use of a coordinate construction to convey the meaning of a subordinate construction. For example, in the statement "Mr. X ate chocolate. Mr. X is sick," the two sentences are simply placed next to each other, whereas it may be that Mr. X is sick *because* he ate chocolate. In other words, there may be a causal connection between the two sentences, though that connection is not indicated by the statement as such. (Chapter 7)

Prolepsis (1) Preemptive remark or statement. (Chapters 5, 12) (2) Foretelling. (Chapter 27)

Qiblah Direction of prayer. The Kaʿbah represents the *qiblah* since the formal prayers are made facing it. (Chapters 4, 5, 8)

Quraysh The tribe that ruled Makkah at the time of Muḥammad. Muḥammad himself belonged to a branch of the Quraysh. (General Introduction, Chapters 3, 5, 8, 21, 24, 27, 29, 35)

Reverse Parallelism Arrangement of several words and phrases in such a way that the first two or more words or phrases are paralleled by the next two or more words or phrases in reverse order (for example, ABB′A′). Also called **Chiasmus**. (Chapters 7, 8, 17)

Sharīʿah The comprehensive Islamic Code of Conduct, governing all aspects of life; sometimes translated as Islamic Law. (Chapter 13)

Sunnah Literally, the "way" of Muḥammad, Sunnah is the established and well-attested practice of Muḥammad that has normative value. Sunnah is accessed through *Ḥadīth*. That is, a study of *Ḥadīth* leads to the determination of the "way" of the Prophet in a given matter. (Chapter 16)

Sūrah A "chapter" of the Qur'ān. (Passim)

Syllepsis Use of a word in relation to two other words in such a way that it properly governs only one member of the pair, the word that would govern the other member being implied or understood. An example is the verb *killed* in "The army killed the rebels and the hideouts," in which a word like "destroy" has to be supplied for use with "hideouts." (Chapter 5). Cf. **Zeugma.**

Talmud Ancient body of Jewish writings, consisting of the oral reports called Mishnah and Gemarah and held sacred and authoritative by Orthodox Jews. (Chapter 23)

Ummah (1) A group of people. (Chapter 13) (2) The worldwide Muslim community. (Chapter 13)

Zakāh Amount of wealth mandatorily given by the relatively well off for the welfare of the poor and the needy and for certain other purposes. (Chapters 4, 15, 22, 27)

Zeugma Use of a word in relation to two other words in such a way that it governs both members of the pair, though it gives a different sense in each case. An example is the verb *broke* in "He broke her fan and her heart." (Chapter 14). Cf. **Syllepsis.**

WORKS CONSULTED

The following is a list of the sources used, starting with the earliest source and ending with the most recent. Only sources cited more than once are given (for a source cited only once, bibliographical details are provided at the place of citation). The short author name—or, in two cases (*Lisān* and *Manār*), the title—by which a source is identified in the notes is given in bold. In the case of the classical authors and of some works, both Islamic and Christian dates are given. For example, in "754/1344," the date before the slash is Islamic, and the date following the slash is Christian.

Abū Jaʿfar Muḥammad ibn Jarīr aṭ-**Ṭabarī** (224–310/839–923), *Jāmiʿ al-Bayān ʿan Taʾwīl Āy al-Qurʾān*, 30 vols. in 12 (Beirut: Dār al-Maʿrifah, 1406–1407/1986–1987; reprint of Būlāq edition of 1323/1905).

Abū l-Qāsim Maḥmūd ibn ʿUmar az-**Zamakhsharī** (467–538/1075–1144), *Al-Kashshāf ʿan Ḥaqāʾiq at-Tanzīl wa-ʿUyūn al-Aqāwīl*, 4 vols (Beirut: Dār al-Maʿrifah, n.d.).

Fakhr ad-Dīn Abū ʿAbd-Allāh ibn ʿUmar ar-**Rāzī** (544–606/1150–1210), *At-Tafsīr al-Kabīr* (1353–1382?/1934–1962?; Tehran reprint).

Abū ʿAbd-Allāh Muḥammad ibn Aḥmad al-Anṣārī al-**Qurṭubī** (d. 671/1272), *Al-Jāmiʿ li-Aḥkām al-Qurʾān*, 20 vols. in 10 (Dār al-Kātib al-ʿArabī, 1387/1967).

Ibn Manẓūr (630–711/1233–1311 or 1312), ***Lisān** al-ʿArab*, 18 vols., ed. ʿAlī Shīrī (Beirut: Dār Ihyāʾ at-Turāth al-ʿArabī, 1408/1988).

Athīr ad-Dīn Abū ʿAbd-Allāh Muḥammad ibn Yūsuf, known as **Abū Ḥayyān** (d. 754/1344) *Al-Baḥr al-Muḥīṭ fī t-Tafsīr*, 10 vols. (Beirut: Dār al-Fikr, 1412/1992).

ʿImād ad-Dīn Abū l-Fidāʾ Ismāʿīl **ibn Kathīr** (d. 774/1373), *Tafsīr al-Qurʾān al-ʿAẓīm*, 7 vols., 4th printing (Beirut: Dār al-Andalus, 1983).

*Tafsīr al-Qurʾān al-Ḥakīm ash-Shahīr bi-Tafsīr al-**Manār***, 12 vols., compiled by Muḥammad Rashīd Riḍā (1865–1935) from lectures of Muḥammad ʿAbduh (1849–1905) (Beirut: Dār al-Fikr, n.d.).

Ashraf ʿAlī **Thānawī** (1863–1943), *Bayānul-Qurʾān*, rev. ed. (Karachi: H. M. Saʿīd Company, 1353/1934; first published 1326/1908).

ʿAbdul-Mājid **Daryābādī** (1892–1977), *Al-Qurʾānul-Ḥakīm maʿa Tarjamah-o Tafsīr* (Lahore: Tāj Company, 1373/1952).

Abū l-Aʿlā **Mawdūdī** (1903–1979), *Tafhīmul-Qurʾān*, 6 vols. (Lahore: Anjuman-i Taʿmīr-i Insāniyyat [vols. 1–4], 1950–1966 and Idārah-i Tarjumānul-Qurʾān [vols. 5–6], 1971–1972).

Amīn Aḥsan **Iṣlāḥī** (1903–1997), *Tadabbur-i Qurʾān*, 9 vols. (Lahore: Fārān Foundation, 2000).

Index

A heading occurring in a subentry is abbreviated to its initial letter followed by a period; for example, "sūrah(s)" is abbreviated to "s." A heading like "Ark of the Covenant" is abbreviated to "A.," and the keyword "language" in the heading "language, style, and literary devices" is abbreviated to "l." "Qur'ān" is abbreviated to "Q," and "New Testament," to "NT."

Lightning Source UK Ltd.
Milton Keynes UK
UKOW04f1516040417
298290UK00014BA/154/P